A Spy's Résumé
Confessions of a Maverick Intelligence Professional and Misadventure Capitalist

Marc Anthony Viola

*Scarecrow Professional Intelligence
Education Series, #2*

The Scarecrow Press, Inc.
Lanham, Maryland • Toronto • Plymouth, UK
2008

SCARECROW PRESS, INC.

Published in the United States of America
by Scarecrow Press, Inc.
A wholly owned subsidiary of
The Rowman & Littlefield Publishing Group, Inc.
4501 Forbes Boulevard, Suite 200, Lanham, Maryland 20706
www.scarecrowpress.com

Estover Road
Plymouth PL6 7PY
United Kingdom

British Library Cataloguing in Publication Information Available

Library of Congress Cataloging-in-Publication Data

Viola, Marc Anthony, 1965-
    A spy's résumé : confessions of a maverick intelligence professional and
misadventure capitalist / Marc Anthony Viola.
        p. cm. — (Scarecrow professional intelligence education series)
    Includes bibliographical references.
    ISBN-13: 978-0-8108-6098-8 (pbk. : alk. paper)
    ISBN-10: 0-8108-6098-8 (paperback : alk. paper)
    ISBN-13: 978-0-8108-6286-9 (electronic)
    ISBN-10: 0-8108-6286-7 (electronic)
    1. Intelligence officers—United States. 2. Spies—United States. 3. Career
changes—United States. 4. Vocational guidance—United States. I. Title.
UB251.U6V56 2008
327.12730092—dc22
    [B]   2008004302

Scarecrow Professional Intelligence Education
Series Editor: Jan Goldman

Communicating with Intelligence: Writing and Briefing in the Intelligence and National Security Communities by James S. Major. 2008.

A Spy's Résumé: Confessions of a Maverick Intelligence Professional and Misadventure Capitalist by Marc Anthony Viola. 2008.

Dedicated to "the 20"

Those hopelessly committed,
entirely too intelligent, and
ultimately disillusioned.

May they learn to just let go,
leave the work to others, and
succeed at their true destinies.

DC-3 Dakota Standing By . . .

Contents

Figures

Tables

Series Editor's Foreword

Since the attacks of September 11, 2001, the United States Intelligence Community has been on a hiring binge. According to some estimates, more than half of those currently employed by the agencies and departments that make up our Intelligence Community have less than six years' experience. Understandably, many of these people are still "learning the ropes" of how to become an intelligence professional. This book describes in a personal way what they can expect as they continue in their profession, and when they decide to leave it. Marc Anthony Viola has been a part of the Intelligence Community for decades, working and teaching his way through the many corridors and levels of our nation's protective services. He is also a perceptive and excellent writer. I can think of no one more qualified to write this book.

Foremost, this book is about surviving the demanding work of what it takes to become an intelligence professional—not an expert necessarily, but a professional. In the following chapters, Marc Viola works his way through his time in military intelligence, on to becoming a civilian intelligence professional, and still later a teacher in the Intelligence Community. The author has worked on both sides of the Intelligence Community, first as a government employee and later as an employee of several companies that did contract intelligence work for the government. Through it all, the author learned some of life's lessons on how to balance your life and your work.

When I envisioned the establishment of this professional intelligence series, I never anticipated that I would receive the type of manuscript for a book which you are currently holding in your hand. Like most books for professionals, most manuscripts I receive focus on how to improve your work by being more effective and efficient; but rarely do we pause to think about the effect this work may have on our mental and physical well-being.

This author has not only provided some extremely helpful tips on how to maintain your sense of well-being, but he has written this book in such a way that even if you are not interested in becoming an intelligence professional, you will benefit from his advice and recommendations. This book is helpful no matter what profession you work in, as well as to those not working in any profession.

This is a funny book, with lots of quotes, charts, and graphics. Humor is liberally sprinkled throughout the chapters, providing the reader with an enjoyable moment and an uplifting experience. This is the type of book that folks like to give as gifts because of both its uniqueness and extremely positive sense of self-improvement; and along the way, you will learn something about what it takes to become an intelligence professional. More importantly, it will help you become a better person.

Jan Goldman, Ed.D.
Series Editor

Acknowledgments

In any transition, participants can feel so detached from reality that they need to turn to others for frequent sanity checks. In my transition from service member to civilian, there were people along the way who helped me remain connected to *terra firma*, and reassure me that my perceptions were not completely off base.

U.S. Navy Lt. Cmdr. Robert "Bob" Peranich has my lifelong admiration and respect as my best military supervisor. I can only aspire to lead with his integrity, strength, patience, and tireless devotion to duty. To me, he will always be, "Sir." I had two additional outstanding mentors along the way. The first was Navy Chief Petty Officer Ron Jost, who (unofficially) inducted me into the U.S. Navy as a bull ensign (the senior ensign under a given command), revealing such closely guarded navy secrets as the inner workings of a Chief's initiation ceremony, leveraging the power of the "boat room," and racing 39-cent hamburgers (after long nights of carousing). My second mentor was MSgt. Doris Carder, whose interpersonal dexterity and social wisdom were matched only by her courage and candor. In ushering my career along the darkened corridors of the intelligence profession, these mentors demonstrated how I might remain firmly human while developing my expertise.

Other colleagues who encouraged me in this endeavor, anxiously awaiting "Marc's book," include Bob Surrette and Daniel Vergamini, and my fellow intelligence-collection instructors at the Joint Military Intelligence College (now the National Defense Intelligence College), Tom Fields, Mark Marshall, Dan Gressang, and Bill Halpin. Dr. Jane Flax provided tremendous insights into the behavioral aspects of transitioning out of the military. Had

I listened to my high school English teacher, Dr. Elizabeth Wheeler, I *never* would have joined the military, and this book would not have been written. Thank you, Liz, for two decades of patient listening, helping, and understanding.

Transforming my collected and analyzed data into meaningful intelligence within these pages were those who extended their assistance in editing and proofreading, including Julia Nesheiwat, Laura Ewald, Donna Finicle, Paraag Shukla, Lt. Cmdr. Anthony Butera, Col. Shelley Bennett (retired), and my editors, Dr. Jan Goldman, April Snider, and Krista Sprecher. Credit for the design of the *Walking 86th Intelligence Group* Patch must be shared with Margaret Matera (former Major, U.S. Air Force Reserve). Credit for the design of the fog ball graphics must be shared with Brandon Well and Sarah Harting. A very special thanks goes to Kathryn "Katie" Walter, whose dedication and superhuman editing talent is matched only by her beauty and goodness. Her assistance was above and beyond the call of duty.

My many thanks go to Harley White for his wit, wisdom, insights, fabulous fashion sense, superhuman patience with my endless questions, and superb customer care overall.

It may sound trivial, but I am also grateful to Apple Computer for designing its Mac G-4 laptop so well. I regard it as perfect technology for the intuitive thinker, and for those who may feel a little out of place employing the so-called technology of the modern world.

During my sabbatical from the Intelligence Community (itself the subject of another book) certain establishments in Washington, D.C., were both welcoming and inspiring in their atmosphere. They include the Hirshhorn Museum and Sculpture Garden, Phillips Collection Art Museum, Cascade Café (between the east and west buildings of the National Gallery of Art), Kramerbooks & Afterwords, Levante's, Science Club, Starbucks at 20th and P Street, Captain Nemo's, Starbucks on Dupont Circle, and Alberto's Pizzeria.

Finally, I would like to thank all my supervisors, colleagues, and coworkers, and especially my subordinates, for putting up with my zeal and enthusiasm over the years. With age and experience, I am now thankful to those who exercised restraint on my behalf.

What is this Book All About?

"The best-kept secret in the Intelligence Community."
Staff member for George Tenet,
director of Central Intelligence (DCI), 2004

The U.S. Air Force spent a lot of money molding me into a successful spy; then it asked me to quit. In common parlance, the word "spy" has many connotations. Most people immediately think of Ian Fleming's James Bond, but the business of spying is actually much more than dry martinis and sweaty mayhem. It is a far broader, entirely sober profession, composed of any number of different specialties. Mine is the art of applying new technologies, or innovative new approaches, to collecting and analyzing information. In the most challenging cases, it requires understanding both technology and people, and this union can yield uncannily accurate understanding of adversaries.

Unfortunately, the Air Force is not really in the business of spying, or intelligence, per se. The mission of the Air Force is "air superiority," the domination of airspace. Consequently, any efforts that do not *directly* benefit air operations are viewed as verging on the superfluous. It is an establishment that strives to put bombs on targets, with the express purpose of destroying them. There are no extra points for studying targets. This philosophy is reflected in how the Air Force views its career specialties. Those who inflict blunt-force trauma on bad guys are rewarded with promotion. Those who see a different value in understanding the inner workings of their adversary are not as highly regarded. As a spy, then, I found that the intelligence field offered little room for upward mobility as an Air Force officer.

After ten years of my cultivating a unique talent in these mysterious arts, military promotion boards informed me that the Air Force saw no need for my specialty. I was asked to leave, with severance, and guidance not to return. Astonishingly, before my terminal leave ever started, the Air Force Reserve came looking for me with an avowed interest in my rare skills—especially one known to insiders as "measurement and signature intelligence," or MASINT. Once in the reserve, I was quickly promoted. Less than five years after being asked by the Air Force to leave because of this expertise, *I represented it* on a presidential commission that cited the many causes of the U.S. failure to accurately assess the likelihood of weapons of mass destruction (WMD) in Iraq. It is no small irony that one cause cited in particular was that MASINT hadn't been employed to contribute to the assessment. As the commission report notes:

> In part because of a lack of collection, and in part because of a general lack of understanding among analysts about MASINT and its capabilities, very little MASINT actually factored into [intelligence] community assessments. There was MASINT reporting on WMD—the National Intelligence Collection Board noted that from June 2000 through January 2003 MASINT sources produced over 1,000 reports on Iraqi WMD (none of which provided a definitive indication of WMD activity). But the reporting did not play a significant role in forming assessments about Iraq's WMD programs. This lack of reliance was no doubt due in part to the tendency among analysts to discount information that contradicted the prevailing view that Iraq had WMD. But it was also due in part to unfamiliarity with, and lack of confidence in, MASINT.[1]

Clearly, something had been profoundly awry with U.S. Air Force intelligence-officer career management in the 1990s.

Yin and Yang

This work is actually the commingling of potentially two different books. The first is about the actual task of a job search. It is a practical guide for leaving the military or government service. The second is about your state of mind, about letting go of the emotions associated with the service. So again, my double-edged approach in this book covers two main areas: (1) conducting a job search, and (2) tending to one's state of mind in the course of transition.

Job-hunting is uppermost in everyone's mind when they leave the service. It is completely understandable. People continue to have financial, family, and personal obligations, so the practical demands of leaving the military are covered here in two sub-areas (a) building your résumé, and (b) mastering the interview process. They are straightforward, pragmatic chapters to help readers leave their present profession for another, newer one in the civilian world. There are many good books out there on this transitional process. I invite you to consult them as well. My hope has been to include observations that go beyond what others already advise.

Your state of mind throughout a transition is often overlooked. The emotional aspects are subtle but substantial, so the topic of letting go of military or government service has two sub-areas as well (a) examining your feelings throughout the process, and (b) shedding new light on a service for departing members to connect and identify with. Few in the military or government like to talk about their feelings. This subject is often viewed as not being manly, and feelings are seen as a sign of vulnerability. Ironically, in the years since my leaving, virtually everyone I have talked to about this subject, no matter how objective, has spoken to me with intense feelings about his or her experiences.

Humans are feeling creatures, so these chapters are designed to focus on the not-so-straightforward perceptions, awkward emotions, complaints, and lingering feelings that people may experience before, during, and long after their transitions. Those leaving the military behind and moving forward in their lives should also know that they are not alone in their perceptions. I hope my observations resonate with your own. As an intelligence professional, I owe it to my former comrades to share my assessments, right, wrong, or otherwise.

The Intrigue of Espionage and the Business of Change in a Changing World

Part of this book approaches the task of transitioning from the military (or government service) as if it were an intelligence operation. It is about applying all the spying tradecraft I learned in the military to the task of finding a "real" job. You, a government or military person, can employ all the tricks of the intelligence trade to a different goal: making the jump to civilian life. This is *not* an evil instruction manual for spying on Americans, nor a book on predatory tactics to manipulate employers. Instead, it is an approach to transition that is both practical and encouraging to the person on the move.

Leaving the protective confines of the military for the dog-eat-dog world of business can feel a little like operating in a "denied area," which is Department of Defense jargon for "an area under enemy or unfriendly control." The outside world can seem hostile, threatening, even adversarial. Well, that is what the intelligence business is all about. It is designed for building knowledge of just such a non-cooperative environment. The Air Force trained me how to collect and analyze vast stores of data and turn it into operational pictures for decision makers. On departing, it only seemed natural for me to swing my professional viewfinder around, point it at the civilian sector, and then document the results. It was a natural extension of doing my job as an intelligence professional. Now the decision maker, in the case of this book, will be the reader, as the collector, the analyst, and the ultimate user of the intelligence.

This book is designed to help people through their transition by showing them the value of observation. It shows how to collect data and formulate usable and actionable information (intelligence) for a job search, how to use the arts of surveillance and reconnaissance, preparation, organization, and serendipity to one's advantage. It is about walking into a job search with requirements already in mind, eyes wide open, and an executable strategy to make decisions about the next phase of life. All of my observations come from my own, first-hand experiences. They are based on events, successes and, more importantly, failures.

There are no dirty tricks in this book, but there are warnings about evil employer tactics and strategies. In keeping with the tenets of good intelligence, the book is designed to inform, educate, and encourage cultivating in-depth knowledge as part of important decision making. The business world can be unfair to the noble breed of warriors leaving the military—especially if they expect the same level of honesty, integrity, and forthrightness that they were accustomed to in the service. The business world can also change people, harden them, and bring out the worst in them, especially if they are not forewarned or forearmed. Journeys out of the military need not be distressing for well-informed decision makers who knows what to expect, and have the resources necessary to make reasonable choices that preserve their well-being.

Ending a Marriage and Divorcing a Culture

It took me seven years to find all the right words to express my emotions about leaving the military. Writing this book, although therapeutic, was a difficult emotional task for me. Every section of this book touched raw nerves and exposed old emotions that I wanted to forget. I wanted to believe that I was strong enough to put those feelings behind me and forget about them. For years after separating, I struggled with feelings of disappointment, regret, disillusionment, anger, loss, inadequacy, and failure, and they just would not go away.

When a person chooses to leave the military, it is usually because something about their experience hasn't been quite right. The more a person wanted to be in the military in the first place, the harder their eventual separation. Separation means adapting to a new and different world, and something can feel lost in the transition. When loss is felt, it is often accompanied by an uncomfortable array of emotions. To do the process of transition justice, this book must also be about feelings, and the ways of dealing with those feelings.

The military functions very well in telling people what is good for them, and ensuring that they believe it. This facilitates all the military's basic needs, but it also makes for an environment that is susceptible to abuses by negligent or malicious people. It can feel like a dysfunctional home or problematic relationship, where abusive people manipulate others for their benefit. In essence, then, separating from the military can be like going through a divorce. When people move on from the service, they may feel the need to grow free of painful bonds to a relationship that failed. I hope this book will help them look inside themselves, perhaps for the first time in their lives, and really ask themselves difficult questions about their own desires and needs, hopes, and fears.

When you operate in a war zone, you don body armor for security, even when in heavily guarded posts or huge support-structure facilities, behind miles of concertina wire and crash barriers. Conversely, in the intelligence business, security is a state of mind. Protection does not come from body armor, concertina wire, crash barriers, guard posts, or even support facilities. Your intelligence uniform of the day might be a T-shirt, jeans, and SPF-50 sunscreen, with very little else between you and the locals.

The one thing you can be sure of is that you are never quite sure *who* has your back. There may be no one to rely on except the shopkeepers, bus drivers, fruit salesmen, or friendly little kids that you have come to know during your stay. You are alone, amidst crowds whose mood might boil over into vehement rage and frenzy at a moment's notice, with no security detail to protect you. Your strength lies in your resolve, in daily tests of will and patience. Your protection comes from blending into the crowd, and keeping your cool while immersed in a totally different culture thousands of miles from home.

When you separate from the military, leaving your base for the last time without an ID card, you might feel the same way: alone, unarmed, and, I hope, unafraid.

Time Traveler Mocha

I have no doubts that anyone reading this book can successfully leave the military and transition back into the civilian world. One purpose of my book was an experimental journey back to the precise moment when I committed myself to separating from the military. I imagined the kind of discussion I would have with my past self, say over a cup of coffee, with only a limited time to share *all* of the lessons learned from seven years as a civilian. I realized that if I only had a short time I would not waste it on details. Instead, I would give myself words of encouragement, and then leave behind this book. This book, then, is an after-action report of my lessons learned—the hard way.

Would I have heeded my own lessons? Outwardly, I was cocky and self-assured in my ability to leave the military and succeed. Deep inside, however, I was scared to death about what was waiting for me "out there" in the civilian world. I felt like I was drowning in uncertainties, and in the absence of usable intelligence I was paralyzed. In such a state, learning the hard way seemed the only option. I now believe that, finally, I have written a book that would have spared me the pain of learning from avoidable mistakes.

Note to the Reader

Throughout this book you will find portions of text set off in a variety of frames or boxes. Some may appear randomly, others may directly apply to the text, but all will stand out amidst the general run of words. These textual asides fall into the following categories:

1. Sayings, slogans, proverbs, adages, aphorisms, and apothegms
2. Mavaxioms

3. Intelligence jargon and other unorthodox observations
4. Figures and tables
5. Letters and e-mail

These widely gathered nuggets are intentionally interspersed throughout the main text in an optically disruptive strategy to break up your reading. Like park benches along a path, they are there to provide rest stops, if you choose, or opportunities to think outside the box about what's inside the box.

While writing this book I had my own epiphanies. In my mind, they were statements or propositions that I regarded as being self-evident. They were not self-evident, however, to everyone else so I grouped them into a special category for which I created a new term. The invented term for such realizations dawning on me in a moment of inspiration or epiphany is the "mavaxiom," whose origin I will leave to your imagination.

Some people hate quotations. If you do, then just skip them. These breaks are also for those who like to open a book and start reading anywhere, or to read chapters in bite-sized chunks. However you choose, my hope is that you enjoy the read.

Disclaimer

I admit it. The intent and message of this book runs the risk of being very misunderstood by many. Citizens need to trust in the integrity of their military. Despite what critics might suspect, I am a strong advocate of the military. Any military, however, is only as good as its people. My concern is for those people who are willing to give their last full measure of devotion to their profession.

If you are out, have chosen to get out, or are about to do so, then I hope this book will help you. Many of my observations may not apply to your own experience, service, situation, or timeframe. I do not expect 100 percent agreement from everyone about my observations. I accept this responsibility, and, since I cannot expect everyone to share my perceptions, I only ask you to take them with "a grain of fault." It means that a measure of healthy responsibility should be applied when reading my observations. Specifically, I realize that I do not perceive omnisciently. My experiences were specific to me, and so they have an inherent bias. Can they apply to someone else? Possibly. If there is a possibility of helping just one other person with the difficult process of leaving the military, does it behoove me try to lend assistance to a soon-to-be fellow veteran? You bet. Will my assistance be without hazards? Probably not, so I accept the fault of not being perfect in my desire to help my comrades. My experiences are bound to differ from those of other military and government-service members. Numerous conversations with others in the service, however, have told me that there are enduring themes, pervasive throughout the experiences of most.

The best intelligence is the product of many parts. In a process called "fusion," many sources are brought together to form a final analytical product greater than the sum of its parts. It calls for elusive problems to be examined from different perspectives, numerous vantage points, and by means of various observables. All are layered to create a composite view yielding an intelligence assessment with puzzle pieces fit in from each for greatest clarity. Knowing this as a career intelligence professional, I concede that this book is not the product of fusion, but rather an expression of the observations of primarily one man: me. I wrote this book alone, and I take full responsibility for whatever raving assertions it makes.

The perspectives and opinions in this book do not represent the views of the United States military, Intelligence Community, or other government entity. They were observed through my filter on the lens of experience, and therefore are situational in their dependencies, circumstantial in their basis. I did not conduct scientific studies or representative surveys. I did not consult with leaders of the community, or successful members of the establishment. They may have their story, but I wrote this book for the individuals whom I call "the twenty." I believe they will identify with my experiences. I hope they gain comfort from reading about them, and knowing that they are not alone in their transition. They are human beings in a sometimes-inhuman business, but they can still walk away from their careers with their dignity and self-respect intact.

Note

1. The Commission on the Intelligence Capabilities of the United States Regarding Weapons of Mass Destruction, *Report to the President of the United States*, Co-Chaired by Laurence H. Silberman and Charles S. Robb (Washington, D.C., U.S. Government Printing Office, 31 March 2006), 166.

Time for Change
A Process of Necessity

"Little growth comes from planned success. Real growth happens when everything falls apart."
— Mavaxiom No. 11

S
ooner or later, everyone leaves the military. They have to; it is the law. Either by the laws of man or by the laws of Nature, everybody who is in must eventually get out. Anyone can relate to this experience. Leaving military (or government) service is a subset of much larger transitional experiences that occur throughout life. But be it separation as an Air Force intelligence officer, enlisted Marine, Navy submariner, government service, or Army combat soldier, the event can present a challenge to the best of us. The observations presented here, and the strategies recommended, are not necessarily trade secrets of the Intelligence Community (IC). However, I did approach the subject of transition as a product of the IC. A hallmark of Americans is their predisposition (as much as their right) to do things their own way, and to form their own opinions. You are encouraged to do the same because you are about to change your life for good. You are not alone, as this is a task that faces virtually all of us at some point in our lives.

If the military is for you, and you love what you are doing then, by all means, please, stay in and continue this noble profession. If, however, you are not happy in the service and can do nothing about changing what you do not like, show some leadership and do something about it.

Whatever the case, if you want or need to separate from the military or government then *get out.* Leave those who want to be there, get on with the job of defending the nation. If this career of service is not for you, then it is your responsibility to yourself to find a path to your happiness and satisfaction.

Ultimately, this is about change. It is not just about leaving the military, but leaving the military *behind* and moving on with one's life. Like any parting relationship, separation from the service is a difficult process of change. It demands that those involved learn, grow, and transform to become new. Each person's experience will be uniquely individual. I can only claim to understand my own, and hope that my observations from along the way will help others in their own journey. Many of the

> "Lead, follow, or get out of the way."
>
> —Thomas Paine

people I spoke with on the route of my own transition told me that my experiences resonated with their own. They were a source of encouragement, validating the importance of sharing my observations with others.

To those of you staying in service, "supporting and defending the Constitution," I say you are heroes. It is no easy task to forego any semblance of a normal life. I salute you for sacrificing your civil rights, and putting your ideals (and your lives) on the line every day. Veterans wish you well in the struggle. Please take no harm from my commentary. You are doing a job that I could not, and I respect you for it. When it comes time for your own departure, I only hope that my observations will help you in your *own* transition. Until then, I leave make only one request. While you are still serving the country, make change for a better military. No institution is perfect, and the one that you are part of can still afford the benefits of your assistance. Aspire to make your place in the service a little better for all who serve with you, if only by small improvements where you have influence. Please be the leaders that the military needs now, more than ever.

Sustainability

Before you can live the so-called American Dream, you will have to consider a few concepts. Perhaps the most underrated, most misunderstood of these, is the concept of sustainability. In the simplest terms, and in the subtlest of ways, sustainability is a new career's capacity to continue providing employment, purpose, opportunity for professional growth, and satisfaction *despite* cyclical changes in the economic forecast. Taking up a new career is like taking up farming, except that you want to plant yourself in an employment field that won't be depleted by expiring contracts, changing company policies, management shakeups, or fickle customers. In short, you want your job to have legs, range, and the time to browse for additions to your credentials and explore differing aspects of your developing self. You must have sustainability so that your skills will endure through changing financial climates. The most important prerequisite is education. If you do not yet have a college degree, then get one first in your quest for sustainability.

My experiences in defense contracting taught me valuable lessons about sustainability. During wartime, defense industries boom. Government money flows, research produces new technologies, technologists develop new systems, and defense contracting becomes a growth industry. Yet as fast as it booms, it can just as suddenly fizzle. Post-war demobilizations invariably feature government clients canceling defense-related contracts as part of government-wide cost-savings. The relationship between government and its defense contractors is inherently symbiotic but it is so susceptible to fluctuations in defense spending that the relationship can sometimes resemble dependency.

This dependency problem challenges individuals and businesses, alike, when defense industries are *no longer* sustainable. To stay in business, defense contractors may re-tool their employees, forcing them to migrate—like hunter-gatherers—to "following the money" to new sources of business they can find. The alternatve is to hunker down and hoard their work to the end, even if it is no longer relevant or useful. In this way, programs originally designed to take years to come to fruition somehow stretch out for decades of development. This is not work. It is a counter-sustainable approach to prolonging the inevitable. Some military and government veterans are drawn to defense contracting by the temptation of making big money, especially in a field that does not necessarily require extensive background or experience. They may become a "systems engineer," and work a range of functions. In practice, however, many of those duties are similar to the functions of a military staff officer.

Good conscience comes into play when evaluating these kinds of jobs. Beyond extending the life of government contracts (at taxpayers' expense), people must ask themselves if they believe in the work they are pursuing. Is it genuinely sustainable, or merely profitable in the near term? Some leaving the military believe they address such ethical questions *after* they find a job. Many seek to first get their "foot in the door," and then worry about the deeper philosophical issues later. Paying the bills is important, but it is also important to get your foot in the *correct* door, the door that is right for you. That door is probably the one that allows you to grow and build something real with your new career. It involves the conscious pursuit of satisfying work that allows you to feel like you are making a difference, versus precariously navigating through the daily bureaucratic obstacles to progress. You must feel appreciated, worthwhile, and empowered, otherwise you count down the days to the rest of your life.

Sustainability is a life that progressively builds on itself, minute by minute, year after year, from the time you leave your old life, and for the rest of your life. It is not so much about permanence as much as it is about answering the fundamental question of what you really want in your life. It is about defining what you value, and what will continue to have importance to you over time. This means building a new life around your desires, instead of around making money. Money is not life; it is merely a means of paying for things in life. The real challenge, then, is asking yourself the *toughest* question underlying the separation process, a question that only you can answer:

What do you really want?

This is a daunting challenge for those leaving the military (or government) because it is the one question that nobody asks you while *in* the service. The military does not ask its members what they want because individual wants are counterproductive to the military's larger mission. Militaries mobilize masses of people and equipment, and then hurl them at conflict, unimpeded by choice. Military culture necessitates squelching individual desires for the sake of the larger organization. Within this kind of culture, people can lose track of what it is that they really want in only a few years of service. Personal concerns are replaced by the needs of the larger organization. Unfortunately, something personal dies in that kind of lifestyle, something creative, individual, and crucially important to sustainability. When people shift out of an all-encompassing military lifestyle, they must also shift philosophical gears in unaccustomed ways, and learn how to live in new ways. This means learning how to support one's own life without a new umbilical to an old form of culture.

When you find yourself in that situation, you must choose for yourself with your own needs in mind. Your needs and opportunities must stretch out, all the way to the end of your life. Pick something that you can cultivate. This is not some form of imprisonment. Instead, it means committing yourself to getting a life, making more choices every day, and opting for something new. This may mean exposing yourself to new things and allowing yourself to try, fail, and ultimately learn from the experiences. Try to explore beyond your comfort zone, try everything possible, and see what fits you best. Change your models of expectation, and allow the opportunities to find you.

Trusting Yourself

You have to trust that you can generate your own sustainable environment. After the military, no one is going to tell you what to do anymore. In fact, they may even ask you, "What do you really want to do?" Prepare yourself. That question could become a swarm that buzzes at you from every direction.

Some people (including yours truly) go looking for an answer, but the answer to the question is not "out there." Instead, the answer is inside, deep inside each of us. You will find what you want by looking inward.

Another misconception (shared by yours truly) is that finding a good job means "striking it rich." Many find rich veins of green dollars in defense contracting, where each new contract resembles a buried treasure awaiting excavation. Many are handsome finds, but many are also not sustainable. Inevitably the vein runs out, leaving you looking for the next big strike. Aspiring to a career of looking for the next big strike may not be the way of answering what you really want.

People who depend upon unsustainable solutions also tend to artificially create a false sense of sustainability in whatever they do. That may involve:

1. Intentionally slowing projects to generate a never-ending need for additional funding,
2. Operating in countereffective ways, ensuring that nothing gets done until new sources of financing have been secured, or
3. Seeking the tacit collusion of everyone else they work with, so that the "slow-roll" is a coordinated group effort.

Sound familiar? Such systems do not seek progress. Countereffectiveness is their goal. Confronting this head on means morally obligating yourself to answering the really big, important question: what do you really want? Your answer is a starting point from which to design the rest of your career.

Chances are that you will not find a perfect fit, and that is okay. It is more important that you find somewhere to place yourself that will not damage you as a person. There is no magic solution to this problem, nor is there a single technique that will work better than others. Instead there will only be one pursuit: yours. This is a uniquely individual pursuit that you will build along the way. It is more important that you look at yourself than at the sequencing of your steps or the actions of others to accomplish their own journeys.

Throughout change, temptation tests all of us. There will be a temptation to quit early, and manage the consequences from there. This temptation is human nature, an attempt to manage the process on terms that we can control because we are not ready to change. Change is hard, really hard. It involves letting go of parts of ourselves upon which we have become dependent. Change, like transiting out of the military and into a completely new career, is one of the most stressful situations we will ever encounter. The temptation is to cut your losses, hedge your bets, and take the first opportunity that presents itself. The path of expediency is the wrong approach, as going from one interim solution to another only adds to the difficulty. You set yourself back just because of being afraid of rolling up your sleeves and really the hard work of building your future. Taking the easy way out is easy, but runs the risk of not being fulfilling. This is a commitment that you must make with yourself. Do not undermine a promising and inherently good venture because you fear the commitment required.

Not for Everyone

My last permanent change of station (PCS) in the military was the clincher. In a desperate attempt to take myself out of an uncomfortable environment, I tried one last move. The time was ripe for me to leave and surround myself with new people. I needed a change, a break from the pressures of not feeling right where I was. I thought it was a matter of literal surroundings, of geography, something I thought a move might be able to fix. But after packing up and moving more than 1,000 miles to a completely different part of the country, I came to find that I was surrounded by all the same kinds of people and situations.

The names and places had changed, but 1,000 miles farther away the military had remained the same. All that I had done, all that I had achieved, all I had become, had suddenly grown incompatible with the environments from one office to another, assignment after assignment.

In the end, all the skills that I had learned in the military as an intelligence officer had the unintended and unexpected effect of allowing me to analyze my dilemma. My professional intelligence assessment was that the military was no longer for me. Regardless of how good I was at my job, how much I contributed beneficially to the team, I no longer belonged there. Soon, I would have no other choice in the matter but to leave. The military is not for everybody, and now it applied to me. I had no other choice at the midpoint of my career. I realized that it was time for me to go.

Military life is about the people. It is always about the people. Unlike all of my previous assignments, my last PCS came with unprecedented observations. None before proved so rich in learning. Perhaps it was because I had come to a point in my life where I was ready to see what had been there all along. I had reached a state where I could no longer ignore the indicators around me.

As an intelligence professional, I recognize that *all* indicators, in one way or another, contribute to solving an intelligence mystery. Some are more important than others. Some indicators may challenge our beliefs and expectations, and some may challenge the way we understand the world. Dealing with these challenges requires a special kind of open-mindedness, and an ability to step outside our own limits.

At my last duty station, uncomfortable indicators were visible all around me. The behavior patterns, belief structures, and ways that others conducted business around me were problematic, and had been all along. Situations became more and more difficult to work in, and I could not understand why. Part of me did not *want* to know because it was becoming increasingly evident that if I did finally understand I might not be able to live with the answers. Why? Because, in knowing, I then would be responsible for acting in my own best interests. If my best interests were truly important to me, it might mean changing my life. I was resisting change.

I recognized that the discomfort was a problem. At first, it was just a mild discomfort, a nagging annoyance. It was not a cause for immediate concern. As is often the case, however, minor irritations have a way of slowly transforming into chronic conditions if left unchecked. Every day I was expending more and more energy to shrug off this minor inconvenience, and it was not going away. It felt as if the entire military was somehow changing all around me in ways that I could no longer live with. The military had not changed insomuch as I had changed while serving in the military. Somewhere over the years, through my many assignments, in just over a decade, I had changed. The change had happened slowly, progressively, and subtly, imperceptible to my own ability to sense change.

My subconscious barometer was reacting to the environment. Some days it was up, some days it was down. Eventually, it became a consistently unpleasant environment that I tried treating symptomatically, rather than as the underlying cause. By way of analogy, it was like an allergy I tried treating with constant antihistamines. I resorted to constant distractions, like adventure travel, extreme sports, overactive dating, and extensive partying to try not to focus on the discomfort. In retrospect, I was so busy trying to distract myself that I was missing the real point of the discomfort. The pain was an indicator. When you are in pain, it is trying to tell you something. If a job really hurts, then to stop the hurting may mean leaving the job.

Both in the military and in every job I have held since, there were telling indicators from "day one." The lesson is to be courageous enough to listen to those indicators, and not let the distractions get in the way. In this way, job search is like an intelligence mission, using important indicators that can be found everywhere. *Seeing* the obvious requires stepping outside normal operating modes, and transcending ordinary experiences. To truly think outside the box you must *be* outside the box; and live outside comfortable norms. Many people want to stay within relaxed and familiar boundaries, but searching for a new job is an uncomfortable process.

A Lesson from Shredding Classified

There is a saying in the Intelligence Community that "the only job that ever really feels *done* is shredding." Generally, after destroying classified documents, there are no more questions, unknowns, variables, or further research required, and there are no more briefings to give. All that remains are dusty white paper bits that supposedly cannot be reconstructed to yield any usable meaning. Crosscut shredders approved for destroying classified documents slice paper into dust specks. "Shred," as it is called, is surprisingly heavy, but has a nice fluffy tactile feel when you run your fingers through it to confirm complete destruction. From this intelligence officer's perspective, it was my *cheapest* form of therapy. You do not have to pay for the relaxation shredding brings.

One of the best ways of shredding large documents is to sequence their pages in what I call underleafing. You will have to forgive me. Underleafing is not a real word. Language is innately limited in expressing all ideas, so I take liberties to creatively expand those boundaries by inventing new words. In my definition, underleafing is a special technique of intentionally inserting pages into a crosscut-type shredder. By placing the second page beneath the first page just before the first page is completely consumed, and the third page under the second page, and so on. Preceding pages guide and draw the subsequent pages into the blades, where they are caught and then guide the later pages (in this case, of a classified document). Entire books can be shredded in no time if their pages are underleafed properly.

Underleafing pages into a shredder creates a pattern of overlapping paper just like that of overlapping roof shingles. Because shingles overlap, they act like a seamless surface, down which gravity conveys rain or snow. Similarly, underleafing creates a seamless stream of overlapped sheets conveyed into a shredder. Only when the feed gets too fast will a shredder overload, overheat, and jam the blades.

Underleafing, by analogy, is an effective approach to your career transition. Before you are done with your military job, feed yourself into the process of finding the next one. Ideally, you want to have that next job all lined up, so that the termination of your military service overlaps the commencement of your next venture. It means paying attention to the passage of time, and sequencing your activities so that your past efforts help convey your new efforts forward effectively. In the civilian sector, job assignments must be underleafed to allow for successful transitions, as now income is directly at stake.

You will probably have terminal leave saved up, and some kind of transition time provided for house hunting and job search. Even so, it is important that you start looking for your next career *before* your military job ends. You need to be looking for it now, while the current job is underway. Naturally, that also requires a little discretion, so that you are not necessarily advertising your joy in departing, which makes for envious co-workers and disgusted supervisors. That is why I also recommend underleafing in the sense of being under, or hidden. Keep your operations clandestine, at first. When your efforts have caught the blades of the next job, the process will convey you along into the next phase of your life.

If you do this just right, your transition will reduce some of the separation anxiety associated with wondering about what you will do next. Underleafing your transition strategy will allow you to know what comes next. When you align assignments and transitions like this, you will have the flexibility to line up other important life events as well, such as much-needed vacation time. If I have any regret about my own separation it is that I did not use some of my eighty days of saved-up and terminal leave to take a round-the-world trip. I overheated my shredder blades and jammed up my own transition by starting my new job almost immediately. All I ended up doing was depriving myself of once-in-a-lifetime opportunities. In retrospect, I realize why that terminal leave is so important. At no other time in your life will you have:

1. Unlimited medical-insurance coverage,
2. Unlimited emergency-evacuation insurance, and
3. A full paycheck, all while you are on vacation.

Most civilian employers do not allow terminal leave. They will liquidate final vacation time to reduce the risk of incurring liability should the employee become sick or injured while on leave. The military, or government, offers the last opportunity you may ever get to actually take this kind of paid vacation. So do yourself a favor: take that trip. Enjoy your time between careers. Just make sure you line up your next job first.

Your Last PCS

Finally, this is *your* transition. Own it, make it an expression of who you are as a person, as an individual. The question of what you really want for yourself must be answered first, before you can move on to any other endeavors with any sense of true fulfillment. Failure to answer this question will not prevent your finding a good job, but it may prevent your finding a new career that satisfies you and leaves you happy at the end of the day. Anyone can find a job, but a job just pays the bills. Your transition runs the risk of being much longer and much more painful if you do not answer this more fundamental question first. So, before attempting forward motion, you must answer the real, big, important question: *What do you really want?*

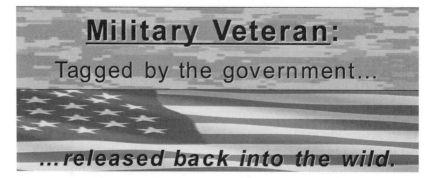

Fig. 1.1. Veteran Bumper Sticker

CHAPTER TWO

Divorced Feelings

"Letting go, really letting go, is letting go of all that is dear, all that is necessary, all that is practical, all that is good, all that you love, all that you hate, all that you envy, and everything that you have. And after you have let go of everything in the world, you find the whole world holding on to you."

— Mavaxiom 21

I remember being asked by friends to describe the toughest thing about leaving the military. There was no single "toughest" thing, really. It was more of a conglomeration of feelings. Some say, "The military is not for everyone." When you start out, you want to believe that the military *is* for you. You want to believe that this is where you belong, and this is who you are. But you change as a person over time when you are in the military. The military forces you to grow up, and in doing so some people grow out of the military. It is not an altogether bad thing to grow as a person, but it sometimes spells the undoing of the thing that caused that growth in the first place. In this, the military is like any relationship. Relationships are built on the zeal and attraction of initial encounters, the excitement and romantic notions of possibilities. Over time, reality sets in, and the participants have to take a couple of steps back and decide whether they can live with the reality of the relationship. What we want to believe comes into sharp contrast with the way things really are, and then we need to decide if that is what we really want.

Splitting the Assets

Although bad things can happen to individuals in the military, the military in and of itself is not a "bad" thing. On the contrary, military service for some is what saves them from the chaotic existence of an undirected life. The military gives people purpose and training. Service to one's country is one of the oldest and noblest of professions. Military forces throughout history have espoused great principles in common: unity, discipline, courage, dedication, and vigilance in service to country.

In some ways, the military saves its members from their own shortcomings. It focuses them, directs them, and builds usable and definable qualities into them. I benefited from much that the military offered, especially by way of professional networking and exposure to new technologies. The military surely benefited as well from my hard work and service, and so neither walked away from the relationship empty-handed.

Everyone leaving the military should think about what the military has done for them. As much as each person sacrifices for the military, each accomplishes and gains *from* the military. The following is an interesting exercise. If you want to be especially judicious, divide a tally sheet into two sides. On one side, list the pluses, or "pros," and on the other, the minuses, or "cons" of military service. List the things that the military enabled you to accomplish, versus the things you can no longer live with.

Some of the things the military enabled me to accomplish:

1. A bachelor of science degree in aerospace engineering, mostly paid by a Reserve Officer Training Corps (ROTC) scholarship.
2. A master of arts degree in business, three-quarters paid by military tuition assistance.
3. A master of arts degree in computer resource management, three-quarters paid by military tuition assistance.
4. A master of science degree in strategic intelligence studies, through assignment to the Joint Military Intelligence College.

Less formally, my service also: led to the Central Intelligence Agency publishing a condensed version of my master's thesis; paid me enough for world travel; paid off my truck (that I drove for more than fifteen years and 229,000 miles, a story unto itself); assigned me to visit, and live in, diverse parts of the country; introduced me to interesting people; cared for my health; motivated me to move on from unhealthy influences; gave me incredible access to the inner workings of the Intelligence Community; and taught me a profession. Obviously I could continue, but the point of the exercise is to realize that there was a lot of personal good to come out of service to my country.

Drawing up the Papers

For better or worse, for richer or poorer, in sickness and in health, there is a sacred bond between all military personnel that civilians cannot understand. Citizens can see aspects of it on television or in movies, but without *living* its familial vows— hating it, loving it—they can only imagine what a life in military service is all about. At times, the military is a domineering foster parent, a constant taskmaster always telling you exactly what is right and wrong for you. The system never ceases telling you what to do, and how to do it. And you listen, at first with resentment, and then because you depend on it. You end up doing exactly what your foster parent tells you to do, and then, just when you begin to wonder why anyone would ever join a family like this, you realize that you *are* the military. You are writing its policy, upholding its regulations and traditions, and mentoring its new children that have just arrived. You do all this because you realize that the military is a devoted partner trying to protect you and take care of you.

If you come to the military from a dysfunctional home, abuse, or poverty, it becomes your new and better home. It gives you the means to move on from everything in the past that ever held you back from being a better person, or achieving more, or just being yourself. The military loves all its children, in its own strange way. It offers tough love up front, showing you the way to belong. And once you belong, you are bonded through vows pledging duty and honor to your country, against the backdrop of centuries of history.

"Reality is frightening enough, without you trying to deceive yourself into believing that it is *not* real."

—Mavaxiom 22

With so much going on in the military, and so many benefits for its members, some might ask, "Why would you ever leave?" Well, everything comes with a cost. For me, the costs began to outweigh the benefits. For others, the benefits are *more* than ample to carry them to their eventual retirement.

As has already been mentioned, there is sometimes a difference between how people perceive something, and its reality. I call the difference "reality dysplasia." Again, this is another invented term on my part. Dysplasia is a medical term, from the Greek for "bad form." It can apply to many conditions. Reality displasia is a condition where the state of the real world is taken over, replaced, or changed with something that is simply not real. I am sure many readers are already getting a mental picture of what I mean. It can be a partial or total loss of connection between the state of things as they actually exist, as opposed to an idealistic notion. Consequently, reality displasia manifests itself as a state of mind where what is actually experienced or seen, especially when it is grim or problematic, is moved from its proper perception and given a more pleasant and believable form. For example, reality displasia often convinces military members that the Uniform Code of Military Justice (UCMJ) has no jurisdiction over his or her sex life. Likewise, reality displasia can reject ideas that are simply beyond the comprehension of an individual's mind. Take, for example, management's insistence on the so-called paperless office environment, which is really just a symptom of a larger, organizational reality displasia.

Before I ever joined the military, I suffered from a reality dysplasia that I attribute to an overactive imagination. I cannot say that the military cured me of the condition as much as it pointed it out to me in repetitive detail. The military is good about that sort of thing. Those in her ranks do not sugar coat their observations of an individual's inherent flaws, weaknesses, vulnerabilities or shortcomings, and for that I am entirely grateful. Some reading this may be making an almost uncomfortable association. Others reading this will have already divorced the military, and their resultant feelings may still echo unpleasantly.

At my final duty station, I spent so much time arguing with my commanding officer and being counseled at his office that I got to know his secretary well. She was a wonderful woman, a little older, and much wiser, at a time of pleasant change in the seasons of her life, and we enjoyed our conversations and occasional flirting. One day she mentioned that many of our conversations reminded her of the sorts she would have at the meetings of her Tuesday-night "social group." She invited me to come along to one, and, at her pleasant insistence, I could scarcely refuse. Her group was actually one of a number of such groups that met at the same time at the local community center. She greeted me at a food table and showed me to a room for newcomers, then she went to another room with the "advanced group."

Laden with free donuts and coffee, I met the many newcomers in my designated room, all of us in chairs arranged in a circle.

As I looked about for attractive women, it struck me that these people, all grown-ups, were veterans of life who seemed a little worn around the edges. They were roughly my age, but appeared to have gone through more challenging times. The women did not look as well made-up, and the men not as confident, as those I was accustomed to in more social settings. The atmosphere was somewhat sobering. I ate my donuts slowly, carefully paying attention to everyone. One by one, in turn, they identified themselves, and related how long they had been married before their divorces.

I was sitting in a divorce group! What was I doing there? I had never been married, let alone divorced. While they continued discussing their feelings, I tried to figure out how to politely excuse myself. Then something odd happened. As each in the circle spoke of loss, sadness, anger, a sense of failure, resentment, and a host of other feelings that I struggled with myself, I began to identify with these people. I could relate my feelings to theirs. As each speaker shared, and my turn came closer and closer, I thought of what I would say, and how to put my experiences into a form that they could relate to.

Then it struck me. I would couch all my experiences with the Air Force as if I were speaking of a marriage. All my references to the Air Force would be to "her," and my references to my military service would be to "our marriage." The result was an epiphany. The skies opened with revelation that the feelings I was having regarding my pending departure from the military were the *same* as those felt by people going through a divorce. I had been married to the military, and I was divorcing. I had taken vows, had sacrificed my time and energies and the possibilities of what else I might have done or become, and I was about to extinguish my vows to the service.

As I spoke, a hand came to rest on my shoulder. I could feel all my emotions bubbling up from a place deep inside that I had not wanted to disturb. But now my deepest feelings were not going to wait for me to come down to get them—they were coming to me. In a mere moment that I could not have expected, I was in communion with others with whom I found I shared a great similarity. My fellow group members had entered into sacred trusts as well, had taken vows to abide by solemn rules and shared expectations. Yet their dreams and their unions, too, had been smashed by unrelenting waves of reality. Their journeys had not reached their anticipated destinations, and now they wanted only to carry on in new, healthy directions, with a better appreciation of what they really wanted. In relating to this group the trials of *my* failing "marriage," I finally found solace. I was going through a divorce of my own.

Stages of Military Career-End Grieving

Somewhere along the way, the marriage begins to fall apart. There are the arguments, jealousies, and anxieties, and then there are the tears. So grieve. Grieving is good for you. In 1969, Dr. Elisabeth Kübler-Ross wrote her now-classic book entitled, *On Death and Dying.* In it she described five stages that people experience when they are terminally ill, and emotionally dealing with the end of their lives. I have adapted these generally accepted stages of grieving to apply to dealing with the end of a military career, in terms that military personnel can relate to their circumstances:

1. First there is *denial and isolation,* where you try to tell yourself that you can make it to the twenty-year retirement. You can do it, on your own and alone, if necessary. You can do anything. That is what the military taught you, right?
2. Then there is *anger,* usually directed at everyone and everything that is military. Your anger may derive from initial feelings of failure, or that others you depended on have failed you. This is when you start blaming everybody in the U.S. Armed Forces. Then, when you get to the point where you can finally see blame in yourself, you move on to the next stage.
3. Next is *bargaining,* when you start wrestling with your doubts. You try to convince yourself that you can make it work by somehow negotiating to improve the situation. You start making "deals" with yourself, and try to "sell" yourself on their feasibility. As Kübler-Ross puts it, "entering into some sort of an agreement which may postpone the inevitable."[1] But this never works. In that realization, the tailspin begins…
4. The next stage is *depression,* which carries you to profound feelings that you have failed. You punish yourself with thoughts that if only you had tried harder, or had done something differently, it "would have worked out." The realization that you are not a military person is a deathblow to some who saw the military as a source of esteem. For men seeking

validation of their masculinity, the realization that the military is not workable to them can be overwhelming. It seems like the end of the world, but eventually the storm passes.

5. The last stage is *acceptance*. Most people want to fly through the first four phases at light speed, so they can get to this fifth and final phase— and for good reason. At this point, you are ready to let go of all things military, and to move on, without regrets, and without sadness. You are ready to move forward with your life. Before you get to that point, however, you must go through the other painful stages first. If you do not, they will come and find you at a time not of your choosing.[2]

In truth, most people will have lingering aspects of denial, anger, bargaining, and depression throughout the process, and long, long after they think it is really over. The trick is in accepting these feelings into your life. The simple truth is that acceptance means acceptance. It means accepting the reality of the situation that the military is not for you. It might have been right for you once, when you were a different person, but that was a long time ago. Time has come and gone, and *you* have changed. Change is the only certainty in this universe, and your stint in the military confirms it. Whether for eighteen months or for eighteen years, the child who enters the ranks does a whole lot of living, learning, and growing after taking the oath. Conditions that once applied then no longer do, and part of acceptance is realizing that.

Acceptance also means accepting responsibility for what lies ahead of you in life. You no longer need to have lingering feelings of attachment, animosity, desires for restitution, or anything other than a vision of your future. Be at peace with the realization that you must go, and go soon. There will be no need to look back; only to look forward. When it is time to go, you will see that your transition will take a tremendous amount of work, but you will be ready to adjust your life to take on the task. Remember, you are not leaving a job. You are leaving a way of life, a calling that few are called for, and that fewer can make it through.

Making my own transition as an intelligence officer, I looked for every checklist I could find. I called every person that I knew (friend, enemy, or otherwise) who had gone before me and asked for advice with all the rigor of a debriefing. I wanted to know the best approaches for making the change, and understand the most successful tactics, techniques and procedures (TTP). Meanwhile, I wrestled with difficult choices and awkward feelings.

In short, I was not sure what to do. My team was not there to help. I felt alone, exposed, and utterly without the support I had been accustomed to in the military. Without any best way to undertake the task, I soon realized that I would have to make it up as I went. For all those years, I had been accustomed to someone else telling me how things worked, and when to act. Now I was going to have to ask myself what I wanted, and figure out how to get it. It was a life-changing paradigm shift.

As was discussed earlier, part of moving forward requires grieving. Thinking that you are too tough to grieve is not realistic. Strong feelings from your military experience must go somewhere, and dealing with them can present an even greater challenge than just finding a job. If you do not allow yourself these feelings, they will find their own way out—and potentially impact you at inconvenient times.

Thank You For Your Service

I found inspiration in my departure from military service by a great leadership figure. He was a general officer who came to speak to our intelligence unit. As we sat in a big auditorium he advised us not to look down on *any* service member who wanted to leave the military. We were all puzzled. This was a general officer, someone we expected to spout the party line, a member of the good-old-boy network, someone in the business of roping in youngsters to serve "just one more tour." A hush fell over the auditorium as everyone paused in anticipation to hear what this crazy old guy would say next. Was he losing his mind? Were we in for some kind of newsworthy moment? For a second, it felt like riding in the back of a school bus that had just gone over a bump, and everyone was in momentary freefall, about to come crashing back into our folding chairs.

The general went on to say that very few Americans actually commit to serving their country. Those who do so are the exception, not the rule. In essence, he was saying that everyone in the room was head and shoulders above their countrymen and women in service to their country. This was especially true for those who stayed beyond their active-duty service commitment. He was thanking us for just being in; reminding us that service, in and of itself, is cause for pride. We were giving above and beyond, and those leaving the military deserved nothing less than thanks from those staying, and receive well-wishes on their new life journeys. Anything less would undermine the integrity of everything the military stands for. Wow. Where was *that* guy when I needed his kind of leadership? Well, he was right in front of me then, and that is when I needed the inspiration.

So, thank you for your service. Accept it as part of your sacrifice and as inspiration to move on. You will need it. Now that you are in the midst of transition, there is a lot of work to do, and little time to waste. You are embarking on a task that may be tougher than anything you have ever done before. Really.

Some people leave the military and have almost no difficulty transitioning.

> "Those who leave the military are oftentimes the ones who *can* make it on the outside. And those who stay are sometimes those who are just too terrified to leave."
>
> — Mavaxiom 23

Others find it daunting. If your transition is difficult, it does not necessarily mean that you have done anything wrong. Maybe you have simply chosen a difficult route upfront that leads to greater payoffs later. Likewise, having had a smooth transition initially does not mean that you have necessarily taken the correct steps. You may have chosen an easier start, and a hard finish still awaits you. Simply put, there is no right way to make a life change of this magnitude. There is only *your* way, the path that you make for yourself. It is an individual journey, an odyssey in the classic sense, that you can make as simple, or as complex, as you require. However you do it, though, make sure you move forward in your life.

Disappointments of a Relationship Ended

My transition was difficult because nothing else made sense to me. All I ever wanted was to be in the military. When the stumbling years of adolescence beset me, I struggled to uncover a rite of passage to guide me. There was no coming-of-age ceremony that validated my progress. Growing up in religious schools, most of my childhood education was based on uniforms, discipline, and conduct codes. It only seemed natural for me to move on to the next level, the military. It made sense in my mind, but not in practice.

The unfortunate truth was that, almost immediately upon entering the military, I knew something was wrong. It was a gut instinct from the beginning, and it lingered for the entirety of my military experience. In truth, as hard as I tried, and as much as I sought to belong, I never quite felt like I really "fit in." I worked with good people. They had come from all around the country, and from different walks of life. Like me, many were given opportunities in upward mobility and made the best of them. We all had our own vision of what the military experience was supposed to be but the day-to-day reality was slightly different. This disconnection led some to disappointment, and then they began to stand out. I stood out almost immediately, and not necessarily in a "good" way. The implicit rule was simple: "Keep your mouth shut, and make it to retirement."

> "If you're not making waves, you're not underway."
>
> —LCDR Robert "Bob" Peranich, U.S. Navy, 1989

One of the more difficult realizations for me was that the military was not looking for agents of change or visionaries. The military I knew valued loyalty, and cultivated those who demonstrated obedience and conformity, regardless of competence. Those who did not conform quickly found themselves in the spotlight.

Those promoted in the military seemed to be skilled at playing the system. Actual talent became lost somewhere in the pages of status reports. Those in charge were just ordinary men and women, prone to the temptations of human nature. They were not necessarily better, they were simply more experienced at politicking. I began to see my superiors in a new light. They were people who made mistakes, and I began to pay close attention to the politics in the upper echelons of organizational rank structure. Seeing these kinds of corporate politics in action, especially at high levels, was disheartening. Watching the dynamics of unnatural selection was cause for concern because the best were not moving up, they were moving out, and those who ascended seemed to do so not on merits but on capitulating to the status quo. Finding a good mentor was consequently no easy task. There were a few, here and there, but I was looking for someone to look up to, learn from, and emulate—not clean up after. Subordinates need leaders to follow. What I was hoping for from the military was not materializing, and the strain of disappointment began to weigh on the relationship

The flaw in my perception of the military was believing in the biographies of its founders. The great warrior-leaders who built the services had long since departed. Any of them in the service today would not last long. They would surely draw so much fire for their uncom-

> "My anxiety stems from a recollection that not so long ago it was acceptable to have people like me burned at the stake."
>
> —Mavaxiom 34

mon personalities that their careers would be short. In fact, some of those leaders actually suffered that fate simply in attempts to push their (rightful) causes forward.

The business of the military is about raining death and destruction down on adversaries. It requires pinpoint focus, and an unwavering integrity by those in positions of leadership. I hoped that the system would prevent pettiness from overriding practical military necessity. But in my mind, this was not the case. Instead, an approved "process," would account for lapses in skill or experience on the part of an individual. These processes were designed to ensure compliance, instead of critical thinking. I felt as if we were being graded on our attendance instead of our contribution. From this example I learned the value of avoiding decisions, and diffusing responsibility.

In the end, my relationship with the military unraveled for a reason that ends many personal relationships: stagnation. I was no longer growing as a person. My maturation became stunted, and my management was getting in the way. It was not that the Air Force was a soulless organization of automatons. Instead, its leadership lacked the courage to trust its own people to imagine possibilities. I was not allowed to try new things, to experiment, or to take risks. Management was too fearful of failure. Risk aversion was the norm, and in such artificially controlled environments, I was never going to move forward with my own development. The environment of zero-tolerance became an environment of zero-growth, and there just seemed less and less for me to look forward to in future assignments. My inability to adjust to the military was a problem, compelling me to move on to bigger and better things.

So, your marriage is over. Tears have been shed, and you have come to accept that leaving is best for all involved. There is no better way to file the paperwork than to be content with your decision. That means accepting that the war is over for you. Leaving the military means letting go; never wearing the uniform,

"Leadership is not a right; and its privileges can only, in good moral conscience, be enjoyed after all other responsibilities have been satisfied."

—Mavaxiom 35

Dear Marc's Boss,
He quits! Why? 'Cause your office is creating negativity, unhappiness, and a huge urge to leave! So he is running away to Lithuania to join the circus!

—From Marc's Friend

feeling the rank, having that kind of camaraderie, or doing anything in a military way—ever again. You have to leave behind the acronyms, dispense with the jargon, stop talking about war stuff, resist the temptation to collect military memorabilia, and get on with your new life. Let go of it now, forever, and for good. It is time to go. You are a civilian.

Notes

1. Elizabeth Kübler-Ross, *On Death and Dying* (New York: Scribner, 1969), 93.
2. For a complete diagram of the "Stages of Dying," see the figure in Kübler-Ross, 265

CHAPTER THREE

The Business-Minded Spy
Understanding a New Mindset
Outside Socialism

"The most beautiful thing we can experience is the mysterious; it is the source of all true art and science. He to whom this emotion is a stranger, who can no longer pause to wonder and stand rapt in awe, is as good as dead: his eyes are closed."

— Albert Einstein, 1930

W hen you leave the security of military culture, prepare yourself for a shock. People on "the outside" focus more on their own priorities, and may not have the same shared interests you were accustomed to in the military. Outside the military is not the same environment you came to know inside the military. Civilians have their own lives outside of work because for them work is work, not a *lifestyle* the way it is in the military.

Corporate Philosophy for Newcomers

Unfortunately, a transition from the military sometimes leaves people feeling as if they have made the wrong decision. Still, our first lesson in life is that the world outside the womb is harsh. There you were, comfy-cozy, floating in warmth, enjoying the surroundings, and the next thing you know, big, strong people were hanging you upside-down in your cold nakedness, spanking you and laughing at your tearful vulnerability. The business world is no different.

> "Work is not supposed to be fun. That's why it's called work."
>
> —Dr. E. Wheeler, 2006

Some people experience withdrawal immediately on leaving the comfort of their military womb. The reason is simple. For better or worse, no one looks after you outside the military the way they do inside the military. Outside the military you are not ordered to go to the dentist every six months. Civilian companies do not have institutions dedicated to morale, welfare, and recreation. Rest and relaxation (R&R) is a government thing. In the corporate world, the only thing that they want is for you to do your job. Period. They want you to work and keep working. In fact, a real challenge for some military people to overcome is the notion that the only reason for their new civilian job *is* to work. Some struggle to understand that employees are only paid for products and services rendered, not attendance. Anything else you do is your business and on your time. No one is going to tell you what to do during your free time, or when to wake up, but you damn well better be at your job, working, and earning your pay.

For some former military (and government) personnel, that prospect can be scary. No more mandatory "all hands" formations or "team-building" exercises will pull people from their cubicles. Those cubicles are there for a reason: to make money. For others leaving the military, this prospect is a refreshing idea, as perhaps now they will have a greater chance of being compensated accordingly for all the work that they did before in the military. Such individuals may even be highly motivated to leave so they can finally do their jobs, without an endless stream of distractions from their tasks.

Clearly, an individual's transition out of the military owes a great deal to how the individual operated while in the military. For those who were "hiding" in the military, their time is up, and now they face the harsh reality of having to work for a living. For those who worked hard to "make a difference" in the military, their discharge is an opportunity to finally unfold their wings and claim the sky as their own.

Many civilian employers are happy to hire military people. With these employers, veterans enjoy a reputation as hard workers, dedicated team players, individuals who wake up early, stay in shape, and do what they are told. In the minds of these employers is a certainty about the benefits of hiring veterans, and military members who understand this can leverage that perception to their advantage. Five important factors are worth remembering:

First—and absolutely foremost—civilian employers constantly seek hard workers because hard workers produce far more profit than slackers.

Second, dedication is extremely valuable. Employers will make more money, over a longer period of time, from dedicated employees than from equally hardworking employees who will soon move on to other opportunities. Remember when you become a civilian, you can once again vote with your feet. If you do not like your job, you do not have to wait around for another duty assignment. You just quit. Of course, when you quit, you also do so without income, medical benefits, or anything else. You are free to go (and do) as you please as a civilian, but you are really on your own. If you are wholly dedicated to an effort, and will see it through to completion, employers will see you as an asset, as an investment. This is so because no matter how wretched the project, dissatisfying the task, or management, or pay, you will not leave until you are done. This gives managers (with employees like you) one less thing to worry about.

Third, most jobs require the coordinated efforts of many people who are (preferably) working together smoothly. Although the team principle is central to military philosophy, it is not as common in the civilian sector. Businesses with a great deal at stake grudgingly send their trusted employees to expensive seminars to build team skills. But civilian employers who hire veterans know that they are getting ready-made team players, and those team philosophies could possibly (and profitably) rub off on fellow staff members. Civilian employers hope for this because the imperative in the minds of civilian employees is to work and then go home. Remember, this is the business world. Dog-eat-dog is not just a cliché. It is do or die in much of corporate America. Managers realize that trust, camaraderie, and cooperation build invaluably cohesive office environments in the long run. Veterans bring this kind of good fortune in a civilian office.

Fourth, employing early-waking military people ensures that at least someone will make it to the office and get things started before others arrive. For a civilian boss, there is nothing like knowing that someone actually likes to be in the office early. Although early rising is routine to the military, it is not a foregone conclusion for civilian employees. Employers hope that the eagerness of veteran employees to arrive early will influence the rest of their

Figure 3.1. Walking 86th Intelligence Group Patch[1]

employees to be early, be more ready to take on tasks, and be willing to tackle tasks longer throughout the day.

Fifth, is the perception of military people as physically fit, in shape, and healthy. Outside the military, both employee and employer pay for health insurance. These plans are expensive, and are more so for people with health problems. Thus it behooves employers to hire healthy and health-minded individuals. Although regulations on physical fitness exist in the military they do not in the civilian world. In fact, employers do little to encourage fitness in their employees, because the prime concern of employers is profit.

Business output is more important than the resting heart rate of its employees. Resting anything is unprofitable to employers; they pay their employees to work, not to go to the gym. Wiser employers recognize that employees who actively attend to their own wellness and physical fitness are long term assets to their work. Health becomes one less thing for a manager to worry about.

A New Sense of Belonging

In the military, everything was "free." I love that word, "free." There is a fantasy-like quality to it now that I have long since departed from the military. Nothing is "free" anymore, especially not in the free-market world of capitalism. You have to work for *everything*. You have to pay for everything. The more you work, the more you get paid, and the more you can afford. It is that simple. This new reality is daunting for separating service people accustomed to the spoils of military life. For those merely contemplating separation, the thought of having to take on the burden of all these new expenses can be a deterrent against ever starting the separation process.

Most leaving the military understand that civilian life is focused on imperatives that are different than the military. The esprit de corps that military members are accustomed to is somehow missing in civilian life. The team concept that military members come to expect as the focus of their sense of belonging differs greatly on the outside. Cohesion at work is something only hoped for by civilians, as opposed to the daily necessity it is in the military. For example, as a civilian you might consider yourself an employee of your parent company, or of the subsidiary you work for, or of the regional office you work in. In other contexts, you might identify your team by the sort of customers it works with, by the goal of its efforts, by its expertise, or even by your particular skill set. Take your pick.

The military *tells* you whom you belong to, and daily reinforces that sense of belonging. In the military people recite the team specialties they are given, such as "I am M.I." (military intelligence), or indicate the unit they are assigned, such as "1 I.D." (First Infantry Division), or echo their given service motto ("Semper fi"), or call out their particular service's acknowledgment ("Hoo-ah!"). There are constant reminders of belonging and purpose in the military. In the civilian world, all your associations, loyalties, pay sources, and so on are much more complicated and much less

meaningful collectively. That can leave many who separate feeling disconnected and without the sense of belonging they had in the military.

Winnowing Wheat from Chaff

In the transition process, you may suddenly find yourself unable to move
forward. The realization of all the new responsibilities you will have as a
civilian may seem overwhelming, but there is hope. Help is available from
a variety of sources prior to being thrown into the fray of the dog-eat-dog
job market. Many are available on base, like the Transition Assistance Program (TAP). This is also a good time to go to the base Education Office
and ask them about the G.I. Bill. You might be surprised what you are entitled to upon separating. Benefits you may never have dreamed of may be
available, and the only reason you never knew about them was because you
were too busy before. Now you have a reason to inquire, and that reason
has become a priority.

Philosophically, it is time to start wrestling with really big, tough questions like "What do you want?" These kinds of questions are a little intimidating at first so a little preparation is probably in order. The answer to what
a person "wants" may require first answering several smaller questions.
Depersonalizing the task can help bypass any psychological brick walls. To
begin, look at the question in a different way.

When imagining what kind of work you want to do, you must also
imagine everything else that will come along with that new job. It is not just
the work, it is the people, the office environment, the location of the work,
and everything else to be encountered in a day. To do this really effectively,
reflect on your current environment with painful honesty.

Based on your current situation, and the follow-on environment you
envision for yourself as a civilian, honestly answer the following two questions:

1. Is there *any* intellectual stimulus for me in this new environment?

And,

2. Can I stand the people I'll be working with—for most of the day?

Intrinsic frustrations exist with *any* job. Pressure to perform, stress,
demands on time, and so forth, will all be present in a new job environment.

There is no getting away from that. The real question for you, then, becomes: can I live with the environment that is already there? No matter how inclined you are to "make a difference," do not expect things to change at your new civilian job. Do not expect to change other people's attitudes or biases or prejudices. The environment is the environment is the environment. Those who go into a new job thinking that they will change things "for the better" or to "their way of thinking," condemn themselves to exponential amounts of work as is necessary. If you carried a heavy load in the military, your load will get considerably heavier on the outside, and there will be no one there to protect you. The rules have changed. There will be no rank structure to depend upon, no underlying system that will catch you if you make a "bad call," and there may be little of the camaraderie so reliably there in the military. Why front-load an already difficult job search with unnecessary stress?—so decide upfront if you can (or cannot) live with the new environment.

After you accept the intrinsic frustrations of your new civilian workplace, your next question should be whether you will get anything out of the job itself. Does the new job offer acceptable trade-offs to the usual frustrations that arise from all work? Can you live with the boring tasks, or will the environment become toxic to you over time? While in the military, many people can plan out an escape to their next assignment before the current one becomes toxic. The unfortunate thing with this approach is that the timelines to toxicity have a trend of getting shorter and shorter with each new assignment. No matter what the job, no matter where the assignment, no matter how the rewards might beckon, the inevitability of burnout make this approach to civilian work impractical, and potentially undermining to your new career.

If that strategy was common for you, then you have an even more pressing need: to self-evaluate your motivations in selecting any future job. This will not be easy because it requires you to acknowledge your interpersonal limitations, your social pain-threshold, and/or your emotional vulnerabilities. These limitations will become a brick wall, and self-defense mechanisms that may reduce your psychological discomforts will get in the way of your ability to function in a new job setting. There is no point in ignoring them now, and it is probably too late to back out of moving forward, so address them while you still have time. You are in this process for good, and you cannot afford to let anything get in the way of your success—most of all yourself.

Some Basic Business Concepts

There are a few basic business imperatives that overrule many of the military's basic principles and driving directives. Realizing them early will help you adjust. They include, but are not limited to:

1. The Bottom Line – If you cannot bring in revenue for a company, the company has no reason to employ (or retain) you.
2. Assets & Liabilities – If you prove more of a liability to your company than an asset, the company has no reason to keep you on its payroll.
3. Delegation – Once hired, do not perform tasks someone else does for you. However (and by whomever) the job gets done, just make sure that it is done right (according to customer desires), on time, and under budget. If it is not, the delegation trail leads back to the one person (you) who caused many to fail. Business teaches you how to take credit for accomplishments, and profit, but it is ruthless in its intolerance of failure.
4. Market Worth – Military people have virtually no idea what their skills are worth on the outside. None. What you do not know about your worth to a company will always equal the difference between what it should offer you as a salary, and what it actually does when it hires you.
5. "Oops!" – This occurs when an interviewer asks you for a salary range. If you name a figure, and the interviewer says, "No problem, we can pay you that," the interview is over. Get up, leave, and do not come back. You blew it; you just *undersold* your market worth. Do not answer their calls for at least two years. Regard this experience as an opportunity to get paid your *true* market worth elsewhere.
6. Profit – It is *all* about profit. Period.
7. Risk – You have not assessed your true market worth until the interviewer's eyes roll, and he or she groans aloud, saying, "No, we cannot pay you that." *Then* (and only then) do you really know the ballpark range of your true market worth.
8. Salary Negotiations – Figure out what "year-end bonuses," "stock options," "out-of-cycle incentives" and "spot promotions" are all about before you ever walk into an interview. If you do not, you will make it all the more profitable for the company to hire you.
9. The Upper Hand – It can be scary to leave the military and start over in a completely new environment. It can be even scarier if you do not know what the hell you are doing. Get smart quick. Do the research

(AKA "intelligence") and seek help from those who have gone before you (AKA "advance scouts"). To be forearmed is even better than to be forewarned, especially where your new salary is concerned.

10. Gross & Net –Your gross is the salary that your offer-letter says you will be paid; the net is what you actually "see" after taxes, benefits, 401K, and everything else are taken out. If your net pay is less than what you brought home in the military, then you blew it. You should have read this book (cover to cover) before negotiating.

11. Overhead – the cost (in addition to your gross salary) that a company bills a client, like the government if you are a defense contractor. Overhead covers the operating costs of the company (its administrative staff, paper, pencils, maintenance costs, and the salaries of its managers). Overhead costs charged to a client are roughly twice the salary cost of the people employed on the contract. That means that whatever you make in salary, your company is also making and applying to its profit margin. Twice the salary is only a rough estimate. Some companies bill three times as much as your salary, or more, depending on the client.

12. Real Metrics – there is only one "real" metric for success in the business world. That metric is usually accurate to the second decimal point and is preceded by a currency symbol (usually, "$") when tabulated. Fail to accurately compile this metric and you are history.

The World's Most Successful Form of Socialism

Long before I ever departed the military, I realized that the military operates in ways that significantly differ from those of the civilian sector. The imperatives of combat necessitate decisive action by large numbers of individuals, all synchronized by centralized control. For obvious reasons, allowing freedom of choice and authority at the individual level would risk disrupting smooth military operations. That social structure seems to run completely *counter* to the very system that the military is tasked to defend: capitalism. If someone is fighting for capitalism as a way of life, then it is probably worth having that someone understand what that fight is all about.

Capitalistically is *not* how the military operates at all. In the military, no one owns anything, and there is no real profit to be realized. In fact, there are specific regulations against it. So, essentially, people who enter the military remove themselves from the capitalist culture they are defending, and adopt a different kind of culture that is more conducive to warfare.

In the past, our rationale for maintaining a large, standing military was to defend the United States and its allies against the threat of the Soviet Union. Ah, the good old days, when global post-nuclear death and destruction made *sense*, along with the clash of political ideologies. To the Soviets, capitalism was demonized as propping-up ruthless banking institutions manipulating consumer populations, enriching the treasuries of corporations who exploited workers, and further enriched greedy billionaire aristocrats who ruled over the proletariat in neo-feudalist fashion. I suspect that the Soviet Union would have loved Enron, had either survived.

It therefore seems ironic that the military, in defense of capitalism, indoctrinates its recruits in a system that most closely resembles socialism. By removing military recruits from their capitalist surroundings and controlling all aspects of their lives in increasingly centralized ways, some might say that military culture resembles the theoretical aspects of America's Cold War nemesis. Since the fall of the Soviet Union, the most successful form of socialism may be embodied in the U.S. military. Why is this relevant to job search? If correct, it illustrates the degree to which military members must transition their mindsets to find their place back in the capitalist civilian society they once defended. Like the Soviet Union, that transition may be messy without good economic know-how.

The more I looked at how the military functions, its values, policies, and theories, the more I realized why returning to civilian life is so difficult. Not only do they change uniforms, they must change ideologies. They go back to capitalism from a system where decisions were made for them. Under socialism, as with the military, the central committees control production, distribution, and exchange. Under capitalism, however, all commerce is in the hands of individuals, often without regard for education, experience, or professional training. So, for example, twenty- and thirty-somethings, by virtue of their computer skills, now run companies while older employees unable to keep up with technological advancement sweep floors.

Those who have spent a career (or even a few years) in the military tend to emerge feeling overwhelmed by a need to "catch up." They are outsiders in their own society, and desperately need a jump-start in the ways of the capitalist world. This strange new capitalist world appears to have no official rank structure, no uniforms, no regulation of behavior; everybody seems to do whatever they want. For some indoctrinated in military socialism, capitalism seems like out-and-out chaos. If you fall into this category, you will have to learn a whole new approach to earning your keep. The skills you bring to the table even at the outset will be valuable, so see to it that you are appropriately compensated.

Note

1. Credit for the design of this unit patch must be shared with Margaret Matera (former Major, U.S. Air Force Reserve).

CHAPTER FOUR

New Shoes
Finding New Footwear after a Tsunami Changes the Landscape

"With pain comes growth, and vice versa."

— Mavaxiom 41

Leaving behind military service is life-changing. It is such a profound event psychologically for some people that afterward they gauge all life events as having occurred before or after their departure from the military—as if it were a great, cataclysmic divide. The period prior to entering into military service has a childhood feel for many, and the time just after separation seems to bear the unmistakable burden of adulthood. Somewhere in the middle we do a lot of growing up. Sure, there are fun and games, but for almost all military members there is a span of time precariously poised between carefree adolescence and the weight of adult responsibilities, worries, and obligations. Growing up comes with many awkward adjustments.

A Wave of Change

Buddhism builds its entire ethos around the point that where there is life there is suffering. In the Buddhist view, it is our attachment to earthly things and desires (or cravings) that are the causes of human suffering. Leaving the military is no different. All that you enjoyed, all the people you

35

cared about, your friends, lovers, co-workers, bosses, subordinates, the desk
you flew or the equipment you played with, virtually everything gets left
behind as you move on to become a civilian. The whole world shifts slightly
in one swift tremor of perception, and all of it originates with you. It feels
as if you are the epicenter of a tiny alteration in the fabric of the universe
that no one else seems to fully appreciate. Trying to hold on to anything
from the past that gave you a pleasurable sense of stability only seems to
lead to further suffering.

Though only a few things truly change during the upheaval of your separation from the military, the energy of the event yields unimagined consequences. On earth, a tiny ripple in the ocean's depths transforms into a wall
of destruction on seashores thousands of miles away. That is the nature of
the change. The energy released by your transformation travels upward, outward, and around, and through all the aspects of your life like a tsunami.
The change might seemingly impact your life at a low level, but then carries
its effects miles inland on the shores of your life.

Anything that you rely on that is not nailed down feels churned up and
heaped on a growing wave of debris. You will look at, and think about, all
that you are, all that you have done, all that you want, all that you need, and
then feel countless fragmentary decisions converging on a point where you
must learn how to move forward in your life. As if caught in a tsunami, you
may find yourself trying to move to safer, higher ground, clinging to almost
irrational ideas of what really makes sense. But not much will at that point.
You may feel the need to grab onto people you can count on, and things that
you trust, to ride out the initial shock of change. Then it will become abun-
dantly clear what still works, what is really important, and what has become
dead weight to you over the years. You will feel stripped away from everything that you knew and will find yourself in disturbing new surroundings
with wreckage all around.

This is normal. Life-changes of this magnitude do this to people. Not
that this bit of news will make you feel much better after a tsunami of change
has turned your organized and predictable military existence into a debris
field.

Your reasons for leaving the military or government service are complex, and individually dependent. For many (like myself), the military
turned out to be completely different than expected. I strove to master my
profession and believed that my expertise would be valued. I thought decision makers would value my contribution, and then I realized that some-

thing else was going on, something that I did not want to be part of. So, I left. When I did leave, willingly tearing myself away from the profession I wanted to be part of was a jarring experience, complete with an immense emotional debris field, and much suffering. Your experiences may vary. I can only hope so.

The New Shoes Do Not Fit Quite Right

One of the common feelings when separating from the military is an uncomfortable sense that the new place "fits," but not quite right. Imagine strolling a beach barefoot after a tsunami, feeling vulnerable and exposed amid the torn houses, broken glass, debris, and who-knows-what all around on the beach and in the surf. You are looking through all of it, all that you were, and all the things you did. The first thing you find is a pair of brand-spanking-new combat boots. This pair is intact because their laces were tied together shortly after purchasing them. You have not worn them since, but now you have no choice. This is all you have, and you are grateful to have a pair of boots. Then you begin sifting through everything else. You start making piles of stuff: awards and decorations over here, fitness reports over there, promotional recommendations to the left, and all your old uniforms to the right. You have got a million things on your mind, and you have no idea where to begin. You do what the military has taught you to do: you start organizing everything you can. You start imposing order on chaos. And then, inexplicably, you begin to notice something that bothers you more and more until it becomes impossible to continue working without feeling pain. Your new boots are killing your feet.

The way you feel with a new pair of shoes that hurt is how it feels after separating from the military. Nothing fits quite right, and there may be a little discomfort. Nothing is going kill you, but even simple tasks take on new challenges amid the chaos. As most military people recognize, you really do not "break in" combat boots as much as *they* break in your feet. The pain of squeezing yourself into an unyielding new life can be similarly daunting. The new life does not appear to give as much as you would like, and you have to thicken your skin against its discomfort. Over time, the shoe softens and your feet toughen. The same is true with transitioning to civilian life. Eventually, the discomfort starts to give, a little at first and more later. Soon, an agreeable coexistence, or *modus vivendi*, is reached and like your boots, your new life turns into a perfect fit. For now, however, time is your enemy.

After the military, people try to quickly reimmerse themselves into what they think is the right fit, and then become overwhelmed by inexplicable discomfort. This is because underlying issues have not yet been addressed. Since the military teaches personal sacrifice, veterans try to persevere through the pain. But now, as a civilian, there is no team, or mission, or corps. It is only *you* in your new life, and your feet still hurt. It seems that everything hurts, but you have no time to attend to the pain. There is so much work to do. So what do you do? Where can you find a new pair of shoes that actually fit as they did in the "good old days?"

Perhaps a better question is to ask yourself whether you really want to go back to the good old days? Were they actually all that *good*? People confronted by change all at once are quick to latch onto something that they know, something familiar, secure, predictable, safe and, most of all, controllable. In this sense, reminiscing will not solve the problems that you experience while in transition. Reminiscing means clinging on to old ways, craving the past, and in the strictest Buddhist traditions, this is critical mass for suffering. And, reminiscing does not answer the really big, important question:

What do you really want?

Think long and hard about that question. Will the same old answer to this question suffice in a new, post-separation tsunami life? The results might surprise you....

A Greek River

Answering the question of what you really want may also require answering other questions in the process. For example, how much do you want to change your life? Is it a little bit, or a lot—and how much can you stand? Only you can know the answers. Ask yourself these questions in the section entitled The Desired Range of Change, which offers some options to consider as well, and examines the outcomes from each. But no matter how you decide, the options will require work. Before jumping to that section, though, here is some philosophical gristle to chew on first.

No change is easy. We can never be completely sure of the outcomes that will ensue from our actions. All too often people think they know what the outcomes of their actions will be. Maybe they have "done this before," and think that it will be "just like the last time." Anyone trusting this approach should be warned that Murphy's Law applies everywhere.

In the absence of knowing exactly what will happen, you should perhaps adjust your expectations and shoot for a desired range of options, as opposed to a specific outcome. If you have a good shot at a job, take it, but what will you do if Plan A fails? Do you have a Plan B? More importantly, would either Plan A or Plan B make you happy? Just because you did those sorts of work before does not mean that they will make you happy in the future. Remember, we all change over time; we grow up and our tastes change, and the things that seemed exciting in the past prove really boring to us later. The process of change requires that you think about these changes *before* you put yourself right back into your original setting. Sometimes people do this because it is "a known," and is therefore "safe." But such choices set us back because they fail to take into account how much we really change over time. The time that calluses our feet and softens our boots is what makes for a perfect fit. It does so by changing all aspects of the fit. Not accounting for the inevitability of such change only invites disaster. These situations also obstruct personal growth and development. People who think that playing it safe will make them happy are looking for a stagnant form of happiness.

No matter how well we think we can navigate the hazards of a situation, we invariably encounter uncharted variables. Even if you could control every aspect of a situation, there would still be something else that you would probably miss. The military changes everyone, no matter who you are, or where you come from. Separating from the military is life changing as well. If you could go back to the hometown you left behind when you joined the military, you would find it somehow different. If no one in that town had moved, no buildings had been built, and nothing else had changed, you would *still* find it different, in one important way. The town would be different because *you* had changed during your time in the military. That town is no longer the same old town that you left because you are no longer the same person as when you left. The transition to a new life after the military is similarly challenging. The same is true for a new job. When people plan their exit from the military, many opt to go back to the field that they knew. But, like the small-town experience, the same job you did in the military will not be the same job you do as a civilian. Technology will change, policies will change, the economy will change, social values will change and, most importantly, *you* will change from who you were while you were in uniform.

So a very important aspect of the adjustment will be in formulating reasonable expectations that take the inevitability of change into account.

For thousands of years, people have pondered this issue. Time, change, and happiness are central to philosophical inquiry. Some 2,500 years ago, the Greek philosopher Heraclitus proposed his own analogy for the process of change. He likened change to crossing a flowing river. In life, he said, you cannot step into the same river twice. He posited that with every step, and as the water flows, you enter a changing stream that has come and gone before you have completed the crossing. Likewise, venturing back to the same (old) line of work, to a similar job that you had in the military that represents a "known," creates a riverbank you no longer recognize. You thought it was the same stretch of water, and maybe your old tracks are in the mud, but something has happened between the two events. Between the crossings, the river has carried sand, and silt, and rocks, and fishes downstream, so that all the conditions that were there the first time have long since changed. Your own transition from military to civilian life might be similar.

Now you are getting a sense of how change affects all aspects of your life. Likewise, I hope, you are getting a sense that adapting to civilian life has more than just finding a job. Anyone can find a job, but not everyone can deal with the range of effects brought on by change. Fortunately, this is not change that you do not have some control over. You can deal with this event by adjusting your expectations, and examining a full range of options. These options have been outlined on the following pages. When you look at them, ask yourself a few questions to get a sense of what it is you want, what you need, how much you can handle, and ultimately how to get to the other side of the river of separation.

The Desired Range of Change

This section is designed to stimulate thinking and feelings about what you want to do, whatever your range of responsibilities. For example, you might find a great job with terrific pay and benefits, but what do you do when you become bored, unchallenged, and just plain unhappy? And then there is the question of bills. Everyone has to pay the bills. There is no getting around them. If you have a spouse and a family, they depend on you to take care of them. That is a responsibility far beyond yourself that you cannot ignore. But, people who are fearful of their separation from the military may just grab at *any* work that guarantees to pay the bills regardless of the job. As an implication later, what good are you to yourself (and those who depend on you) if you implode from work stress and can no longer function?

Some people try to rationalize their decisions, regardless of whatever it is that they really want. They will say things like they took the job to "get their foot in the door," but then will move on to something else. Some people choose a huge company that runs exactly like the military, just because they know what to expect—even though they hated the military. In considering your options, and the degree of the transition you really want to make, contemplate the plausible range of change that you might desire, as compiled below.

Unreasonable Expectations

People join the military for any number of reasons: patriotism, family legacy of service, job opportunities, college scholarships, you name it. Sometimes the expectations going in are not realistic, exacerbating the separation process later. For example, some people join the military hoping to find a new family. Perhaps the home they left behind was not healthy, or helpful, or even stable. What their family lacked to promote their personal growth is sought after in the military. Perhaps they left behind an abusive environment, and the military became an escape for them. Whatever the case, military service can be more than just a job for some, it becomes a new home, and this makes the task of separation more complicated because the military quite likely *is* their source of emotional stability. Removing them from that source of stability does not just feel like chaos, it is chaos for them. Since the military is not a lifelong profession, it is inevitable that this source of stability will have to be removed eventually.

For me, the military seemed a natural surrogate for stability, discipline, purpose, and rational authority. I expected time-tested pragmatism to be the driving imperative to national security. In this I thought that my values would align with the values of the military. In this way, I was willing to commit and sacrifice to sensible and coherent principles. Even this would succumb to disappointment. Specifically, my disappointment related to the Pareto Principle, or 80-20 rule. Simply put, the 80-20 rule asserts that 80 percent of the work in an organization is done by 20 percent of its people. Those driven, meticulous, committed people go out of their way to ensure the smooth functioning of *everything*. They do so because they believe in

Table 4.1. The Range of Desired Change

1.	**Complete Change** "departure"	New line of work • Leaving your military specialty / training behind • Starting at the bottom of a new learning curve • Lower wage, or no wage – learning everything from scratch • Medium financial risk, low personal risk
2.	**Radical Change** "security"	Same line of work, but new employer • Going from government to defense contracting • In the middle of a familiar learning curve • Higher wage – maybe teaching others • Low financial risk, high personal risk
3.	**Revolutionary Change** "ownership"	Starting your own company • Much more work on your part • Applying everything you have learned, the way you want it • No wage, in debt – investing in future success • High financial risk, medium personal risk
4.	**Real Change** "joy"	Same line of work, but more satisfying J-O-B • Know yourself and be very discriminating with job offers • At the top of a learning curve, the way you want it • Higher wage— maybe teaching others • Medium financial risk, low personal risk
4a.	**Substantive Change**	• More agency over your own work • Ownership / latitude / creativity in what you do
4b.	**Qualitative Change**	• Making a difference / making change • More rewarding work / happy with contribution
4c.	**Quantitative Change**	• More money ($$$) • Less work? Fewer hours? More vacation time?
4d.	**Good Change**	• Better quality of life / commuting / etc. • More energy / less stress

the institution, perhaps even depend on it like a family. But they soon come to also believe that if they do not do the work, no one else will. Those in what I call "the 20" feel obligated to carry the load for the lazy, the uncaring, scheming, irresponsible, incompetent or just plain incapable, lest the organization suffer. All of you in that 20 percent know who you are, and know exactly what I am writing about.

Those in "the 20" also know that this level of devotion to the institution is no easy task. When you truly believe that those in positions of leadership will reward this extra level of effort, and that recognition never fully materializes, you are posed with a moral dilemma. On one hand, you are duty-bound to obey those above you. But on the other hand, when leadership fails to reward you accordingly, you struggle to understand why. Since twenty-percenters are inherently self-sacrificing, their inner turmoil can only go so far before affecting their physical and psychological health and well-being.

I know all about the 80-20 rule. I am a recovering member of the 20 percent. Over my years in the military, I learned painfully, slowly, and unremittingly how tiring it became to incessantly clean up after others, especially those in positions of authority who disregarded the value of my contributions. By the late 1990s, it appeared to me that the military was looking for careerists, not contributors. Those with a knack for taking credit for other people's work were getting promoted. As the military thinned because of downsizing after the end of the Cold War, the percentage of careerists seemed to increase. Consequently, detecting, locating, tracking, identifying, and characterizing the threats that these careerists posed to twenty-percenters soon took on added urgency. Fortunately, careerists emit observable "signatures" that provide quick and easy telltale indicators of their presence. These indicators are listed below.

From my perspective, careerists lack altruism, the ability to provide real encouragement, or a capacity to inspire people. Fortunately, careerists did not tend to hang around very long. They always seem en route to their next career-enhancing assignment, usually before ever fully learning their current job. Somebody has to take up the slack left by these people. It was a constant problem in my time in the military, which then seemed forever understaffed and overtasked against too many requirements. As the workload went up and the supply of bodies went down, our confidence in authority began to falter. Where was the leadership to focus our mission, prioritize our efforts, and limit our diversions into frivolous activities? It seemed that the main concern was not on doing the job well, but gaining recognition for promotion.

Telltale Signatures of a Military Careerist

- Leaves work by noon Friday, regardless
- Attends training courses clearly unrelated to responsibilities
- Attends all organizational functions held during duty hours
- Serves on all planning committees, in all action cells, at all costs
- Goes out of the way to speak to and hang around senior staff at all functions
- Rarely can be found, or seen functioning, in primary job responsibility
- Somehow has worked "everywhere" and knows "everyone"
- Stays generally less than a year on any given job or assignment
- Moves to next assignment before achieving competency in the current one
- Claims the ability to learn "anything" in less than six months
- Is constantly on a "learning-curve," without any depth of experience
- Is "too busy" to contribute to ongoing efforts, but somehow . . .
- Volunteers, fundraises, and attends community events while on duty
- Displays almost superhuman capacity to cut corners and avoid work
- Lives by "checking the box" and CYA (cover your assets)
- Never wears only the upper rows of service ribbons on uniform
- Carries a clipboard when not driving or eating (the dead giveaway)

I expected the military to be *different* than civilian life. In fact, I was counting on it because I needed to know that "somewhere" there was an environment founded on timeless principles and standards. This was an unreasonable expectation because I put so much dependence on it in the first place. Instead of stability, discipline, and purpose, the military became a game of musical chairs. Careerists endlessly circled around promotion opportunities for the next chance to sit down and put their feet up. These people know who they are, and they will be my most vocal critics.

Family

All you can reasonably expect from any profession is an opportunity to learn new skills and perhaps add to and enhance them for others. Professions normally do not provide people with unconditional acceptance and love. A profession is about satisfying objectives and accomplishing goals, not maintaining the emotional tranquility of its members. In this way, the military cannot be a substitute for family. Those longing for lost nurturing or upbringing should *not* go to the military looking for a home.

Can the military function as a surrogate to family? Sure, especially for those serving together in combat, where all have a vested interest in caring about the emotional state of their comrades. In wartime, the military can be more family than its members may ever know. They will be "friends for life." Yet when war ends, the circumstances that brought individuals together cease to exist, and the surrogate-family members scatter.

For most, the military is a job, a profession—and perhaps even a calling for some. As I have felt, it can be like a relationship where you and the institution share great experiences and emotions. But a vocation does not produce hereditary offspring. Your posterity may seek to enrich their lives in the military, but this union is radically different than one with a spouse. A family comprises people who love you, completely and unconditionally. They do not expel you for misbehaving. Although a family has its own customs, if you do not follow the path of the rest a healthy family will not disown you. Likewise, a healthy family does not require you to prove your worth, or force you to endure trauma as a means of acceptance. A well-adjusted family accepts you for who you are, truly does care about what you have to say, and asks you what you think. A family is *unconditional*.

Note that I used words like "healthy," and "well-adjusted" in describing these family traits. I assumed that this was a prerequisite for the term "family," but also recognize that it might *not* be the case for some people. They may read the previous paragraph only to acknowledge that their childhood and family life *was* very much that way. This raises an interesting point. If your childhood was conditional, maladjusted, or emotionally unhealthy, the demanding and stressful life of military service might actually make sense to you. In fact, it might seem appealing or, dare I say, "normal," because this is how you were raised. If this was the case, then it raises an even bigger dilemma. If the military truly resembles family to select members who had "unorthodox" emotional upbringings, then the transition to the civilian world may be even more challenging.

The Twenty-Percenters

Imagine that you are among the twenty-percenters, or "the 20," meaning the 20 percent of the people who do 80 percent of the work in your organization.

You are the kind of employee who does not need incessant prodding by management. In fact, you probably embody all the traits that bosses find pleasing in their workers. You are passionate about your profession, always seeking improvement, and helping others without a second word. In fact, your very sense of self-esteem is linked to how well you do your job, how much of a difference you make, and how many people you can help by the end of the day.

Twenty-percenters do not just join a profession, they internalize it and *become* that profession. On their job they display depth of knowledge, confidence, and self-assurance. This comes across as strength, just the kind of armor that the military values. But behind that armor, something else may be going on. Over time, some twenty-percenters create a strong, confident, almost impenetrable front devoid of kinks. No matter how thick the armor, however, underneath it lies a soft-squishy human being. Like everyone else their heart shelters vulnerabilities. They just have learned how not to show them, nor ever admit to them. So anything that may prove a vulnerability to their profession remains buried, deep beneath the armor so that they may continue deriving worth and value from their profession.

Unfortunately, what the armor conceals is often simple insecurity. No matter what success the twenty-percenters achieve, no matter how much they work, they may never entirely feel a full sense of satisfaction. What they do not understand is that they may never feel enough satisfaction from their job because emotional worth never has to be proven in the first place. This is their fatal flaw. They were emotionally worthwhile all along. They just never felt this, and tried to achieve that through external actions.

So why is this emotional psycho-babble important to the separating military member? The reason why may be overwhelming for some, so prepare yourself. In truth, no matter how strong such an exterior feels to the wearer, there are some who can see it a mile away. They know it exists, and more importantly know how to manipulate it. In effect, some among you know that the twenty-percenters are striving for emotional acceptance and are willing to work themselves to death to achieve it.

Who are these unscrupulous individuals, who would willfully control others via psychological vulnerabilities? As an intelligence professional, I am authorized to disclose the following, highly guarded secret. Describing such emotional distinctions between people may appear overly sensitive, but consider the following. Manipulating people is a vital component of the intelligence profession, and is relatively simple and expedient once you understand an individual's psychological vulnerabilities. But with this power comes responsibility. Like a weapon it must never be used without cause, and especially not on friendly soil. To penetrate a collection target and gain useful information often requires influencing an adversary's sensitivities and emotional weaknesses. All are fair game on the ideological battlefield of spying. But the use of such tactics against one's own comrades (or subordinates) constitutes a betrayal of trust and a misuse of professional power. One of the reasons why I focus so heavily on the confluence of leadership, trust, and service is because managers are *supposed* to be looking out for their people. In the military, those people are busy looking out for the enemy. Hampering your own people (who are watching out for the enemy), by manipulating their trust, is in my mind akin to sabotage. And yet, it is an all too common occurrence.

For example, some managers would tell me that they worked me harder than everyone else because they knew that they could expect more from me. How nice of them. There are entire categories of unscrupulous managers who manipulate their subordinates' insecurities to achieve their goals. They find the temptation to take advantage of emotional vulnerabilities sometimes too great to resist, especially when their poor planning requires last-minute clean-ups and fixes. Their employees find themselves lured by the promise of opportunities to make a difference, and are eager to contribute, and hence become easy targets.

> "The more I tried to please others, the more they wanted to be pleased, and the *less* they cared about me."
>
> "In a world of employees who seem to just not care, people who do care come at a premium."
>
> —Mavaxiom 43

Managers may never know exactly how much trust is conferred to them via the authority of their positions. Delivered right to the carpet of their offices are people who depend upon them. The ultimate employees are among 20 percent requiring little or no maintenance, care, or feeding because they are on the endless search to make a contribution at any cost. All managers need to do is set such people to the task, step back, and reap the rewards of their hard work. In too many cases, that is exactly what happens.

One of the most unprincipled management techniques is to provide virtually no feedback whatsoever to a twenty-percenter. The perception of a twenty-percenter is, "Well, I guess I didn't work hard enough; maybe if I try *harder* they'll notice my contribution." At this point, the barbed lure is embedded so deeply into the individual that any tug by management will yield more work. But there is no need to do so. The less feedback to the subordinate, the more performance insecurity generated, yielding ever-greater output of results. This can go on until the inevitable employee meltdown.

This meltdown can have several possible outcomes. In the first, members of the 20 percent become members of the 80 percent. By now underachieving, they find less is expected of them, and consequently they no longer work as hard. This is passive-aggressive behavior at its finest. The problem is that this option simply transfers the burden to others. In the second outcome, employees aspire to and strive for their own authority. By becoming manipulative, aping the managers who abused them, they hope to protect themselves from other ruthless individuals preying on vulnerability. This also is an inappropriate outcome because it continues the cycle of abuse. It also adds layers to the psychic armor that ultimately leaves its wearers emotionally unreachable. The third outcome leads to a higher moral ground. This is not the easiest option. It involves absorbing a great deal of negativity, and not reacting in ways that harm others. It requires tremendous patience, resilience, and faith in people. If these demands become too great, circumstances might require contemplating a change in employment.

Your Responsibility to Yourself

In a perfect world, subordinates should be able to trust the lawful orders of their military superiors. In the real world, however, all people are subject to the shortfalls and temptations of human nature. So what *should* a member of the 20 percent reasonably expect from a job? The following is an experiment for those evaluating their current situation. Think about your superiors, and ask yourself the following questions:

1. Can I trust my superiors to act in my best interest? Think about that. It is an important question. It asks if your environment feels safe, and is a place where you can grow without threat or emotional hostility. Based on the behavior you have experienced thus far with your superiors, ask yourself if they would put their interests before your own. Has there been some personal or professional gain for them (rather than the team

or organization) that your participation could have afforded? If so, what was in it for you? If you can trust your supervisors to not take advantage of your vulnerabilities, you have indeed been fortunate.

2. Can I exercise my skills, and do I do so? This doubled question seeks to clarify whether your natural talents and abilities are valued. Consider whether you have been prompted to underachieve by being over-tasked, but underchallenged, in your duties? What have you learned from your work? Does it help your career progression, or are you stuck with work at which you have long since demonstrated proficiency? What can you really hope for from this work? Does it meet any personal or professional needs? Are your being encouraged to be a professional, or are you just going through the moves and doing someone else's dirty work?

3. Am I satisfied working the job? This is an important question because, at the end of the day, if you do not get any satisfaction out of your job, then something is seriously wrong. Do you have the ability or freedom to use your time constructively, and do you actually achieve anything acceptable to yourself, or have you just been wasting your time?

The first two questions ask if you can trust your management to *not* take advantage of your vulnerabilities. The third question asks if you feel useful in your job. They are important questions that you have to ask yourself in any job, military or civilian.

This job examination prompts one final question, and that is, "What makes a good boss?" Any intelligence assessment of a battlefield points out all known threats, their dimensions, and intended targets. Thus far I have tried faithfully to execute an assessor's role. Another side to an intelligence report points out "friendlies" in the area that might lend assistance. My own encounters with great leaders assured me of their enduring presence, here and there, scattered amid the careerists and bureaucrats. Setting them apart from the others were traits that for the most part demonstrated how human they were. For example, the more compassionate leaders were happy to set me loose on projects. They trusted my abilities, only occasionally needing to tug gently on their figurative bungee cord to see how I was doing. Those were the bosses who allowed me room for creativity. To me, they were not bosses or managers; they

"Leaders know how to trust their people."

—Mavaxiom 44

really were leaders. They inspired me to take on more responsibilities and "own" more of my stake in a mission. The best bosses pushed me to make more of myself, seek further education, and outside activities. They had the faculty of giving me room to take risks, experiment, fail and, most importantly, to learn. These leaders were capable of trusting. They were secure enough in themselves to let go, and allow others to shine. They were a pleasure to work for, and with. They made the service worth serving, but they were the minority.

CHAPTER FIVE

Trauma
Returning from the Crash Site

"The right to search for truth implies also a duty; one must not conceal any part of what one has recognized to be true."

— Albert Einstein

One of my final obligations in the active-duty Air Force was to lead a search and recovery (SAR) team in the swamps of Florida. A list had circulated through the intelligence center requiring volunteers for additional duties. One duty in particular, searching for lost aircrew following air mishaps, was the kind of additional duty that no one *ever* imagined would be called, until it actually happened.

At the outdoor pool on base, swimmers doing laps stopped in mid-stroke, looked skyward. Unexpected aircraft swooped in for emergency approaches at our otherwise sleepy base. One by one, warplanes circled above, taking their turn in line to land. Few could imagine what their arrival signaled. By the time darkness descended, a full-scale recall was in effect at homes all around the area. Personnel reported to the base that evening in combat attire, with one week's worth of additional clothing. From there we were promptly shipped off in blue school buses to points unknown south of the base.

As it turned out, one in the formation had crashed during a training exercise. The area was remote and virtually inaccessible by road vehicles.

Nonetheless, it was our job to undertake the recovery. I was one of three team-leads, and for the next week our SAR teams hacked through midsummer heat, humidity, and Florida's deep swamps. We had been transported, if only briefly, from suburban American comfort to an experience that few forgot. The citation that accompanied a later award to me encapsulated it well:

> While assigned to the Search and Recovery Team . . . Captain Viola went above and beyond the call of duty to deploy to [the] crash site. His fortitude and cooperation enabled the team to meet the demands of a grueling Search and Recovery operation to recover the remains of the deceased pilot. Despite the pathogenic and parasitic hazards of the Okeechobee swamp environment, identified as "worst-case scenario" conditions, Captain Viola risked his own well-being to wade through hip-deep water and dense foliage to locate remains, prevent further decomposition, and ensure identification of the deceased. Captain Viola's disposition and efforts contributed to unprecedented team cohesion while facilitating an operation praised for its smoothness by on-scene mishap investigators.

Out of respect for the deceased, I will relate only aspects of the operation that illustrate the effects of stressful circumstances on service members. At one point in the week, I stopped wading to get my bearings and take a drink of water. As I did, I noticed a strange glare from the swamp waters around me. I stared down through the reflection to see the unmistakable brass casings of 20 mm cannon shells under my feet. I was standing *on top* of the dispersal field of the downed aircraft's unexploded ordnance. As others unwittingly approached me, I ordered everyone to halt in place and look around them. Fortunately, I was the only one standing on, or near, cannon shells. After a few tense minutes, explosive ordnance disposal (EOD) personnel arrived and flagged off the area around me, reassuring us that the shells were stable, and escorted me from the area. It had been a minor part of a much larger event, demonstrating how quickly military members can find themselves in harm's way.

After only a week, many of us began to feel the affects of the stress. That intense week had been a discontinuity in the pace of our normal experiences. It was a spike of emotional demand that exceeded the bounds of civilian experience and forced us to operate in a different emotional mode. To me, it felt as if I had been gone a month. If we had stayed much longer the effects might have been more lasting. Such is the case for veterans suffering from post-traumatic stress disorder (PTSD).

Post-Traumatic Stress Disorder

The problem with such experiences, especially as they relate to service members, is that they are alien to the lives we leave behind, and to the lives to which we return. When we depart, the world continues on its merry way, but we change, even in a short time. Depending upon the trauma one experiences, the degree of change can produce stress too great to handle emotionally. Psychologists call this post-traumatic stress disorder (PTSD). It is an injury that leaves no visible scars, none that are physically discernable to others anyway. Others may perceive us as acting differently, and saying things that are out of character. We may seem unlike the person they knew before. It is as if a different person has returned from the traumatic experience, and the unfortunate truth is that we *do* return different.

PTSD is so misunderstood partly because people fail to acknowledge the validity of PTSD itself. This misconception is complicated by cultural biases that stigmatize dealing with emotional issues as unmasculine or as a sign of weakness. Unfortunately, such views only exacerbate the underlying truth that, at the simplest levels, trauma affects all that it touches. Crash your car and, no matter how perfect the repair job, the car never quite feels "right" again. On a deeper level, there is something potentially more upsetting about a traumatic event. As career clinical social worker Donna Finicle describes it, "Our sense of safety is disturbed," so that our idea of what is safe versus threatening becomes overwritten by new survival imperatives.

Long after we are back to apparent health, we may be plagued by recollections of a time when we had lost all control and felt helpless. That moment, the moment of impact, remains so frightening that we must repress it in our memories. The mind blocks it from consciousness, we surmise, to protect our ability to continue functioning in a high-threat environment. Soon, our short-term memories of the event may blur, but not the associated feelings.

One of the more notable aspects of trauma is how it seemingly distorts our perception of time. An instant in trauma can seem like an eternity. Just as in *Alice in Wonderland*, the rules of reality seem suspended in a different time, a discontinuity in the flow of time from our "normal" world. All that made sense in that moment, only made sense in *that* reality. As Finicle puts it, "This is a kind of tunnel vision that is part of the survival mode, which occurs in traumatic events." The seriousness of PTSD cannot be understated. It is neither psychosomatic, nor a reflection of an individual's inability to deal with a situation. Each PTSD occurrence is a unique reflection of someone's experiences and trauma. Since few can directly share another's experience, PTSD sufferers may be left feeling isolated, and many, in fact, are left to recover alone. When I asked Donna Finicle for her advice on dealing with this situation, she stressed that "coming out of that isolation and finding a support network are key aspects of healing from trauma."

If you are a PTSD sufferer, it is essential to your well-being that you recognize that you are not alone, and that others can help you. The aftermath of war or traumatic experiences has a range of effects on soldiers, medical personnel, support staff, civilians, and on others with whom the seriously affected individuals interact. Learning and relying on coping skills can make all the difference for many affected by their experiences, often seriously and for long afterward. As Finicle describes it:

> Sometimes the effects do not show up until much later, and sometimes right away. Exposure to the threat of death over a period of time and witnessing it, individuals go into survival mode, with emotional numbing initially. Other problems develop that affect sleep and interfere with daily functioning .... Relationships are impacted adversely, with emotional distance and a desire to isolate, angry outbursts, and other problems....Couple, family, and friend relationships are placed under a lot of stress from the changes. Marriages can fail and children may develop problems in school. When families and survivors understand more, they have the possibility of working together better and weathering the difficult times.

To get a sense of how anxiety affects daily activities we will use a simple analogy of a common occurance. Imagine going to a new specialist for a first-time medical evaluation. You have a referral from your doctor, you make an appointment, and your insurance company will cover the procedure. Reason impels you to follow through with the appointment, but somewhere deep inside trepidation arises. No rational explanation accounts for these feelings. Instead, it is a struggle with irrational emotions. Your mind begins employing defensive tactics. At your appointment, you physically go through all the moves, doing whatever the health professionals tell you to do. In that vulnerable moment with a complete stranger you feel unprotected, without identity, and alone. As your anxiety threatens to overwhelm you, you find yourself simply disconnecting from the event. Rather than displaying embarrassment, humiliation, or helplessness over a simple procedure, you repress your feelings through the duration of the event, and for some time afterwards. Some people behave as if physically absent, or as if they somehow do not exist, and, in an emotional way, perhaps they do not. Their body is examined, they answer questions, but their feelings are locked away, protected in a safe subconscious place. These temporary absences of feelings seem to protect people, but also make it easy for them to "shut down" later and avoid other experiences in reality.

As a means of coping with anxiety, some people do *exactly* what they are told, and frequently their responses may appear almost robotic. Their demeanor will be polite, but their actions will be expedient, clearly in an effort to make their unpleasant experience pass as quickly as possible to its conclusion. They immediately submit to situations as if attempting to emotionally hold their breath. They let go of their "present mind," forgetting the here and now, and focus on completion. Concentrating on someplace elsewhere that feels safer can be a dangerous mode in which to operate. People in this emotional mode carry themselves away from the uncomfortable present time by projecting reality forward into a "future time." It is a safer place that they never reach because they continue projecting the present to the safer future. Even when it is finally safe, and they want to live in the present, their minds continue projecting forward.

Some rationalize their defense (or "coping") mechanism with thoughts like, "I should have been better prepared for this kind of situation," and "I will never let this happen to me again." This takes the focus away from the here and now, and eventually they may forget how to live today. People who employ such coping mechanisms may also not seem comfortable accepting praise, experimenting with new things, partaking in frivolous activities, sitting still, or simply finding simple joy in the day. Everything is in a defense state of forward projection, like a manic race to some distant state. The sooner they finish any given task, the sooner they can get "away" to someplace where they can feel better.

As was described earlier in the medical appointment analogy, individuals employing this coping mechanism may seemingly submit unconditionally in conditional environments. Since not emotionally present they may do what they are told simply to expedite the completion of tasks so they can leave on time. In such a submissive state, they unintentionally risk exposing themselves to abuse and disappointment by unscrupulous coworkers or superiors.

This is where family, loved ones, and true friends become important for those suffering from PTSD. Perhaps the only setting to reasonably expect unconditional treatment is in a loving environment, with people who allow us to be as unconditional as we need.

Military people, especially those who have been in combat, can identify with the state of emotional disconnection just described. Some, whose coping mechanisms were set into motion by traumatic experiences, live large portions of their lives (sometimes years) feeling this disconnection. Present moments slip almost unnoticed into the past. One day you may wake up and say, "What have I been doing all these years?" Those moments are gone, and you can never have them back again. The imperative, then, is to address PTSD and its effects now, so that you get on with living your life.

The Gift that Just Keeps Taking

Dealing with PTSD requires attention from trained and qualified professionals. My own experiences with such services attest to the fact that there is a broad spectrum of care available, from lackluster to exceptional, and everything in between. Good care is invaluable, and very individual dependent. Whatever the caliber of care, it is best received as soon as possible after the onset of PTSD.

The shocks I received at the crash site were both mild and short-lived in comparison to the experiences of others who endured months or years of combat. Mild and short-lived experiences seem to produce what I think of as an "elastic deformation" of the psyche. Aircraft, by way of analogy, sustain loading and stress in flight, inducing parts to deform slightly. Passengers sometimes nervously watch a large range of flexing in the wingtips of their airliner in flight. Wings are designed to give and take in ways that distribute stress throughout the airframe, and maximum loading ultimately comes down to the design, and the materials from which they are made. Stress applied that an object can recover from results in "elastic" deformation, while stress applied that an object cannot recover from results in a "plastic" deformation. Plastic deformations are effectively permanent after which an object will never be the same again.

People are structured with similar features and limits. Humans were designed by nature to withstand considerable stress. Likewise, societies are designed to provide give-and-take, distributing the applied forces of stress throughout their membership. Stress that the individual can recover from produces, in my view, an "elastic" psychological deformation with temporary effects. Like my own return from the crash site, people can return to normal functioning despite the trauma. My experiences left me slightly shaken, but I was able to quickly return to the normal flow of society. Stress that an individual *cannot* recover from results in a "plastic" psychological deformation, leaving them unable to return to normal social functioning. Unfortunately, the effects of plastic deformation from a catastrophic trauma reshape an individual in ways that are beyond the individual (or society) to return to his or her original state. After a plastic deformation, the individual is never the same again.

It is important to note, that elastic deformations may also have long-term effects. Some psychologists believe that even if individuals recover from traumatic experiences, they may be more likely to develop PTSD at some later point in their lives. This will be discussed further in a later section that talks about "triggers."[1]

Service-Disabled Veteran

Because of how elusive PTSD may be to diagnose, veterans run the risk of not getting the benefits they deserve when they separate from the military. The following section should aid members who may have questions on how to receive such benefits. PTSD falls into a large category of "service related disabilities." Most military people do not like the word, "disability," believing themselves somehow unworthy if they happen to have one. A way of overcoming this mindset is to think about high-performance machinery. In the same way that a race car or aircraft needs to be properly serviced to function effectively, so too does an individual. Structural problems are easy to spot, and therefore deal with. Electrical and avionics problems, well, that is a whole other issue that takes a lot of time, patience, and solid expertise to resolve. This is why vets need to undergo the proper screening immediately after returning from combat. It is the best way to ensure the healthiest possible future. Failure to identify possible problems can often result in burdensome costs later in life.

For military personnel, one essential form of screening is therapy. Unfortunately, there is still a stigma attached to that word. Overcoming that stigma is in the best interests of the service member. Soldiers think that therapy is emasculating, because it is perceived as an inability to deal with one's own problems. Well, back to the avionics analogy, you would feel uncomfortable with an amateur mechanic rewiring your navigation system, right? Your friends and family might be able to help, but if none of you really know much about avionics you could do more harm than good. Another stigma associated with therapy is that it is a sign of weakness. Soldiers are supposed to be tough and resilient. Well, if Mafia tough guy Tony Soprano can go to therapy, then *you* can go to therapy too. Enough said.

From my own experiences with the Veterans Administration (VA), I have drawn up a few important guidelines that I think should be followed when making disability claims at the end of your military service:

1. Keep track of timelines. When did you first notice symptoms, and when did you first seek help for the issue. Track reoccurrences and continuing issues.

2. Keep a file of documentation on physicians, diagnoses, recommendations, and treatments. Do not depend on the military filing system alone. Make your own copies (ideally directly from VA originals) that you keep at home.

3. Be proactive and aggressive about disability issues. Do not wait until you are out of the service to demonstrate duration or seriousness of a medical issue. The following is an excerpt from my own disability claim that was denied because I could not show that the condition persisted. It also illustrates the value of keeping good records:

    > review of the evidence within the service medical records does not substantiate that the veteran was ever diagnosed with a chronic knee disability. The veteran was seen once . . . [and the] chronicity for this condition has not been established as the evidence of record does not show that this condition has persisted. His service medical records are silent regarding any symptoms, treatment or diagnosis of bursitis to either of his knees. Therefore, entitlement to service connection is denied.[2]

4. Use the proper wording and approved phrases. I had to figure out what those approved phrases were the hard way, through trial and error. This last excerpt is from my own (approved) VA claim. It is the result of hard-earned intelligence collection. Veterans should exploit this feedback so they can take full advantage of the benefits they are due from the VA:

    > Where emotional disabilities are concerned (depression, dysthymic disorder, etc.), the following are key indicators to have documented in your service record before you separate, or that can be

substantiated by a licensed psychologist/psychiatrist: residual symptoms present which interfere with his or her ability to form social relations, disrupted sleeping patterns, chronic sleep impairment, occupational and social impairment with occasional decrease in work efficiency and intermittent periods of inability to perform occupational tasks (although generally functioning satisfactorily, with routine behavior, self-care, and conversation normal), depressed mood, anxiety, suspiciousness, panic attacks (weekly or less often), or mild memory loss (such as forgetting names, directions, recent events). An even higher disability rating (50 percent) is warranted for the following symptoms: flattened affect; circumstantial, circumlocutory, or stereotyped speech; panic attacks more than once a week; difficulty in understanding complex commands; impairment of short- and long-term memory (retention of only highly learned material, forgetting to complete tasks); impaired judgment, impaired abstract thinking; disturbances of motivation and mood; difficulty in establishing and maintaining effective work and social relationships.[3]

It may seem that I do not agree with how the military functions, but in truth I truly respect the *individuals* who commit themselves to the profession of arms. I respect their bravery and integrity and, more importantly, I respect the fact that these people volunteer to be there. They knowingly and willingly sacrifice their free will and freedom of choice to make a difference in places around the world where most Americans would never venture. Providing them the information they need to move on with their lives is the least I can do to help.

Triggers That May Cause a Resurgence of Associated Feelings

I asked Donna Finicle to outline the types of effects one might expect with PTSD. She said these could be, "permanent psychological, physiological damage as well as neurological damage." On a different level, namely the veteran's spirituality, PTSD can inflict a different kind of damage. This "soul murder" is where an individual loses faith in goodness. Such damage has a way of resurfacing at times not of our choosing. Finicle went on to list the kinds of triggers that may cause a resurgence of associated feelings. I have paraphrased them in a form that most veterans can understand:

1. *Memory*: This includes assistance by any of the senses (smell, sound, touch, etc.), as well as recollections from reading about particular incidents, in stories, in movies, and so forth. The time of year in which trauma happened can also have an effect; people can have anniversary reactions to their individual events.

2. *Sense of Safety*: At times when an individual again does not feel "safe," there may be a triggering back all over again to life and death (or near death) trauma incidents. These include situations where individuals perceive they have no control over their situation or environment, personal safety, professional well-being, etc.

3. *Age*: In our aging process, reminders of mortality and other such reminders may trigger earlier trauma. Examples include confronting cancer (or just the possibility of cancer), heart attacks, strokes, injuries, fears of toxic exposure, and so on.

4. *Media*: Sometimes called "armchair PTSD," it is triggering back to earlier trauma while watching and hearing about war on television via news sources, television shows, sounds, photographs, personal contacts, etc.

5. *Stress*: We are triggered back to the earlier trauma by daily events in our own stress and life situations that leave us feeling helpless, out of control, unable to act, or otherwise.

These are not new sources of trauma, but potential triggers in our everyday life that can reopen old wounds unexpectedly. Life is different from wartime, but random events can accidentally trigger us back to the earlier trauma. Those with PTSD soon become sensitive to "everything" as possible triggers—causing them to withdraw from the overstimulating world all around them. Anything that reminds you of the trauma can become a trigger.

The Military is at War; Civilians are at the Mall

Another issue to deal with after returning from combat is that things might look different to you when you come home. For those who have experienced combat trauma, the most difficult transition is often the one back into civil society. This can have unexpected effects on veterans thinking that "peace and quiet" are all they need. The behavior of those who have lived their entire lives in the comfort of suburban safety can be overwhelming to returning veterans. In fact, to some veterans, it can be down right infuriating. Military personnel have the sometimes unique privilege to see how other people around the world live; many who do not grow up with all of the comforts afforded to citizens of prosperous nations. Many Americans see documentaries about poverty and violence abroad, but have never experienced it firsthand. In fact, many Americans have never even ventured outside their own borders. These factors can lead to an incredible disconnect between the experiences of military personnel and the reality of civilian life back home.

Veterans from Iraq and Afghanistan describe this feeling of disconnection as "no tolerance for stupid." It is a poignant mantra that describes their complete lack of patience with Americans who do not take the time, or care, to treat veterans with the dignity and respect that they (or anyone, for that matter) deserve. Understanding that these feelings exist and why they exist is important for both separating military personnel and civilians alike. The more I reflected on the difficulties soldiers endure, the more I realized how frustrating their fellow citizens could be on their return. In many ways, what service members do is completely taken for granted by civilians. When I separated from the military, it was a challenge for me to understand the behavior of ordinary citizens all around me. Many seemed "phony," and standoffish. The more I shared those observations with other military and former military friends, the more I began to perceive a divide between two extremely disparate camps. In one camp were people who put their lives and their convictions on the line everyday. They were immersed in the realities of the world. In the other camp are civilians who appear to be oblivious to the realities of the world, and committed to the pursuits of their own indulgent interests. Confronting this divide can leave some veterans disappointed and disillusioned. The result can be an awkward, defensive mindset, known as a "fugue state."

A fugue is a state of mind during periods of transition, as an individuals' consciousness is being realigned to adapt to the new environment. That "in-between" period is where the awkwardness happens. For example, persons in a fugue state may begin asking themselves strange questions like, "This is not *my* house; do I live here? Do I *work* here? Who *are* these people?" It is not forgetfulness, as much as a feeling like stepping outside of one's old life and not understanding how it could be in one's current life. The individual is reacting to his or her sense of disorientation. As such, he or she might be tempted to go into a highly protective state. They may try to manage their anxiety by creating distractions. They may also attempt to isolate themselves from those around them. Sometimes this involves fixating on perceived differences between themselves and others. So in the discussion above about "no tolerance for stupid," veterans might adopt an "us versus them" mentality with their own citizens. It is a form of defensiveness that becomes a way for people to cope with the difficult realities of transition back to the civilian world.

A fugue state between the world of military self-sacrifice and civilian indifference can leave former military personnel wondering why they ever served, and why they put their lives on the line. Was *this* what I was fighting for? I pondered this myself after reentering civilian life. To illustrate why many civilians might not be able to relate to the experiences of combat veterans, I decided to include an e-mail from a colleague and friend who was working in Baghdad. Her e-mail was a stream of consciousness *so* striking and touching that it demanded a few days from me to digest. In it, she describes the kind of mindset that is required to get through the day in a place that knows no stability or reliability. She painted an incredible picture of why any delusions of ignorance were quickly erased by the day's next attack . . .

```
— Original Message ———————————————
From: SB
To: MAV
Date: Mon, 25 Jul 2005
Subject: News from the Eastern Front . . .
    Yes, sometimes it's hectic, but sometimes it's just,
hmm . . . I'm looking for the right words. Because it's
such a different reality here, I don't have the ready
words to describe the situation even from a logical or
emotional level. Sometimes the "hectic-ness" lies within
me . . .  To say there are times I just need to sit, just
walk the halls, and collect myself, is an understatement.
    It can take at least thirty minutes to two hours rid-
ing in a car to get to the Green Zone or go to the Minis-
ter of Interior's office. We've made this trip twice a
day for several days at a time . . . The onslaught of
tension and stress from not knowing from minute to minute
where the bullet might come from is real, too real some-
times. Think of the troops doing this for 24 to 36 hours
at a time . . .
    Our Iraqi bodyguards are in the front of the car, and
riding in the car behind us. I'm in the back seat, AK-47
in my lap at times, scanning, continually scanning . . .
waiting for the bomb to drop. No one said don't talk, no
```

one had to . . . There's only one focus and that's scanning the eyes and actions of anyone, any car, anything
coming close. It's an "easy" day when the traffic keeps
moving. When it stops, or gets congested due to the U.S.
Army blocking all the roads, it's a death trap for all of
us, anyone on the roads.

Some days I can blow it off easily, other days the
residue remains in my system longer. I can't tell you why
or how. What I can tell you is that at times it's hard to
sit down at a computer, in an office, in an Arab palace,
and act normal, type a cheery email, and sip a cup of
coffee.

Other days I make jokes about my blond hair causing
traffic jams and blown-out tires, as they hit the road
medians looking at me. However, the next day the Iraqi
secretary buys me a floor-length black crepe covering
with a matching scarf to reduce my chances of being kid-
napped by other locals in need of money.

White slavery, drug trafficking, etc., is moving into
Iraq faster than you could believe; reminds me of Bosnia-
Kosovo all over again. Didn't we, the world, learn anything! And my God, that was only a couple years ago. When
you destroy a society's infrastructure, you've got to
replace it immediately with another one, or the mugs,
thugs, and bullies take over! This is not rocket science.
It's classic sociology 101!

I've rambled enough for now. It's Sunday, but that's
the first day of the week for the Iraqis, so I need to
get back to work. I worked until 11:30 p.m. last night.
Went to church today . . . gave our support to the
British troops who are here with us, sharing in the
tragedy of the attacks on London.

Nothing more moving than walking through concrete
bunkers, surrounded by 14-foot concrete T-walls, into an
empty doublewide trailer . . . to attend an Anglican
service, receive communion, and pray for strength to live
another day and fight for peace.

Keep America free while I'm gone!

———————————————————

My friend's email emphasizes the divide between civilian America and America's military defenders. For those who have sacrificed for their country, the letdown of perceiving the apathy, shallowness, or pettiness of those they protected may be overwhelming. My advice to vets is try not to let it get to you. The more I obsessed over it, the more consuming it became, and the more it cut a disappointing wound in my faith in my fellow citizens. The willful ignorance of the person on the street as to what is going on in the outside world, and the disregard they may have for the consequences, can make the task of transition back into civilian life all the more difficult. A perception that may arise in combat veterans is that the behaviors of those who defend and those who are defended are diametrically opposed. I suggest not trying to view the values of either side as opposing. This only contributes to the "us and them" defensive posture. Try, instead, to view everyone as having a *range* of possible values and perceptions. Others will have different levels of dedication and commitment from you, and that will require your leadership if you want them to change.

> "Prosperity is nothing without posterity."
>
> —Mavaxiom 51

In the end, I found good news in my friend's e-mail. I realized that her bravery restored my faith in my fellow citizens. Her integrity gave me hope to care deeply about the well-being of others, despite living in an insane world. Her actions, and the actions of those like her, strengthened my determination to keep up the fight, and try to make a difference myself.

Notes

1. From discussions with Dr. Jane Flax, and Donna Finicle. My own observations/ experiences in the military suggest that service members who came from abuse, broken homes, or troubled childhoods, may have increased susceptibility to PTSD. As Donna Finicle comments, "They are survivors, coming out of Chaos into the structure of the military; trauma on top of trauma if they go to war."

2. From the author's disability claim, Department of Veterans Affairs (VA), Washington Regional Office, Washington, D.C., August 27, 2001.

3. From a VA support document accompanying the author's VA disability claim.

CHAPTER SIX

Your Résumé

Action in Words from a Noble
Breed that Shirks Self-Praise

"When you possess treasures within you, and you try to tell others of them, seldom are you believed."

— Paulo Coelho

What is a résumé, really? Unless you already know exactly where and when your next job is going to be, your résumé is the *single* most important tool for your job search. Think of it as a summary of who you are, what you can offer a potential employer, and your suitability at that next organization. Your résumé has to accomplish all that in fewer than two pages.

Employers find employees via résumés. A résumé speaks on your behalf when you are not present to sell yourself. It is your advocate, stating your case to potential employers. Truly, if you screw up your résumé, your job search becomes infinitely more challenging. If it says inappropriate things in your absence, you cannot be there to set the story straight. So it is crucial that you develop your résumé to work for you as your first, best ally. No need to worry; I will provide you all my lessons learned.

After I left the military, a number of friends continued to ask me about my transition. We swapped intelligence with each other on what it was like "outside." In many cases, those who remained in the military saw me as an advance scout for their own plans to depart later. They had just not reached the point of signing their paperwork and committing to the act of leaving. In the months that followed my leaving, a curious band of onlookers devoured my every e-mail. They eagerly took notes on everything I did; regardless of whether it had been a misstep or a success. Now, with hindsight, I can share all the successes.

Believing in Yourself

Successful résumés are a matter of attitude. Ultimately, the people hired are those who *believe* that they will be hired—and their résumés communicate their belief. Your résumé has to make it clear that you believe in yourself and your abilities. It must communicate that in clear, concise, and simple language. Consequently, your résumé must be written in English, not a linguistic mélange of military terminology, catchphrases, and acronyms. More than anything else, *you* have to write your own résumé. No one knows you like you do. Likewise, no one else can believe in you the way you need to believe in yourself.

You *do* believe in yourself, right? If you do not, then you approach your job search crippled by a faltering confidence in your own abilities. This will not help you adequately document your work experience, accomplishments, and great deeds. If prospective employers cannot readily acknowledge a candidate's worth from reading a résumé, then that résumé is not going to do what it is supposed to do. So, you *really* have to believe in your abilities—and make sure your skills leap from the page.

A friend who was still in the government, but wanted to apply to a civilian company, asked me to review her résumé. Many résumés are too long, rambling beyond the two-page limit. Hers was less than a page. The following was my impression of it:

```
— Original Message ————————————
From: Marc Viola
To: Job Seeker
Sent: Monday, 10:01 AM
Subject: RE: Résumé & Self Praise


I'm looking over your résumé. The problem is not con-
tent. Instead, the problem has to do with the inherent
shortfalls of this savage little planet.
```

I recognize something in you, just from knowing you. You are of a noble breed that shirks the task of self-praise. Others cannot see the halo that surrounds you, and the light that precedes your entrance into a room.

Therefore, to gain the attention of the ignorant majority of barbaric employers out there, you must descend to a level of evolution long since abandoned by your kind. It will require you to stoop to their level.

You must strike together stones, where once you used a lighter. You must partake of animal flesh, where once you consumed only carefully selected macrobiotics. This is a primitive world we live in, so you must speak to the natives in utterances that they can comprehend. You can continue to lead as a transition figure in this world while still satisfying the distasteful customs of the savages.

So please, beef-up your résumé!

Look at your performance appraisals, cite awards, echo the descriptions of your talents made by friends and co-workers, and (most of all) plagiarize (an intelligence term for "borrow with extreme prejudice" from) other résumés like mine. I know, it is their way, not yours. And quite unfortunately it is *their* world, not yours. Play the game, and your life will be easier to live down the road.

I have great faith in your superior talents.

Marc

My friend was skilled and capable, but she simply did not know how to give herself credit for all the great things she had done in the past. The danger in not incorporating enough in your résumé is that the person receiving your résumé does not know you at all, in most cases, and will not understand the depth of your experience. You are sending your résumé to a world of strangers. It is not that they are bad people. They just have nothing to go on but what you have written. If you have done great things, and do not record them, your résumé will not sing your praises. Only two pieces of paper (at a maximum) can do that.

Getting Started

There are many suitable candidates for jobs who are not hired because they never get their résumés into circulation. Unless you are going back home to a family business, or are part of the trusted inner circle of a civilian company that does not require résumés, you are going to have to write one. If you know people inside a company, they cannot do anything without a copy of your résumé to pass around. In today's electronic age, résumés must also be in electronic form, or they are of limited use. That is because most people will want to send your résumé around as an e-mail attachment. You can delay the inevitable as long as you like, but eventually you will have to produce an electronic version of your résumé.

The highest praise of your skills by friends will fall on deaf ears unless you have something to show them visually. Humans are a visually oriented species. Only two pages might be a confining challenge for some people, especially if they have had a long and distinguished career. For others who have been in the service only a short time, it can be equally challenging to come up with the material to fill two pages. No need to fear. This chapter will help *both* parties, and there are two exercises to help you get started.

Exercise 1: Your Spy Mission

This is, as we call it in the intelligence business, a collection mission (begin humming James Bond movie theme or the intro to *Mission Impossible*). If you decide to accept this mission, you will carry out the dangerously involved and highly focused task of collecting, processing, and exploiting a large cache of missing documents that are vital to the creation and survival of your résumé. You must find *all* of your personnel file documents, if at all possible, regardless of condition or location. These documents may be heavily guarded behind unscrupulously complacent bureaucrats or chaotically mismanaged administrative technicians apathetic to your cause. Neither will easily surrender the information that you seek.

This means that your mission may require you to employ human intelligence (HUMINT) tradecraft. Remember, you must obtain a *complete* copy of the contents of your personal file. You must use whatever legal resources at your disposal to spot, assess, influence, and ultimately recruit human resources (HR) or administrative personnel who will assist you in getting these documents. If you or any of your collection operation is caught employing anything but legal tradecraft, this book, the author, and the publisher will disavow any knowledge of, or take any legal responsibility for, your actions.

Intelligence Collection Requirement [REQ 086-07]

The collection requirement [REQ 086-07] states that you must obtain "usable copies of all unclassified documentation from one's own military records for federated exploitation at one's own domicile, in 8 1/2 x 11-inch photocopy, or decrypted electronic softcopy format."
Such documentation should include:

1. Performance reports ("fit reps" to navy personnel)
2. Evaluation forms
3. Awards and decorations
4. Promotion recommendations
5. Education records
6. Official transcripts and diplomas
7. Training courses and certificates
8. Standardized test results
9. Letters of recommendation
10. Certificates of appreciation
11. Articles you have written
12. Articles that mention you by name
13. E-mails thanking or praising you
14. Security applications and background forms

Accomplishing this collection operation may require your displaying an upbeat and professionally good-natured disposition to your bureaucratic target, a technique also known in intelligence circles as employing "false flags." Limit your contact with your target so as to not arouse suspicion. If the target begins to monopolize your attention with tales of an unfolding divorce drama, listen, but do not put your emotional well-being in danger. The intent is to win your target's trust and confidence, in hopes that they will either provide you with a full copy of your records, or allow *you* to copy them yourself. You will probably not be allowed to leave the premises with the original folder. All you need are good-quality copies for this mission. If standard forms of tradecraft prove ineffective, intelligence professionals worldwide recommend employing a special preparation of roasted and ground cacao seeds and sugar, known commercially as "chocolate." It has proven *hugely* effective in the past against targets of either gender.

After securing all your documents, or as many as possible, you must organize them in some way. Try using file folders, an accordion folder, or in document protectors, but *never* hole-punch the original documents. However you file them, identify your document categories, or natural groupings, with tabs or dividers. Then sequence the contents of each chronologically from the most recent first to the oldest last. That will help you prioritize your résumé skills and related information; with your most recent achievements right up front.

After all your intelligence collecting and processing, you must now exploit the data. This is the tough part. Essentially, it means documenting your biggest successes from past work. Start with the most recent stuff and work backwards. Every time you intend to use an acronym spell it out *completely* first, then put the acronym in parentheses immediately afterwards. This may seem pointless now, but it will be useful later as you begin to cut and paste résumé sections. You cannot predict where you will first use a term in your résumé until you are done with the final edits, so spelling them out each time will prevent one being accidentally used without being introduced. Then later, you can introduce it first, and then collapse all subsequent usage to solely acronym form. This will also help you when you need to consolidate your two-page limit. If you cut corners now, a good résumé will probably not follow.

Exercise 2: Your Vision Quest

Just when you thought you were already working hard, I have another major project for you. Exercise 2 may be as important as, if not *more* important than, Exercise 1. In Exercise 2, we return to that "really big, important question;" the question that ranks up there with "the meaning of life." It is a question that will determine your direction for the remainder of your life. You must ask yourself this question, and seek its eventual answer:

What do you really want?

Drink a martini (shaken, *or* stirred). Meditate on a mountaintop. Watch the sunset. Take a long, long trip to nowhere in particular. Ask your priest, pastor, minister, rabbi, mullah, imam, guru, or the homeless guy on the

street, whomever it is you need to go to for learned spiritual advice. Ultimately, though, there is only one person who can answer this question: you.
It is also not a question that your brain can necessarily answer. You cannot
rationalize the answer, no matter how much you think your answer makes
sense, no matter how practical or pragmatic the seeming outcome. This is
not a rational question, so (by definition) it cannot have a purely rational
answer. The answer must come from a place deep inside that has probably
been closed off and dormant for eons. But it is there, buried, like an ancient
tomb needing to be found and opened. Find the truth that is "you," the *real*
person deep inside. Only that person, from within your true self, can answer
this question, and you will only be able to learn the answer by listening to
your heart.

Capturing Opportunities in Words

Sudden demands for new employees put pressure on organizations to hire
people quickly. For candidates to effectively take advantage of emerging
opportunities requires that they be ready to respond *as* the demand arises.
Preparation is the key to functioning effectively on "alert" status. Like a military mission, you must have an up-to-date résumé ready and waiting,
armed with devastating verbiage, and standing by for immediate action. It
also helps to know someone on the inside who can streamline the process,
but we will talk about that later.

When a large corporation absorbed the small firm I worked for, queries
about job opportunities poured in from my friends who were still in the
service. It was a perfect time for them to inquire because more jobs had
become available than there were employees. There I was, given an incredible opportunity to see the hiring process in action. I had an exclusive, insider
view of how résumés are "racked and stacked." I was actually involved in the
vetting process of potential candidates. Amidst this bonanza of job openings, and this rare vantage point to observe how résumés were screened, I
was struck by a number of observations.

Let me set the scene for you. As an office screens résumés of perspective
candidates, it follows a time-honored corporate procedure. All those trusted
in the inner circle of the office gather in a room away from the rest of the
offices and seat themselves in a circle of chairs. They block out time, say two
or three hours, to focus *solely* on résumés. There will be no calls, no e-mails,
and no interruptions, just so they can focus on the task at hand. Everyone
shows up with a big mug of coffee, candy bars, water, soda, or whatever it

takes to power through the session. The ugly truth is that employers hate this process. Those who must screen résumés would be happy if new employees simply "appeared." They would be happiest if they could press a button to produce competent employees at their disposal. Instead, they have to *find* promising candidates within stacks of résumés. The importance, then, of having a great résumé should now be clear.

Everyone in the 21st Century office still has to sit down and painstakingly sifts through stacks of paper-copy résumés. It is a tedious task to complete. The methodology is simple: each person gets copies of the same 50 or so résumés and chooses the best. Then everyone compares his or her picks from the stack. My observations suggest the following ways to make your résumé stand out and be selected:

1. Vital Data. Put your name on your résumé in any way you choose, but put it clearly. You have options. Generally, the convention is first name first, last name last, entirely in capital letters or title case. Some people include their middle initial; others spell out their middle name. It is a free country, so it is up to you.

    This is where the decisions on aesthetics begin. It seems silly, but people can agonize over the simplest things. There is a reason, though, when it comes to résumés: they are an expression of who you are, and the aesthetics speak volumes. Since the military was never big on your expressing anything, your adopting an artsy mindset can be a little daunting. In my case, I just could not resist the urge to evoke Roman history with my name in full: Marc Anthony Viola.

    Next, provide an address, telephone number, and e-mail address where your prospective employer can find you readily. Reliable access is crucially important. If in doubt, or moving, use your parent's address, or someone you trust with getting in touch with you immediately. Make sure your e-mail address name is simple, easy-to-remember, and non-offensive. While you are in the job market, be certain you can quickly check your e-mail, from *anywhere*. Timing to respond to inquiries may come down to hours. E-mail services are usually free, and permit remote access, and, if you hyperlink your e-mail address on your résumé document, it will be easy for anyone reading it to reach you quickly and easily.

2. Stapling. Companies typically bind copies of submitted résumés in stacks of 50 by either a giant staple or binder clip in the upper left corner of the pages. Think about that. If your name is up in the upper left-hand corner, it will be rather difficult to dig it out. Not good, because it

requires extra effort, extra energy, more time, and the people reviewing all the résumés are tired. If your résumé threatens to make them work a little harder, they may just move on to the next one. Do not give them any additional incentive.

It sounds like a cop-out, but people are only human. Reviewing résumés can be drudgery for people whose day-to-day jobs involve doing other important things. They might not want to go through the trouble of tracking down your contact information, or understanding what you are trying to say. Anything that you can do to make the work easier and more enjoyable for the screeners will be greatly appreciated by them. Since we generally read from left to right, put your name and contact information in the upper *right*-hand corner, far, far away from the big, bad "staple of death" or its cohort, the "binder-clip of doom."

3. Pages. No one screening résumés is going to read more than two pages. Period.

4. More Pages. Most people do not even read the second page. In fact, if they get to the middle of the first page it is a lot.

5. Duplicate Information. A second page can be accidentally torn off, lost, misplaced, misfiled, miscopied, or added to someone else's résumé. This can be a problem. What do employers do if they actually *like* your skills but cannot find the second page? Worse, what if they like the second page but cannot find the first page with your name on it? The solution: put your contact information on each page as a "header," so it will print on every page every time. It is really that simple.

6. Readability. Only the first few résumés in a stack will be fully read. This is good for you if your surname is Aaron or Anderson, as the stack is usually alphabetized. Mine was always towards the bottom of the pile, so I had to work harder to make it eye-catching. People screening résumés revert from reading to scanning to get a feel for each candidate's skills and experience. Consequently, you can expect someone to devote only about thirty seconds, to a maximum of two minutes, to screen your résumé. Really.

7. Summary. Power-pack all of the reasons why they should hire you on the upper third of the first page. I suggest you add the title, "Summary," atop the list of your career and skills and accomplishments, right under your name.

8. Security Clearances. If you worked in intelligence, or any field that required a security clearance, and you wish to continue such work, list your clearance immediately over or under your summary. Also indicate

if you had an accompanying polygraph test. This is an important qualification that can be a deal-breaker for some employers. Most companies in this line of work will not consider hiring anyone without a current security clearance. As important as having a clearance itself is its shelf life. Security clearances only last about five years. The process to investigate and adjudicate security clearances is long, exhaustive, and very expensive, and employers generally do not want to pay for them. Ideally, you should leave the military in the *same* year that your clearance has been approved. This will give you roughly four years to take advantage of the clearances. After that, an employer or their client will have to pay for your investigation and adjudication. That cost is in the tens of thousands of dollars, so a recent security clearance date on a résumé is money in the bank for a prospective employer.

9. Education. Right below your summary, list your education—highest and most recent first, lowest and earliest last. "Education" is not "training." Training is listed in a later section. Education means accredited schools where you received some kind of degree. So you would list PhDs, most recent masters' (MS, MA, MBA), bachelors' (BS, BA), and associates' degree, in that order. After each, list the specialty, and indicate the dates that you received them. If you did particularly well (3.0, or better) in a program, you might also want to list your grade point average (GPA). Finally, if your thesis was published, or turned into an article published by a professional journal, list that as well if there is room.

10. Follow-through. If you submit a résumé to a company while still employed, and that potential employer contacts you, it is only fair and courteous that you listen to their offer. Regardless of whether you are happy at your current job, let an outside employer discuss their opening with you. The discussion will provide you with invaluable intelligence on how your résumé was perceived by the company. It is free feedback on the current market demand for your job skills and what you might earn elsewhere. With nothing to lose, and only more information to help calibrate future résumé targeting, you can ask for whatever salary you think you deserve (or the market will bear) without the fear of rejection.

In the intelligence business, this kind of feedback is called BDA, or battle damage assessment. In its simplest sense, intelligence planners and "targeteers" employ BDA to ascertain whether a target sustained the desired effect. Total destruction is not always intended by an attack, so understanding the subtle effects can substantially aid future planning of precision guided munitions (PGM) strikes. In a larger sense, targeteers might want to deny use of the target by the enemy, degrade its performance, or disrupt its operation over a certain period of time. Assessing the accuracy of an attack requires good intelligence after the fact. Following through on the impact of your résumé should be no different. How will you collect this necessary intelligence? Talk with the company; get "ground truth," by interviewing with them. Think of your résumé as your own PGM (or "smart bomb"); interviews will be your way to carry out résumé BDA.

You have enough now to put together the header of your résumé. What the remainder will look like is up to you. You will have to choose fonts and sizes for your text sections. Again, these are the things that you should decide, because if your résumé is not an expression of who you are, then what is? Having said that, I will also add that the intelligence profession has a long and proud tradition of not wasting its time trying to reinvent anything that others have already suffered to produce. If you are entering the job market, then time is short and you have higher mission imperatives than font sizes. So I encourage you to copy mine. Go ahead, do not be ashamed. You are just copying my format. Everything else you will have to design for yourself. In the past I volunteered that format to a military husband-and-wife team who were interested in working at the company that employed me at the time. I told them, "If you already know that *my* format worked for me, then it will probably work for you, too." It did; the company hired both of them. The company liked my format, so it was one less targeting aspect they had to worry about. And yes, they were targeteers.

Improving Your Chances

When you send a résumé to a company, there are a number of different routes that it can take to getting you a job. Some are better than others. Chances are the person who will get you a job is someone you already know. You do not know them really well; they are just an acquaintance. Maybe they were someone you met on a previous assignment, or at a conference. The point is that they know of you. Maybe they met you once through a friend, or talked to you briefly over lunch with you. In my case, some were actually former students who went through my military classes. Whatever the case

Sample Résumé Header

First line of mailing address   *NAME (Arial Narrow 18)*
Second line (all Arial narrow 12 BOLD)   emailaddress@wherever.com
000-000-0000 (home)   000-000-0000 (mobile)

CLEARANCES

TOP SECRET // Current SSBI (2007) / Polygraph (2007).
Willing to relocate, live and / or work overseas.

SUMMARY (Arial Narrow Bold & Regular Text *Never* Smaller Than
Type Size 11)

- Highly respected and sought-after expert in high-level, broad-spectrum
  . . .
- "Impossible to replace" pioneer expanding use of new and cutting-edge
  . . .
- Requested by name in senior advisory roles . . .
- Acclaimed public speaker, impressing customers and leading dialogue
  on . . .
- Top-tier leader and trusted advisor to decision makers with informa-
  tion derived from . . .
- Widely cited authority on . . .
- Consistently delivers results with superior abilities in . . .
- Proactively anticipating customer needs by . . .
- Initiates groundbreaking new approaches to . . .

EDUCATION

MS, Scientific Stuff, Spy University, Washington, D.C., 1995 (GPA 0.00)
MA, Businessy Stuff / MA, Computer Stuff, Satellite Campus, College,
    1990 (GPA 0.00)
BS, Engineering, New Englandy University, 1987 (GPA 0.00)

EMPLOYMENT

2007 – Present: . . .

Men Seeking Women

Marc Antony seeks Cleopatra. Disillusioned Roman officer seeking peer in a spirited Mediterranean enchantress for long cruises and passionate dialogue. Expect you to be fraught with contradictions: cat-lazy with pouncing energetic outbursts, self-driven but seeking advice, self-sufficient but needing nocturnal embraces, overly able with bouts of self-doubt. Had enough of attending to affairs of state? Let's run off and make beautiful music together. Riches of the Pharaohs a must. Elizabeth Taylor likeness a plus.

what is important is that they already had a good feeling about you. You would be astonished by how far an intangible little thing like "a good feeling" can go towards getting you a job. Just knowing someone who works at a civilian firm is a major advantage over all other applicants, all other things being equal.

It is worth noting that it takes months (yes, months) to go from your résumé being "in the system" at a company to starting at a new job. That is because your résumé must first be processed, circulated throughout the company, and referred to the right office, before ever being noticed by the right people. Those people are the ones who know how to apply your skills to their needs, and are interested in your résumé. After that, it has to be in the right office at the right time—meaning when that office has an opening to fill. You can see that this whole process is like trying to hit a moving target. Many technologies have been brought to bear by companies to ensure that the right résumé is applied to the right job, at the right time. In the end, though, it can all come down to luck. The important thing for you is improving your chances of getting your résumé on the right desk at the right time. One of the best ways to ensure that moving target is being tracked on its flight path is with a little help from those who know you.

By the time that office realizes your worth, contacts you with its interest in your skill sets, interviews you, negotiates your compensation, gets you to accept and sign its offer letter, and you actually arrive on your start date, months can elapse. If you need security clearances transferred, then your start date may be even later. The message is, "Do not wait for the right time." The right time to get started was yesterday.

Do not worry, more help is coming . . .

CHAPTER SEVEN

Cultivating Kudos
The Not-So-Fine Art of Praising Yourself

"Information moves at the speed of light. Bad information moves *faster* than the speed of light, fast enough to go backwards in time, preceding its own introduction and replacing the truth."

— Mavaxiom 71

You already have more than enough raw material to build a fantastic résumé. All of the chronicled history of your exploits and great deeds are buried deep in the endless formwork of the military's bureaucratic behemoth. You are about to learn what data-mining is all about. Remember your intelligence-collection exercise from the résumé section? Now it is time to sift through all those papers and put that data to good use. This process is a cycle, also known as the intelligence cycle, or, to employ the entire mouthful, the tasking, collection, processing, exploitation, and dissemination (TCPED) cycle.

T: Tasking

The first step in the intelligence cycle is tasking. You have already been "tasked" in the previous chapter to identify gaps in information in your personal file. Your tasking was derived from unmet requirements to write and strengthen your résumé. Everything in the intelligence business revolves around gaps in information and unmet requirements. The same is now true for you. You probably still have some gaps in information you need to fill, and a lot of other unknowns to make sense of in the job search campaign. To start with was to complete the task of assembling your up-to-date file of your employment records. Recalling your previous collection requirement [REQ 086-07], you needed to:

"Obtain usable copies of all unclassified documentation from one's own military records for unfettered exploitation at one's own domicile, in 8 ½ × 11-inch photocopy, or decrypted electronic softcopy format."

Documentation includes:

1. Performance reports ("fit reps," to navy personnel)
2. Evaluation forms
3. Awards and decorations
4. Promotion recommendations
5. Education records
6. Official transcripts and diplomas
7. Training courses and certificates
8. Standardized test results
9. Letters of recommendation
10. Certificates of appreciation
11. Articles you have written
12. Articles that mention you by name
13. E-mails thanking or praising you
14. Security applications and background formwork

C: Collection

The second step in the intelligence cycle is collection. This is where you actually get the information. For any number of reasons, mostly legal, I do not want to know exactly *how* you collected all of your employment records. What is important is that you understand the difference between overt, covert, and clandestine means of collection. You may have employed any or all of these approaches in exercise 1: your spy mission.

1. Overt – Collecting information in plain sight of others, where it is readily apparent to others that you are gathering materials. Overt means being conspicuous in action, and relying on those involved to willingly participate and do their jobs. They may even assist you in the act, and

feign being customer service oriented. An example of an overt collection operation might sound like this,

"Can I help you, Sir / Ma'am?"

"Yes, I would like high-quality copies of all my personnel records, please."

"Coming right up, Sir / Ma'am. Would you like color copies, or only black and white? I can also provide those data files to you in soft-copy, and burn them on to a CD if you like, Sir / Ma'am."

Do not rely on the customer support representative to have taken their prescription psychotropic medications, and be so helpful on the day you conduct overt collection mission. In fact, it is more likely that you will have to contend with what is commonly referred to in intelligence circles as a "non-cooperative target."

2. Covert – A hidden operation whose outcome might be realized after the fact, but is not revealed or acknowledged *beforehand*. Afterwards, those upon whom a covert action has been carried out are likely aware of its occurrence, but probably do not know the identities of the perpetrators. This is like ransacking a person's office and leaving it a complete mess when you have found what you are looking for. You do not just burn the bridge; you blow it up, and leave a trail of "Death Cards" in your wake.

3. Clandestine – Secrecy in action so sublime that it rises to an art form. After a clandestine collection has been accomplished, those upon whom the act was carried out will never know that it even occurred. No search will be made for perpetrators and no fault will be assigned because, in the minds of all concerned, nothing ever happened.

Your methods of collection, the tricks of your trade, are referred to in the intelligence world as tradecraft. Your tradecraft is *your* business. If it becomes the subject of your bragging, be careful whom you tell. Bragging always risks undermining future clandestine efforts. What is important is that you have the information you need to draft your résumé. By the way, this is what is really fun about the intelligence business. As a collector, the opportunities to flex creative muscle and design all manner of interesting approaches for acquiring information can be a labor of love. In addition, realizing that you enjoy being creative in your problem solving can help in not only finding a job outside the military, but also the right kind of job. Some military skills, such as medical corps and information technology, transfer readily to the civilian world. Other military fields, like intelligence, require a little more imagination in placement. That is where creative problem solving will come in handy.

P: Processing

The third step in the intelligence cycle is processing. This is the grunt work of intelligence, the unglamorous, unheralded, and hard part of clarifying collected data. At this point, the mass of gathered documentation, also called "the take," is not yet intelligence. In fact, it does not yet qualify as information. Right now, it is just data. The processing step turns raw data into usable information that eventually becomes intelligence. Before that can occur, the take needs to be organized into a coherent and usable form. Yes, formatting is required.

Organize, as a verb, requires, implies, or otherwise describes action. That means you have to go through every file, folder, envelope, drawer, and cubbyhole; and assemble every document, report, photocopy, and printout; every word typed or scribbled on paper, table napkins, and the inside covers of matchbooks, and do the following:

P1. Establish an Original File

This is something that everyone forgets. Once a collected item has been edited or modified in any way, you no longer have an original to return to as a reference. Under *no* circumstances should you *ever* modify these original documents. Remember how hard it was for you to obtain them in the first place? Once you are out of the military, just getting back on a military base can be a challenge, so you must have everything you need before you leave.

Protect these originals as if they were rare museum documents. Ideally, use top-loading document protectors that are "archive-safe." If you have a beer stain on your last performance report, air it out completely, and then put it in a document protector. Pretend George Washington signed these documents, and now they have been entrusted to your care. Treat them, I repeat, as museum documents. For that reason, *never, ever hole-punch originals.* You will have to keep these documents in your care and protection for years, probably decades. The same is true for electronic media. Floppy disks are obsolete, and any valuable information you might have on them should be transferred immediately, with backups, to reliable recordable disks, hard drives, or on-line storage servers. Scanning documents is a good idea as well, as a backup to your originals. Because they are so important, and so universally accepted, take exceptional care of what you have collected.

P2: Make a Workable Copy

After you have secured all of your originals, make copies of everything. The image clarity of a copy, of a copy, of a copy is much worse than that of the original document, and gets worse with every such generation, so be sure to keep track of which is an original, first-generation copy, second-generation copy, and so on. That is another reason why having unmodified originals organized and easy to access is so important. By the way, one of the reasons why the military likes signatures in blue is because blue makes it easy to tell an original from a black-and-white copy.

A straightforward way of organizing your originals is to file them in document protectors with tabbed dividers in a three-ring binder. The fourteen document categories listed in your tasking requirement suggest titles for your divider tabs. Then, make copies of everything, and put the copies in a second binder. You can hole-punch the copies, and jot notes on them, highlight important quotes, make references to other documents, and so on.

The processing phase is where you sow the seeds of later success, if you do it well. This is where you establish categories of information, and methods of organizing, that will make all later analysis quick and easy. The descriptions of all your skills and professional greatness will be discovered in the writings of others, characterized, and made easily retrievable. In the past you had to mine this flattery from a thick bedrock of obscuring admin-o-babble. From now on it will be at your fingertips.

P3: Extract Usable Information

Now find the nuggets, the gold in them thar' performance reports. Give yourself time, and trust your abilities to find what you need. The key is to prevent accidentally overlooking something in the process of looking for something, which may be very obvious. Chances are you have so much to sift through that, if

> "If this was easy, somebody (else) would have done it by now."
>
> —The Sage Consultant, 2006

you miss something, it could be a while before you return to its location again. So, be careful, be thorough, and do not hurry your data mining. Like gold rushers panning the creeks in old California, sift carefully to see the possibilities in what initially may look unpromising.

E: Exploitation

The fourth step in the intelligence cycle is exploitation. This is the investigative work of intelligence, where an analyst rolls up his or her sleeves, stares at the mountain of data, and then makes sense of the chaos. Analysts know that it only looks like chaos at the beginning, and beneath the confused tangle of disheartening "noise" an underlying order awaits recognition. That order emerges slowly, gradually, painstakingly, in bits and bytes that amount to no more than pieces from a jigsaw puzzle.

Then, as is usually the case, long after everyone else has gone home for the night, it happens. Maybe it will be in the shower. Maybe it will be at the gym. Maybe it will be there, under the low-hanging desk lamp, just as you begin to drift off into a warm, dreamy nap. The tangle will loosen. Those are moments of epiphany worth waiting for, the moments that keep intelligence analysts in a thankless business long after they have otherwise wanted to run from their building screaming bloody murder.

Exploitation requirement [REQ 069-07] necessitates that you:

Dissect data: document by document, line by line, word by word, and combine, unite, unify, merge, amalgamate, integrate, join, band, team, and link with information from other sources and methods to produce a softcopy output-product of your skill-sets.

The final output document will include:

1. Dates of performance
2. Organization or agency (customer) of employment
3. Accomplishments and improvements achieved
4. Measurements of improvement ("75 percent increase in . . .")
5. Unique talents employed
6. Specialized skill sets

Now get comfortable, settle in, and focus. Spread out all the papers (on the floor if necessary), get out a felt-pen highlighter, and start reading—

everything. Every reference that defines you as "better than" others requires highlighting. Be judicious. Too much highlighting can complicate the process of isolating specific references, as will become more apparent later, and for now you may want to categorize what you highlight by using various colors. Do not get carried away, or your pages will start looking like a Christmas tree. You can also employ underlining—and bolding or italicizing—but, again, don't produce a Christmas tree. Produce sense of it all.

This is information management, albeit on a personal level. Remember that, in exploiting the data, the order hidden in these individual references is, in fact, a map of yourself. It is like a torn-up and scattered topographic atlas of your being, contouring your strengths and weaknesses, and revealing your seasons of growth and harvest. You have to reassemble the pieces, plot the coordinates point by point, reference by reference. You have to determine where each landmark has its place, in black and white, on two pages of paper—two pages that you will call your résumé.

D: Dissemination

The fifth step in the intelligence cycle is dissemination. This is the point in the process where you are ready to send out your résumé. How you do this, and to whom, will be the subject of later examinations. For now, it is essential that you pay attention to the following recommendation: *Do not send out your résumé until it is time.* Any errors in your résumé now can do more damage than you can possibly imagine. In the Information Age, bad information can completely undermine the most important quality in any job search: your credibility. When you trip over your credibility with an error, especially a spelling error, you could fall into an employment sinkhole. Facing the horde of applicants for a single job, employers look for something, anything, to make the process of *eliminating* candidates easier. Do not give them any ammunition. So, before you do anything hasty, go back to the exploitation phase of the TCPED cycle and give it another iteration.

> "No plan ever survives first contact."
>
> —Anonymous combat veteran

Nothing is perfect the first time through, so repeat the cycle several times. Each time your résumé will become a bit clearer, a bit more concise, and ultimately a bit better all around. That is why this is a cycle.

Borrow, with Extreme Prejudice

Officially, the Intelligence Community does not steal anything. Stealing is a word with such narrow connotations. Perhaps a better way of categorizing our next subject of discussion is "liberating," or "freeing" good ideas from repressive regimes. Yes, it is about borrowing, information-borrowing. After all, why reinvent effective résumé wording that has already been conceived, designed, researched, developed, tested, evaluated, and mass-produced? If something works, adopt it quickly. Or, in other words, adapt your résumé or face employment extinction.

Borrowing is what you need to do when you are at a loss for the right words to describe yourself in your résumé. Over time, each new version will get a little better. Like any engineering design, your initial résumé will likely be inadequate for all circumstances. You need to pay attention to what works, and what does not. After enough iteration it will be ready to send out to the world.

> "You adapt or you die."
>
> —Howard Stringer,
> CEO, Sony Corp.

What follows are broad based and generally descriptive phrases and partial sentences, that you are free to use for improving your résumé. The important thing is that you modify them to fit *your* skills, accomplishments, and experiences. The first list comprises personality-based attributes. The second list is a wholesale compilation of flattering comments that a reviewer might want to see on a résumé. Make good use of those comments to liven up your résumé and document the praise you deserve.

Personal Traits

These were compiled from performance inputs, reports, suggestions, and personality tests during my military service and my post-military civilian employment. Any time you can directly cite favorable comments from superiors, customers,

> "The easy way is not necessarily the correct way."
>
> —Mavaxiom 62

and others, do so by enclosing what was stated about you in "quotation marks," coupled with an action verb to catch the viewer's attention.

1. Tends to perceive the whole, responds to unfolding trends quickly . . .
2. Deals with material intuitively, inner-directed . . .
3. Comprehends abstractions, and sees subtleties others may not notice . . .
4. Learning style is naturally dynamic and flexible . . .
5. Continuously adapts to new situations, categories are temporary . . .
6. Self-directed and skilled at moving easily from project to project . . .
7. Active and searching, continuously seeking and processing, producing energy . . .
8. Tends not to categorize, instead integrates into the whole of the experience . . .
9. Overlooks differences, works well in diverse environments . . .
10. Knows exactly where things are, how to relocate or recall . . .
11. Talented visual learner, best when sees materials and relationships . . .
12. Organized, precise, focused on details, and logical . . .
13. Emphasizes the functional and pragmatic . . .
14. Processes information rapidly, constantly organizing and structuring . . .
15. Unique ability to see what needs doing and gets it done . . .
16. Can see where situation is going before others . . .
17. Well-defined goals . . .
18. Strong visual preference, highly visual learner . . .
19. Organized, structured, detail-oriented, and logical . . .
20. Absorbs environment, selecting out details . . .
21. Simultaneously embeds details in context . . .
22. Can comprehend an overall perspective with added nuances of meaning . . .
23. Prodigious rate of inputting information . . .
24. Can process multiple inputs comfortably, without experiencing indecision . . .
25. Able to focus on more than one aspect of a situation and push for resolution . . .
26. Can tolerate ambiguity, always seeking completion . . .
27. Able to work through problems in a logical sequence, with options available . . .
28. An active learner, yet reasonably logical and disciplined . . .
29. Can "size up" situations and take in information rapidly . . .
30. Remains predominantly functional and practical . . .
31. Abstractions and theory are secondary to application . . .

Input Suggestions

These were also compiled from performance inputs, reports, suggestions, and personality tests from my military service and my post-military civilian employment.

1. Program created was best that anyone had seen in his or her career . . .
2. A powerhouse team member . . .
3. Technical-skills master who marches at a fast pace . . .
4. Leader with boundless initiative, vision, and accomplishment . . .
5. First-rate team-builder and leader . . .
6. Rated as the organization's best leader . . .
7. Places enormous trust in those he leads . . .
8. Vast arsenal of professional talent . . .
9. Exceptional officer with brilliant future . . .
10. Absolutely Herculean work . . .
11. Exceptional leader who takes care of his people . . .
12. Overcomes challenges by sheer force of will and persistence . . .
13. Developed and implemented numerous strategic planning efforts . . .
14. Responsible for revolutionary new technical training programs . . .
15. Directed efforts for new database applications of . . .
16. Operationally developed and deployed . . .
17. Served on hand-picked team . . .
18. Recognized for revolutionizing long-standing intelligence analysis . . .
19. Hand-picked for several high-level staff positions and critical programs . . .
20. Trusted project manager . . .
21. Developed the best information distribution system in . . .
22. Recognized for making best use of evolving computer system . . .
23. Initiated historic intelligence study . . .
24. Revolutionized standing 20-year analysis of . . .
25. Served on the premier organizational team for . . .
26. Built best strategic-threat briefing in team's history . . .
27. Used multi-media for dynamic enhancement and learning aids . . .
28. Developed landmark study and briefed worldwide . . .
29. Ground-floor understanding of . . .
30. Organization's presentations "guru," a master at charts and graphs . . .
31. Published on several occasions in open press. Topics include . . .
32. Acknowledged for "thinking outside the box" . . .

33. The commander indicated that individual was . . .
34. Created revolutionary information fusion and management function . . .
35. Led the largest effort in the organization's history . . .
36. Published on numerous occasions . . .
37. Excellent writing and speaking skills allowed . . .
38. Expeditious communication of strategic visions . . .
39. Assignments include a spectrum of . . .

Being the God of Your Own Creation

While you document your past greatness, you are also building a new future. That future is currently uncertain, and potentially very threatening. Do not despair; there is reason to hopeful. As Dr. Jane Flax puts it, "the worst that can possibly happen already has." Think about that. Now think about your current situation. You find yourself in the aftermath of an event that leaves great ambiguity. There are so many decisions ahead, and you do not know where to begin. The military safety net is gone, and in its place are so many unknowns. Fortunately, the dark clouds of mystery will soon give way, and shed light on a completely new world of *your* creation.

Leaving military or government service means having to follow the course that only you can create for yourself. It will allow you to be true to who you really are, versus what had been deemed acceptable by higher authority. Even in the worst situations, starting over from scratch *gives* you the power of ultimate creation. Being the source of your own creation allows you license to make yourself the way you want to be, not the way others tell you to be. So, prepare yourself for a brave, new life where you will fail a little, succeed a little, and create a whole new person in the process. This is the chance like no other to create a new you.

Separation anxiety is to be expected, and is normal. Do not limit your possibilities just because of natural apprehensions. Even if you hated the military, anxiety about separating will probably still happen. Your real courage will come in allowing that fear to be there

"When our dreams are finally realized, we are not the same people we were when we conceived them. We can only hope now that we will be the people who can later enjoy what we dream of today."

—Mavaxiom 73

while still taking the steps you need to leave the military and succeed as a civilian.

Fear of the unknown makes people react, instead of act. They let uncertainty distract them from what they really want, and what they really want to do. It sometimes manifests itself as a completely irrational fear that they will somehow fail in their transition, and end up "homeless." You may *feel* homeless because you are leaving an institution that has been like a home to you, but you are only leaving behind what you once were. Now, you are standing at the edge of a frontier of your own discovery. Claim that new land in your name.

CHAPTER EIGHT

Being Heard

Just Because You're Correct
Doesn't Mean People will Listen

"It was the best of people. It was the worst of people."
— Mavaxiom 81

What does it mean to have a profession or to be a professional? Perhaps being a professional means you are trusted when exercising your skills; that you are an authority in the field. The military bestows professional "specialties," "skills," or "identifiers" on personnel after certified training and education that builds minimum required standards of performance. But some people are better at their professions than others. Those striving to be better recognize that the minimum standards established by the military do not necessarily encourage them to do better. By contrast, others in the military seemed to aspire to no more than those minimum standards. In this way, there was reason to expect no less, and hope for the possibility of being pleasantly surprised by more in the outcome. A form of comfort comes with these kinds of expectations, a sense of security in aspiring to the minimum. For those striving for more, such expectations almost required *underachieving*, something they simply could not do. Maybe you are just such a person, and are now seeking a greater sense of fulfillment from a life outside the military.

Supply and Demand

On the outside those who are comfortable underachieving probably will not contribute to a company's continued success in the marketplace. They will also not advance far, or last very long at that company. Conversely, those with the drive to apply their skills will find themselves much sought-after via the process of supply and demand. When the supply of particular skills is low, and the demand is high, businesses can reward those skilled with higher pay. Much-needed skills translate into higher wages for those positioned for the market. In short, the market as a whole, reflecting the demands of consumers, creates incentives for people to become experts in particular fields. This evolutionary process is an adaptation to the needs of business.

The military, by contrast, demonstrates a very different approach. It attempts to predetermine its future requirements for particular professions. This can be dangerous, because it relies on anticipated manpower-focused predictions that may *drive* future skill developments, regardless of the changing environment. This high-risk investment might yield high returns, but high risk can also result in huge losses. In the business world such loss results in insolvency, bankruptcy, and financial ruin. In war fighting the results may be even worse. So the danger of this kind of arbitrary approach to skills is that dictating future requirements is wrong. Such decisions can fail to take into account unanticipated external factors, and unforeseen future demands. For example, one can only imagine what the demands were for specialties such as counterterrorism and WMD intelligence on September 10th 2001.

Another example was the Air Force's decision in the late 1980s to eliminate "targeteering" as one of its career specialties. Someone, somewhere, was under the impression that training people to *target* weapons was a waste of the Air Force's time and money. Perhaps this was because so many in the Air Force believed that precision-guided munitions (PGMs) were so accurate that the

> "Maybe you can put a PGM on a dime, but first you need to know where the dime is."
>
> —Unofficial targeteer slogan

need to cultivate weapon-aiming talent on the part of its intelligence cadre would no longer be necessary.

Inevitably, when faced with the preparations for Operation DESERT STORM, the Air Force attempted to track down every individual who had ever so much as picked up a protractor in anger, and designated each person as a targeteer candidate. Perhaps a world superpower can afford to do this, but it would spell defeat for lesser militaries, and economic collapse for competitive businesses. The lesson learned lost on the targeteers was that their economic worth had skyrocketed. Had a similar situation arisen in the private sector those with expertise would have drawn gigantic salaries. For the targeteers, however, being so in demand meant that they would be very busy, but far from duly compensated. And for their troubles, operational counterparts often looked upon targeteers as merely combat "support."

> "Never, ever, under any circumstance use the word 'support' in your resume, or your correspondence.
>
> Providing support is for undergarments, not people. You either *did* something, or you did *not*."
>
> —Mavaxiom 82

So what does all this have to do with your job search? Taking these lessons to the process of transitioning to the private sector, it becomes clear how failing to recognize your own economic worth can have damaging repercussions to your civilian pay. In addition, when you are not reasonably rewarded, compensated, or incentivized for your skills, the shortfalls may also erode your sense of self-worth. People generally join teams to contribute, and when they no longer feel that their contributions matter, they soon wonder why they are on the team. People like to feel valued, and it is management's job to figure out how each person's productive value will yield the biggest return to the organization. When professionals generate that return, they should be given recognition as an acknowledgment by management that what they do is, in fact, important to their organization.

Military cultural norms stress humility, and often people sometimes leave the military with a gross underestimation of their abilities and worth. For the purposes of your farewell to the service, then, it is important that you learn how to recognize and verbalize your economic worth.

Being Paid Seriously

Typically, you must prove your worth to potential employers, who apply the concept of return on investment much more pragmatically than their military counterparts. You must sell potential employers on your estimation of your worth in terms that they can understand. That means describing your skills in civilian terminology, and your worth in terms that will be compensated accordingly.

Some civilian employers believe it is in their best interests to keep you in the dark as to your economic worth. They might be friends, people you trust, people who smile, shake your hand, and rave about how great you are. But then the profit imperative enters the equation, and those who once watched your back may be watching out for something else as civilians. When the principle of scarcity is applied to salary, some managers are willing to manipulate employees' misperceptions of their worth. They may not pay employees properly for their skills, especially if those employees do not understand their own worth. Newly transitioning veterans are particularly vulnerable to such tactics. Management may underpay employees, gambling that they will not discuss their earnings with other employees.

When I left the military for civilian life, I was astonished to see how intelligence-community secrecy paled in comparison to the secrecy surrounding employee salaries. I think salary ranges are kept so secret, in part, because of the gross disparities that arise when pay is used as an incentive for different employees. Some employees are happy with annual raises. Some need carrot-and-stick bonuses. If an employee is happy with less than what other employees expect, management can reasonably ask, "Why pay more?" That is business. Although powered by economic necessity, business makes room for those who do not necessarily deserve more, but receive more than others.

Being Taken Seriously

For intelligence professionals, not being taken seriously is an occupational hazard. In some cases, it can be a struggle just to speak. When analysts are not given an opportunity to air professional opinions, they begin to question their own relevance. Such is the case when decision makers consult intelligence inputs as an afterthought. In addition, if managers reward those who tell them what they want to hear, being the bearer of unwanted news can make for fewer career opportunities. What can a job seeker learn from a profession?

It becomes impossible to explain all the complexities to decision makers if intelligence was never part of the process. When management stops asking for advice or ceases to heed warnings, the outcomes are frequently self-fulfilling "intelligence failures." The key element, then, in these dealings is trust on both sides.

From my own experience as a trusted advisor to decision makers, subordinates can take a number of approaches to maximize their ability to be heard. Foremost is recognizing your role as a subordinate. If you want to be trusted, you must earn the trust of decision makers by sheer force of performance. Do your job. If your job is as a subject matter expert, then ensure that the decision maker knows what you do. They are not the experts, so that will mean that in addition to informing them, your job will also require *educating* decision makers. Education is no easy task with decision makers who have little time. So, when writing a report or giving a presentation, anticipate that the decision maker will likely:

1. not read it, or
2. read only part of it, or
3. read it, but not understand enough to do something about it.

That means that you have to take up the slack, and fill in the gaps to reinforce the message. With that mindset, you can also write in ways that will encourage decision makers to want more by not only educating, but also entertaining their interests. The bottom line is that your job of warning decision makers is an ongoing and demanding process.[1]

Keep in mind that decision makers are in the business of action, and dislike uncertainty, doubt, or details that cloud issues. That makes intelligence intrinsically problematic for them because intelligence gives them more information, making their decisions all the more difficult. It is easier for them to make decisions with less information in the hope that nothing goes wrong. They may pretend they were unaware of available intelligence beforehand if something does go wrong, or simply blame their advisors in classic fashion. But if the information was present, and communicated effectively (as described above) then the final responsibility for so-called intelligence failures rests with those who take action.

In business, overlooking professional advice can result in real financial repercussions, so the difference between good leaders and bad managers is if they pay attention. But leaders blossom few in fields weedy with bad managers, making the job of advisors all the more challenging. All you can do is your professional due diligence. As a subordinate, advisor, subject matter expert, or intelligence professional, the burden is on you to package the information in digestible ways that will be heard and understood to a degree sufficient to make sound decisions.

Sometimes Management Is Just Not Serious

When you are paid seriously, you are taken seriously— an aspect of the commercial job market that seems to confound most newcomers, especially those entering from the military or government service. Even those well-established in jobs have persisting issues with salaries. Understanding your place in the pecking order demands intimate and ready assessment of your economic worth—the learned skills and natural talents you contribute to a company. No one else is going to volunteer your economic worth to you. You have to look out for yourself now, and the intelligence you gather will make all the difference in advancing your civilian life.

In the military, everyone knows everyone else's earnings—they are listed by time in service and grade. In the commercial world, the bounds of your compensation are those of your imagination and enterprise. The survival of your standard of living and the money to pay for your dreams hangs in the balance.

I was a workaholic while in the military, and for some time thereafter. A good work ethic is a healthy thing, but I took it to an extreme. Working too hard, especially for the wrong reasons, can be problematic. I tried to turn lemons into lemonade, but every night I arrived home wondering why I felt empty and unfulfilled by my work. Being told that I was the *only* person who could solve work crises was validating at first, but eventually left me feeling

Management Seeks Employee

Unscrupulous boss seeks workaholic for long hours on projects sane, well-adjusted individuals wouldn't dream of taking. Does your idea of being challenged mean doing everybody's dirty work? Do you strive for non-stop rescue operations? Can you discreetly troubleshoot management blunders? Equal-opportunity employer seeks over-qualified individual (with no social life) as on-call fix-it person. Must raise the bar on output standards while reducing salary costs. Do we have work for you!

unsatisfied and unrecognized. My customers loved me, but the shaky chain of command back to my superiors left me wondering if my worth was truly being communicated. Was there something else I should be doing to ensure they understood prior to my impending performance appraisal? In the past, I had learned that if I did not speak up as my own best advocate that I only had myself to blame if my bosses were unaware of my contributions. In one case, I set up a meeting and detailed my accomplishments. I showed my managers that throughout the year my work directly contributed to a favorable review by our clients, and that I:

1. Met and exceeded all client expectations,
2. Delivered "over and above" anticipated client results,
3. Established productive relationships with new mission partners,
4. Expanded the use of our products and services,
5. Overcame the toughest challenges to advance client needs, and
6. Did so, often, with little or no notice.

Plainly stated, I knocked the clients' socks off. I demonstrated more than just good skills in the execution of my duties. I consistently contributed the highest-valued products and services to our most senior clients. Our customers often referenced our positive impact on their mission, and our commitment to shoot for greater results in the future. Clients regarded my contribution as being nothing short of outstanding; I was a "top-tier" performer. I pointed out in e-mails that previous clients were still asking for me, by name, to provide services that they regarded as "impossible to replace." My past year had set a milestone for positive client feedback. So our consumers got it, but, somewhere between them and my superiors, the echoes of their approval had faded to silence. I felt I needed to point out all this directly because I no longer wanted to rely on a hope—common to many competent but unrecognized people—that my superiors got it as well. I believed that my results should be given a commensurate "outstanding" year-end review.

I was taking no chances, as I fully appreciated the need for being *directly* involved in the recognition and compensation process. My reasons included the following:

1. Direct involvement ensures that management recognizes the worth of your contributions. Management can become so removed that they

never get the customer feedback necessary to accurately assess employee accomplishments warranting pay increases. When management is not keeping track with performance measures, it is time for you to proactively assert your accomplishments to management.

2. When it is difficult for customers to provide direct feedback to your company's management, it is important to seek ways to convey their comments. Try forwarding e-mails or voice messages, to expedite the process of your evaluations. If an "outstanding" rating will yield a bonus, communicating evidence for that rating takes on new urgency.

3. Company management rarely transcribes all accolades from customers to staff, especially when and where they are bestowed. This is especially true if you work at separate locations from your management, and makes it all the more necessary that you find ways to pass along customer accolades to your bosses frequently.

4. Managing your own career and compensation are parts of your daily job. If you are not up to speed in these areas, then your have incorrectly prioritized your duties.

If you have to work too hard to keep your management in the loop, then there may be a larger problem. The company's job—perhaps its most important one—is to take care of its good employees. *That* is why management is paid more than their employees. The higher pay is for the hard work required to retain you and keep the customers happy. If your management does not embrace this belief, then it is dangerous to also assume that your management is taking you seriously.

When management continues to fail to take you seriously, it may be time for you to assess if irreconcilable differences exist at work. If you truly take responsibility for your own career well-being, then the only way to deal with the situation may be to vote with your feet. If you are not happy, you can do something about it.

"If you have to ask how it is done, you will never achieve acceptance. Those in the inner circle do not earn their way in; they are *invited* in."

—Mavaxiom 83

I-Dos and I-Don'ts

Work environments become toxic for common-enough reasons, but other, more individualistic variables also figure in such equations. After leaving the military, I felt I had more control over my life. I began to think more seriously about my role in creating the right kind of work environment. I considered my issues with the kinds of people, jobs, and environments that had been toxic for me in the past. With the skills I had learned as an intelligence officer, I began to record, examine, and categorize all these issues, looking for trends, and analyzing the results.

I saw that my perceptions fell into two general categories: I-dos and I-don'ts.

Although sounding like marriage and divorce vows, my list titles had application in my job search at the time because they elicited emotions from deep inside that I could never verbalize. Verbalization was the key. To express those intensely personal wants, needs, and desires was half the battle. Putting them on paper gave me a target to strive for, and guidelines for what to avoid. I realized that if I did not answer each I-do, I might wind up stuck in the I-don't list.

Try something similar for yourself. Imagine the work environment you would like, versus a work environment that would be toxic. Think of the places, the people, and the jobs. Make a list of numbers, say one to twenty, skipping a line between each, and then just start writing. Try not to worry about grammar, or logic, or a plan. Just write. Keep writing. If an idea begins to spill over, just create a new number for it. Do not try to organize anything quite yet. Just spit the ideas onto paper (or your computer screen) as either an I-do or an I-don't. Do not let anything stand in the way of capturing ideas. Return later to worry about analyzing patterns, and for now think of yourself as a vacuum cleaner collecting up all the ideas you possibly can.

If the two lists sound whiny, self-centered, and petty, then you have done it *correctly*. In fact, that is why you are doing the exercise. For the moment, try not to let your conscience bother you on this exercise because you are trying to accomplish much more than just complain. What you are trying to do is get to the heart of your wants and needs, and also identify the "deal breakers" that get in the way of your ability to concentrate on the job. So indulge yourself for a few moments. Completeness is of the essence; restraint is of no concern. This exercise is selfishly all about you. It is your wish list, so be as demanding as you like.

I-Don'ts

These are the results of my own lists. I-don'ts were first, as they were easier to identify from all the frustrations accumulated over past military and civilian jobs.

1. I don't care about the administrative details:
   - a- I don't want to fill out forms
   - b- I don't want to plan staff meetings
   - c- I don't want to schedule or coordinate conferences
2. I don't want to waste time focusing on the things that are not the skills focus of all my training, education, and experience:
   - a- Spreadsheets
   - b- Monthly reports
   - c- Timecards
   - d- Expense reports
   - e- Other related administrivia
3. I don't want my skills wasted putting out fires:
   - a- Emergency planning and reactive staff meetings
   - b- Rescue operations for office meltdowns
   - c- Cleanups for bad management decisions
   - d- Task reprioritizations
4. I don't want to wait anymore for people who cannot make decisions
5. I don't want to have to pay my dues anymore, especially to people who do not care about my well-being
6. I don't want to have to prove my worth anymore, especially to less-than-competent managers
7. I don't want my know-how to be ignored, not listened to, or not taken seriously
8. I don't want to waste anymore time commuting:
   - a- More than 30 minutes each way to work everyday
   - b- Endlessly paying tolls on highways to avoid traffic and/or tickets
   - c- I want to enjoy driving my car for pleasure on the weekends

I-Dos

Then came I-dos, which were surprisingly more difficult than I thought. The reason why is not completely clear, but may have to do with expressing wants and desires, but not wanting to sound needy. Unfortunately, because of the nature of this exercise, the only way to really get inside your personal wants and desires is to actually allow yourself to *be* needy and demanding. It is a way of giving yourself permission to ask for what you want.

1. I want to learn
   - a- I want to travel to other parts of the world
   - b- I want to encounter new cultures and languages

2. I want to focus on the "big picture," strategic issues rather than on attending to the specific details (that requires extra effort on my part)
3. I want connectivity with the rest of the Community / world
4. I want my office tools to work, and not to keep breaking down:
   - a- Computers
   - b- Printers
   - c- Phone connections
   - d- Internet connectivity
   - e- Intranet connectivity
   - f - Copiers (color / black and white)
5. I want reliable colleagues and managers capable of high-end performance:
   - a- I want to feel that my assessments are taken seriously
   - b- I want to feel that my contribution counts
   - c- I want to know that my opinions matter
   - d- I want to be listened to and consulted for my professional know-how
6. I want administrative assistance that is more detail-oriented than I am (like my tax accountant) for:
   - a- Administrative forms
   - b- Spreadsheets
   - c- Monthly reports
   - d- Scheduling
   - e- Room availability
   - f- Equipment trouble calls
   - g- Timecards
   - h- Expense reports
   - i- Performance input formats
   - j- Bulk typing
   - k- Troublesome bureaucracy
   - l- Nagging requirements
7. I want both home and work to be near public transportation, so I can:
   - a- Live inside the city
   - b- Work inside the city
   - c- Use my car primarily for pleasure driving or weekend use
   - d- Commute via train or bus
   - e- Have safe and reliable transportation during inclement weather

Lists like these are important because pouring wants and desires onto paper enables people to learn things about themselves that might not be obvious. For example, I could not write my I-dos nearly as quickly as my I-don'ts. After years of service, just thinking of my own needs first was a challenge. In a new civilian reality, though, all the rules have changed. If *you* do not take care of yourself, who will? If certain things in your work environment are a source of toxic frustration, they will impact your ability to do your job effectively, and potentially hurt your advancement. Should you ignore them? My answer is, emphatically, "No!" If you are not happy in your new job, then you have failed to transition effectively. It is *that* simple.

In a more practical sense, though, lists like these help focus you on the kinds of jobs that you want. This is an exercise in fulfilling your individual need to be happy. The lists can turn your personal desires into tools that enable you to demand more for yourself. They become expectations or thresholds not to fall below, because you have already acknowledged that this is what you want. So there is no need to punish yourself further, in an environment that you never liked in the first place. You have served your country. To move on to a new life you have to create an environment that you can thrive in. And before you can create anything, you have to know what you really want. So, it keeps coming back to the big, tough question: what do you really want? Look at your own lists and think about them. Keep coming back to them. The minute you betray yourself by not seeking what you *know* you really want, that old toxicity will begin percolating back into your system. In the civilian word, there will be no assignment detailer to save you from your next lousy job. Only you can save yourself now.

> "Don't ask the question, unless you're ready for the answer."
>
> —The Military Pragmatist

Note

1. This concept is central to the teachings of Dr. Jan Goldman, National Defense Intelligence College (formerly the Joint Military Intelligence College) at the Defense Intelligence Agency (DIA) in Washington, D.C.

CHAPTER NINE

Walking on Water
How to Prevent Becoming Your Own Worst Competition

"All happy families resemble one another, but each unhappy family is unhappy in its own way."

—Leo Tolstoy, *Anna Karenina*

It seems odd that those who deserve to receive praise do not always know how to accept it. I agree that humility is a virtue, but I also recognize a misconception among the humble that their management has judiciously acknowledged their worth. The noble view is that we should not preoccupy ourselves with our own recognition, nor seek approval no matter how tempting the offer. In ways that many have already experienced in the military, and certainly out of necessity in the civilian world, I pose the following questions. If you do not keep track of your accomplishments, *who will?* Your boss? Your coworkers? Your peers? Your competitors?

As you begin to make important decisions about your career advancement, recognize that you will be doing so on your own. It takes a special amount of willpower to overcome innate modesty, to stop what you are doing, and take the time to document your accomplishments, particularly while events are fresh and relevant in your head. This almost seems contrary to the principle of "service" that you left behind in the military.

In a world where strict accounting of limited resources sets the tone of business, many believe that there is only so much to go around. These people live by the principle of scarcity. This view is a defining characteristic of certain kinds of management (and mismanagement). Managers who perceive a scarcity of resources respond by hoarding what they have—whether assets, people, or even their people's skills. That pathology goes well beyond a simple desire for control. Hoarding can involve a complex intertwining of greed and narcissism, a need for both possession and self-aggrandizement. That means that the same behavior that constricts the actions of subordinates also manifests an incessant drive by overly ambitious managers to win favor from superiors. It can turn the modern office environment into a perverse adult version of musical chairs, where careers are at stake. In the middle of this maelstrom is the employee, freshly transitioned from the military and wanting to get on with his or her new life.

Walking_on_Water@Work.Com

If your management thinks that you "walk on water" because of your capabilities, then you probably *are* that good. Being in that position, means that you take what you do seriously. You take pride in your work and know that the praise puts you in the precarious position of possibly screwing up and plummeting to the bottom. It is as if the mere acknowledgment of accomplishment might mock the mythological Fates and destine you to doom. So, you shirk from praise because you fear it might encourage you to slack off and not perform as well. Or perhaps you fear that your success will establish new standards that you cannot maintain. Any of those reasons demonstrates conscientiousness to a fault. The only thing you fear more than your own failure is success. This is why overachievers can become their own toughest competition.

It becomes apparent why overachievers need to *relax*. They need to stop racing around on fire, listen to, and start writing down, all the good things that people have had to say about them. This means you. Well, why are you just sitting there? Start writing it all down! Yes, now, and from now on…

What follows is a list of some of the persuasive ways that you can word your descriptions of yourself and your professional talents. Note that words describing action, which means verbs and adverbs, are particularly important in introducing your list topics. Even more than well-chosen nouns, verbs will add vividness and life to whatever you write.

Action-Oriented Descriptions

These examples were drawn from performance inputs, reports, suggestions, and personality tests from my military service and civilian employment, as well as the military's own Transition Assistance Program (TAP). Any time you can directly cite praise from superiors, customers, and others, do so by enclosing them in "quotation marks." Note the use of an introductory verb, to catch readers' attention, in almost every instance.

1. Acquired _____ technologies years before other offices . . .
2. Advanced _____ technologies by . . .
3. Advised principal representatives to the _____ Committee . . .
4. Anticipated customer demands years in advance of . . .
5. Applied state-of-the-art expertise of _____ to . . .
6. Averted potential security compromises by . . .
7. Capitalized on several new business areas for organization . . .
8. Captivated senior staff members with thorough familiarity of . . .
9. Captured customer buy-in with . . .
10. Commanded technical skills of . . .
11. Consistently demonstrated "superior ability" to surpass customers' expectations . . .
12. Coordinated enterprise architecture requirements for . . .
13. Cultivated a rare talent in the organization. . .
14. Directed additional guidance for . . .
15. Delivered the "best briefing to date" on . . .
16. Demonstrated the model approach to customer needs by . . .
17. Developed a novel method of _____. . .
18. Ensured timely, accurate, and up-to-date capabilities . . .
19. Expanded the reach of customer interaction beyond . . .
20. Formed an education / training / outreach program for . . .
21. Improved the customer's technical capabilities X percent, by . . .
22. "Impossible to replace" hand-picked member of the team . . .
23. Constantly demanded by customers to . . .
24. Instructed internal and external customers . . .
25. Intervened on behalf of mission partners reluctant to change . . .

26. Introduced imaginative solutions for future program issues and requirements . . .
27. Investigated a tremendous new capability to . . .
28. Revitalized an advocacy program on all current, proposed, and future . . .
29. Launched the new customer outreach program for . . .
30. Leveraged other areas (teaching courses, council member, etc.) . . .
31. Marketed new capabilities with overviews and tutorials . . .
32. Negotiated and resolved long-standing mission partner issues with . . .
33. Originated and tested a customer-oriented road map for . . .
34. Overcame significant budgetary constraints by . . .
35. Pioneered the connection between other communities...
36. Promoted future systems. . .
37. Produced excellent, timely examples of the various capabilities . . .
38. Published subject matter expert on . . .
39. Recognized the need for . . .
40. Recruited numerous quality individuals for . . .
41. Single-handedly executed a ground breaking . . .
42. Solved a difficult task with the customer that . . .
43. Standardized the principal-briefer program . . .
44. Stimulated new approaches with new ideas and information . . .
45. Verified with hands-on experience . . .

Other Values Enhancing Your Reputation

The following were also compiled from performance inputs, reports, suggestions, and personality tests from my military service and civilian employment.

1. Loyalty: Demonstrates complete loyalty to the company. Always looking for ways to expand business and enhance the company's bottom line. Actively pursues new talent with skills or knowledge of potential value to the company.
2. Commitment: Devoted to accomplishing the task at hand. Demonstrated conviction in pursuit of the best course of action to accomplish goals.
3. Team Player: Establishes good working relationships and promotes cooperation with co-workers, supervisors, and customers.
4. Dependability: Totally reliable. Embodies a tremendous reputation for technical knowledge throughout the community.

5. Professionalism: Seeks and accepts responsibility. Logically approaches decisions and demonstrates awareness of their consequences/implications. Fair and ethical.
6. Competence: Produces the expected quantity and quality of work, on time, within budget constraints.
7. Organization: Simplifies issues. Effectively lays out complex concepts to customers.
8. Initiative: Anticipates problems and proposes alternative solutions. Generates new ideas and recommends modernizations and improvements.
9. Drive: Visualizes new ways to make things happen. Not satisfied with the status quo. Envisions what can be accomplished, and pushes to achieve it. Passionate professional.
10. Innovation: Conceives new or modified approaches. Not bound by past solutions or approaches. Thinks strategically.
11. Adaptability: Flexible and responsive to change. Adapts to changing situations and seizes opportunities. Always acting to ensure continued successful contract performance.
12. Customer Focus: Makes the customer the first priority. Responds to customer needs. Builds and maintains good relationships with customers.
13. Communication (both oral and written): Creates accurate reports. Shares information with others. Actively listens to customers and mission partners. Articulate and clear.
14. Influence: Promotes ideas persuasively. Shapes the opinions of others and overcomes resistance. Builds consensus for action and negotiates beneficial solutions to problems.
15. Reputation: Well known and highly regarded throughout the professional community.
16. Connections: Superb contacting and establishing influential new contacts.
17. Results: Sets high standards. Strives for constant improvement and drives for results.

What Are You Worth?

It became clear in my first year of civilian employment that I had seriously underestimated my economic worth. As I cannot say too often, this is common among military people. Getting your salary, vacation, and other forms of compensation to balance with work is a real challenge for people who have spent years in the service. As I stumbled through the process of discovery, I realized that I could bring my training as an intelligence professional to bear on this job search. It was essential to identify the assets (and liabilities) at my disposal in my skills arsenal, and how to structure them in a coordinated campaign plan.

When trying to figure out your economic worth, there are several approaches you can take. A person's compensation is a function related to a number of factors:

1. Job Knowledge – Your compensation needs to be commensurate with your contribution (knowledge, training, education, experience, skills expertise, natural talents, security clearances, accesses, contacts, and other assets).

2. Local Cost of Living – Your compensation needs to be commensurate with the local housing market and standards of living.

3. Given a Credible Voice – If you want to be taken seriously, then you have to be paid seriously. Professionals are entitled to a professional opinion. The more seriously that opinion is taken, the more "voice" that person has professionally. Likewise, the more seriously that opinion is taken, the more a company will spend on that employee. To keep both sides of this equation equal if you are paid seriously, then you will be taken seriously.

   If your office environment is frustrating because management does not listen to your observations or suggestions, the problem may not be you. It may be deficient management. If they are spending a lot of money for your services, then the last thing they want to do is ignore the cost of your input. If you are not paid enough to be taken seriously at the office, then you probably will not be taken seriously.

4. Additional Skills – Your compensation should reflect any rare, difficult-to-develop, or much-in-demand skills. Any skills that place you above and beyond your peers can make a difference when it comes to pay. So, for example, a master's degree is generally worth an additional $10,000 per year. In addition to its obvious educational benefits, an advanced degree also demonstrates the employee's ability to commit to a long-term project, follow through with extra demands, and complete involved tasks. These are all very desirable, but not generally advertised, reasons for employers to pay their employees more.

5. Capacity for Transition – Sometimes compensation is commensurate with your ability to leave your company and go somewhere else. For

people trapped in a stair-stepped promotion cycle, the only way to get a good raise is to leave your company and start somewhere else at a higher salary.

Leaving a job is prohibitively stressful, and employers know this. They bank on their employees being too anxious to uproot and move somewhere else when they get frustrated. I have listened to friends complain about their jobs for *years*, only to see them continue to stay at the same job that they said was killing them. In truth, I have done the same. People are generally more scared to leave than stay and endure the torture. When confronted by the prospect of the unknown, people often choose to manage their employer's shortfalls and the accompanying stress.

When people negotiate their salaries, employers sometimes try to convince them that they should be happy with their pay, and even feel lucky that they have it so good. This is no consolation if they still feel awful at the end of the workday. They may find themselves spending most of their weekends regrouping, decompressing, recuperating, and recovering.

I actually had a girlfriend break up with me because of how much my work week changed me. She liked me on Mondays, but hated me by Fridays. I went through a Jekyll to Hyde transformation every week, and it drove her crazy. I had less and less energy to enjoy my life at the end of the day, and I was bringing my frustration home with me. Waiting for such events to serve as indicators is no way to gauge your job satisfaction.

Unfortunately, people dread starting the job-search process so instead, they hunker down to survive their current situation. Job search takes so much effort, and can be so stressful, that most people shelve any plans of looking elsewhere until their environment becomes toxic. In doing so, employees play right into the hands of management. Managers know that people fear the very idea of pulling up stakes and relocating elsewhere. They know that their employees are far more inclined to complain about their jobs and do nothing to improve their situation.

Leaving your job only when it becomes intolerable is the wrong time to go. The time to leave your job is when you are at the top of your game, when you are still happy with yourself and comfortable with your contribution. At this point your negotiating strength is at its greatest, and you are able to wait for the most agreeable terms. The worst position to negotiate from is when you absolutely *need* a job.

Reacting to Your Situation

The feeling of stepping off into the civilian world can leave many disoriented, like free-falling from the rear of an airplane and seeing ground rush. Things seem to happen so fast. Safety mechanisms that were once there, like a ripcord, have not automatically engaged to slow your descent and anxiety builds. The "pucker factor" goes up, and your adrenaline is pumping. Soon, your looming transition is beginning to affect your sleep. You are beginning to worry about undefinable "things." To be more precise, "everything" is on your mind. The one thing that is not on your mind is the one thing that should be on your mind: what do you really want to do with the rest of your life?

> "Managers need only be capable of enduring employee complaining."
>
> — Mavaxiom 91

To answer this question, you need to look inside despite all the external distractions. You need to take the time and make the space for yourself to sit still and think about where the rest of your life is going. This is a vulnerable state to be in. Change is plummeting at you. Friends, colleagues, loved ones will lend their opinions, and their suggestions may help. You may find yourself wanting to do what they say because it "makes sense." A warning: be careful to do what is best for *you*, and not what is best for somebody else, If you take someone else's path, instead of your own, you run the risk of finding yourself unhappy down the road. Those who you trust and know very well might be able to lend a little steadiness to your increasingly stressful situation, but they might not know what you really want. They might care, and they might do anything for you, but they cannot make up your mind for you. Only you can do that. And now, more than ever, you need to be true to yourself because your whole life is changing. Be part of the central component of that decision-making process.

Basic human-fear responses compel us to react to change in a number of different ways:

1. Fight—Stand and take on the threat.
2. Flight—Run like all get-out and only look back when you think it might be safe.
3. The null set—Do nothing and see what happens next.

Unfortunately, *none* of these options are sensible for use in your situation right now. As you continue plummeting, you may realize the following:

1. Fight—There is no threat. Unemployment is a reasonable concern, as is taking a job that is not for you. To overcome these situations requires finding the right job.
2. Flight—In the analogy, the C-130 you jumped (or were pushed) out of is over another state by now. Go ahead, look back up at it. What do you see? That plane is now a dot on the horizon, the crew is closing up the cargo platform, and waving "Bye!" In simple English, soon the military will be gone. The earth, however, is getting much, much closer; and getting more so with each passing second.
3. The null set—You are about to hit the ground really, really hard. If you choose to do nothing, you are liable not to feel anything—ever again. I know what you are thinking; "Hmm, that actually sounds like a good plan right now." Now, that is no way of dealing with a crisis. The military taught you better than that. Right?

Well, the answer is, unfortunately, "No." The military probably did *not* teach you how to deal with the situation of knowing what you really want. They told you what you should want, and you had to believe them. Now it could be a confusing proposition.

The military's Transition Assistance Program (TAP) is a great class for service members who are separating. The people who teach that classes all deserve medals for what they do for departing military members. I soaked up all I could in those courses. I paid very close attention in my classes because I was scared to death about my plunge toward separation. As an intelligence officer, I went through the TAP course as if it were a professional mission. I collected and analyzed all the data I could. Then I went through it again, just so I could interrogate all the instructors. I set it up like a full-blown intelligence campaign, complete with my own targeting requirements.

I was scared, Cold-War-Strategic-Air-Command-24/7-global-nuclear-annihilation scared. Every indicator on my anxiety "big board" was lit up and flashing as if I were personally preparing to go "nuclear combat, toe to toe with the Russkies."[1]

Then I found a job.

It was "a" job (not "the" job). I could relax and back off from DEFCON-1 (the U.S. Defense Condition rating for all-out war). In my analyzing my situation I realized that the source of the stress I was experiencing was not from what had been expected. The stress had come from something I had completely overlooked. The stress had come from inside of me, from a failing to understand what I wanted after the military.

The rationale goes something like this: in combat situations, you do not stop long enough to think about anything. Your training and experience teaches you how to act before you ever get a chance to think. You want to act before the enemy does, and the only way to ensure this is by reducing decision making to pure muscle memory. You train, and train, and train until you can do your job in your sleep. But a new threat requires a whole different approach. For all the training you received, all the skills you learned, and all the ways you know how to combat your adversary, the thing that was missing was how to stop and think about what you really wanted. This is what makes getting out of the military and moving onto your new life a challenge.

It is difficult for proud, hard-working service members to conceptualize anything from their skills "tool kit." The military teaches you discipline, self-control, superior personal and professional standards, so what could possibly be missing? Being unprepared is something that the military goes out of its way to avoid.

How can you possibly find the job that is right for you, if you cannot answer this question first?

What do you really want?

The Effect(s) of Change on You

When you transition, you may perceive that things are going badly all around you. The good news is that even though you feel out of control, you might actually be on the right path. I know this sounds counterintuitive, but try to remember that despite even a desire to leave, the military has been a place of stability. You have been comfortable in your rut, and you have probably been in that rut for some time. Leaving that stability means that you have to relearn even simple tasks all over again. In that learning process, mistakes will abound. This is a good sign, because it means you are learning. In other words, "Don't panic!"[2] The fact that things do not fit the way they used to validates that you are firmly in transition.

You are on the right path. The pain you feel is from shedding old skin and exposing the new skin underneath to the elements. You will feel the biting cold, the unrelenting wind, the pounding rain, and the burning sun. You may also feel the warm caring touch of others you are close with in a way that you have never felt before. Revel in the change. This is *your* transition.

It is also your own life, so take good care of it. As is pointed out on every airline flight, "Put your mask on first—then put the mask on the small child." Passing out and flopping over into a child's lap is cause for losing major cool points during an in-flight emergency. The same is true for your health during transition. Taking care of your own needs first is essential for ensuring the well-being of others who may depend on you. At this crucial time do not take chances with your health. So, if you begin to notice unusual or compulsive behaviors in yourself, or a resurgence of unhealthy habits, pay attention to them.

The process of transition to a completely new career takes months, if not years. Holding out that long without suffering adverse effects is impossible. So be good to yourself, and take care of your own needs. Get plenty of sleep (eight hours a night is recommended). Eat healthy foods and take time to enjoy yourself with the things that give you pleasure. Do not wait for bleeding gums or hemorrhoids to be your wake-up call.

Along the way, stress can take on stealthy forms. Sometimes it moves from one part of the body to another, just to reduce its own acuteness. It can start out as a nagging cold, and then a few weeks later it is a rash that seems to linger beyond reason. It could manifest itself as increased eating, or a sudden weight loss from *not* eating. Stress might manifest itself as a gradual increase in late-night clubbing, drinking, general partying, or promiscuity. Likewise, it may make itself apparent with increased alcohol intake or an antisocial propensity to *not* go out at all. Either way, you need to pay attention to your habits, and notice any subtle changes.

One of the telltale signs of stress is an alteration to sleep schedule. In my case, I know I needed sleep so I tried all manner of different sleep aids. True to my intelligence training, I began documenting the before and after effects of both over-the-counter as well as prescription sleep medications. I conceived a metaphor to describe how those medications made me feel. The figure is an actual entry from my sleep journal I made to capture the mental image:

The lesson from the experiment was that every person's individual physiology and body chemistry reacts differently to each different kind of medication. No two people are quite the same when it comes to medications. Sometimes the only way to know for sure is to test how a medication reacts with your system by carefully and methodically evaluating its effects over

"The sensation of waking up after a night on some sleep medications feels like waking up after a shipwreck."

Figure 9.1. The Feeling from Some Sleep Medications

time. Just because someone tells you that the medication is what you should be taking does not mean that it will sit well with your body chemistry. Many different factors play into that equation. Knowing yourself, and your own body's sensitivities, is central to making an informed decision. No one else can do that for you. So before you blindly follow another person's recommendations, even a doctor's, empower yourself to make the best decision possible. See for yourself if the medication helps relieve your symptoms of stress, or just contributes to further complications.

If you get too caught up in what you are doing, you may need to turn to trusted friends, family, or even professionals for input. Trusted loved ones are *not* the enemy, especially if they start telling you things that you do not want to hear. What they say might seem spiteful or malicious, but this is because transition makes people feel extremely vulnerable. As your whole world changes, it might be a challenge to recognize that not everyone is out to get you, or working against you. It might be because your defenses are up, and you are sensitive to every indica-

"Stress kills."

—D. Welles, 1990

tor. Your subconscious is on high alert, and may try to read between the lines, and see threats that might not really be there. So pay attention to yourself, now more than ever.

Finally, as your life changes, so will you. When people change deep inside, it is reflected in a change to the way the world outside appears. Do not be surprised if your friends, co-workers, supervisors, maybe everyone who you knew in the past, begin to seem somehow "different," more, and more, every day. It may seem like an uncomfortably indefinable quality at first, something you cannot quite describe in words. Later, it may become so intense that it is difficult to interact with others in the same old way. If this happens, try not to be alarmed. Change brings about unusual, and sometimes unsettling, new perceptions of the world around you. This does not mean that they are a threat to you, or that you do not belong. It may just be a defense or coping mechanism. Your changes in perception may also signal that you are seeing the world through completely new eyes. Shifts of this magnitude only reinforce that you are changing fundamentally, at the core of your being. Ready yourself for this possibility, and the possibility that your life will never be the same again.

Notes

1. An expectation of B-52 bomber pilot Maj. T. J. "King" Kong (actor Slim Pickens), in the Kubrick film, *Dr. Strangelove.*

2. A much-repeated counsel in the Adams comic science-fiction novel, *The Hitchhiker's Guide to the Galaxy.*

CHAPTER TEN

Changing Values
The Twilight of Childhood Ending....

"You never realize how bad you felt until you start to feel
better. It reminds you never to take your health for granted."
— K. Walter, 2006

V alues inspire a person to grow. Finding a place that will accept and
encourage your growth is not a foregone conclusion. That place—
one that shares your values—might not exist. To do so you might
have to create the environment that will suit your value system. You must
have a job that will pay the bills and ensure your economic survival in the
Capitalist Theater of Operations (CTO). Intelligence preparation of the bat-
tle-space (IPB) would be incomplete, however, without addressing the non-
material aspects of your transition.

Self-Generated Values

After I left active duty, I took the skills I developed in the military and rejoined
our capitalist society. Although many believe that making money is the key to
success, others—idealists, perhaps—believe that making a difference is more
important. Reconciling the two viewpoints can be a challenge to some leaving
military service. In the absence of reconciliation, veterans usually find themselves contemplating military service attributes worth holding on to, that no

longer apply in civilian life. Of course, making money is important. You need to pay for life in a capitalist society, but you also need to live. Living requires immaterial aspects, even if immersed in a materialistic way of life. As I thought about the things that were still important to me as a civilian, I began to also notice things I had taken for granted in the military.

My realization came years after separating, while pursuing my favorite pastime. Scuba diving requires many of the same attributes that made me feel "connected" in my military experience: teamwork, dedication to others in challenging projects, and practical communication. As part of my rescue-diver certification, I committed those attributes to action and word. They were immaterial expectations that I valued long after military service. When I wrote them down, they became what I call my "dive-buddy motto."

> "A trusted bond exists on *every* dive. Communication is the key, even if feelings are hurt—even my own"
>
> —Marc's Dive-Buddy Motto

This motto was important to me because honest communication is not always easy, in the military or civilian life. It takes a special courage to say, "I was wrong," even if only to yourself. Now, as a civilian, I needed to be honest with myself to make sure that all the important lessons learned from my military experience would find their way into my new civilian life. Likewise, now is the time for you to be honest with yourself because from here on out it is *your* future.

I strongly believe that your value-system is essential to your transition. So, again, back to the really big, important question:

What do you really want?

Let me stress that your value system reflects whatever is important to you, not what was imposed upon you by the military. For years, your superiors, supervisors, and peers imposed a set of common values on you and expected you to adhere to them. Soon you will be on your own, detached and isolated from the military. Without any dictation to you of "approved" options, you are now posed with endless possibilities. It is freedom-of-choice, and only you are responsible for the outcomes of your choices.

You may find yourself in a civilian population with ideals and beliefs wildly divergent from your own. The environment may seem strange, threatening, or even frightening. This is normal; it is all part of readjustment to civilian culture. Feeling out of place and disconnected is a sign that you are changing, evolving, and adapting to your new environment. And this, too, shall pass. You are operating on your own power, and handling your own replenishment. Have faith, and trust in your own abilities; you will make it.

Take what you learned in the military, along with the values from your family, religion, friends, mentors, movies, books, school, and so on, and confirm the strength of your *own* views. Focus on your own needs so you will have what you need for the challenges ahead. This may sound difficult, especially since you are accustomed to a professional doctrine based on service and self-sacrifice. Now, as a capitalist, you are in a system of self-service. The spoils of the free market are only available if you ask for them. No need to get greedy, but a time and a place exists for you to demand what you deserve. For example, in relation to your new job, ask yourself the following:

What is in it for me?

Applying a little self-service in this regard will help you determine if this job is a reflection of who you are as an individual. Obviously, for some in the military, adjusting to this new reality will require more effort than for others. Think of it this way: the closer you are to receiving what you really want from your new job now will help reduce more of your career distractions later.

Operating Security

The civilians you will work for and with will probably have *completely* different imperatives than those in the military. They will already be looking out for their self-interests. The new imperative is now called "profit" and it is the engine driving companies to live, grow, and prosper. Anything that adds to that prosperity is a good thing. Anything that hinders the smooth functioning of the firm is a problem. Consequently, no one necessarily cares about your well-being in the same ways that you were accustomed to in the military. No one will require you to exercise daily. No one will order you to have medical checkups. That is all *your* responsibility, and as such attending to your needs only gets in the way of your company achieving a greater profit. You have to take care of yourself, and not let it get in the way of the company's bottom line. Work is about keeping up with what they are paying you for, and the rest is your responsibility.

The solution to this dilemma is to take charge of your new situation. Create an outcome to your transition with an environment that reflects what you want and allows you to achieve the results intended. Part of this process of change requires creating a way of cultivating your natural talents, and making yourself more valuable to your new company. The skills you have learned in the military will actually assist you in this endeavor. However, make sure you understand (and accept) that anything you do that may interfere with your company's goals will not be looked upon favorably. For example, if you want to complete your degree, or go on to an advanced degree, but the new job prohibits that pursuit, then accept it upfront. This job may only serve as a stepping-stone so that you can eventually reposition yourself into another job that will allow you to complete your educational goals. As with all such strategies, control the dissemination of such information. Anyone at this job who has any knowledge of your plans could disrupt your eventual success. Planning any clandestine operation of this nature requires good information security (INFOSEC) and communications security (COMSEC). Be careful in your e-mailing, as all are potentially legal records. Phone calls can easily be eavesdropped in a cubicle farm.   Any phone message you leave anymore is converted to an audio file that can easily be forwarded to suspicious managers. Take your calls outside with your cell phone on "smoke breaks," and employ other good operational security (OPSEC) practices.

Ultimately, only you can decide what you want. Only you will know what makes you happy. A successful choice is the job that gives you the most enjoyment and the least aggravation. If it does not turn out that way, do not get discouraged. Remember, you now have the freedom to choose what you really want.

The Cage

In today's high-paced, competitive world, people are so caught up in what they are "supposed to do" that they never get around to doing what they really *want to do*. In this regard, the military's requirement of self-sacrifice is above and beyond the calling of the average citizen. It never ceased to amaze me how heavy my uniform always felt when I was wearing it in public. Every action, every gesture, every nuance seemed to carry with it the risk of interpretation and judgment by the civilians around me. In any public setting, with no other service members around, I *was* the military. Those in the military must uphold higher standards than their civilian counterparts. For example, the military lifestyle requires adherence to its own legal system, the Uniform Code of Military Justice (UCMJ). In time, these limits become your life, and the lifestyle becomes almost "comfortable." In time, the same will be true of your new civilian life, but not without a struggle.

The odd thing about an institution is that those who submit to its norms are usually only tied to that institution by their own choosing. At any time, they can choose to do otherwise. A problem develops when we become so comfortable with the choice that we stop choosing. It becomes easier to keep plodding along. Even if the circumstances are unpleasant, it seems easier to endure the discomfort rather than confront the unknowns of change. As a testament to how such approaches to change entrench themselves, service members need only look to their own military assignment system. The viewpoint that attrition is a viable approach to change is so evolved in the military that it is exemplified in an almost comical manifestation.

The "Who-Will-Be-Reassigned-First?" Game

A military culture coping mechanism that relies on attrition

In any military assignment, there are those who simply do not get along. It may be a subordinate and a superior, coworkers, peers, "bad blood" from past assignments, failed relationships, you name it. Since military members often feel that there is very little that they can do in such a situation, many defer to what they see as their only hope for rescue—the military assignment system. Somehow, some way, someone will be reassigned to a different office, deployed, sent to training, participate in an exercise, or, if you are very lucky, have a permanent change of station (PCS), preferably to the other side of the globe. Eventually, somebody will PCS first.

People continue functioning in objectionable situations, believing they can "make it work," rather than trying something different. Being institutionalized by military culture can make the prospect of change so frightening that even people who hated the military have difficulty leaving.

Years after leaving the military, I found myself in jobs that made me very uncomfortable. I did not realize what was happening, but kept finding myself in similar circumstances over and over again. Then I began to notice recurrent themes. As a trained intelligence professional, I decided to do my own analysis on the subject. I examined each of my supervisors since leaving the military, and voila! Answers began jumping off the page so quickly that it became embarrassing that I had not seen them before.

Subtle, but important, connections appeared from manager to manager that should have alerted me. Instead, I "stuck it out," in classic military fashion, and kept trying to work through all the issues. I always had the latitude to opt out, but did not. The question was, why? Why did I endure unsatisfying jobs for any longer than necessary? Why did I wait until I had to leave because the job was adversely affecting my life? And most importantly, why did I accept the job at all? My rationalizations at the time were common to those of many people. I was concerned that leaving might (a) cause friction in the organization, or (b) upset the customer. There I was, being the military guy again. I was (a) concerned about my fellow team members, and (b) focused on the mission. Regardless of the inevitability of my departure I put up with the situation until I could not stand it any longer.

The message from this analysis is that in all cases I had a *choice* in the matter. I could have chosen a different path at any time along the way. Instead, I coped with the situation, dealt with it, in classic military fashion. And, in classic military fashion, instead of cutting losses and regrouping else-

Table 10.1. Manager History

Boss #	Time Span	Manager's Style	Former Military	Rating of Experience	Why I Left
1	18 mo	In absentia	Yes	OK	Realized I was being underpaid
2	18 mo	Everything is an emergency crisis	Yes	Agonizing	No real raises
3	18 mo	"Let's talk …"	Yes	Confined	Much higher offer; corporate culture
4	12 mo	In absentia	Yes	OK	Company reorganization
5	12 mo	"Deal with it."	Yes	All used up	Self-imposed sabbatical

where I dug in deeper and kept fighting. The problem with this kind of strategy is that when you finally get to the point where you are ready to leave, the process of job search becomes a crisis. This is the worst time to go looking for a new job. You are burned out, tired, and scarred from the past job experience. You may end up accepting less salary than you deserve just to get out of the old situation. Starting a new job requires you to be at the top of your game, not when you feel broken down and used up. The consequence of such a strategy is potentially a worse outcome than the last situation.

When it is time to leave the military, you must leave. Military people, including those disgusted by their experiences, may find themselves in a similar situation as described above. If you left the Department of Defense, only to find yourself in a defense-related job, no matter how good the pay it may be more of the same. If the military wore you out then jobs that require the equivalent of a suit uniform for employees, hierarchal management structures, and strict adherence to a chain of command, might not be the answer to your job search. It may be "what you know," but that might not be a good thing. You may find yourself plagued by bosses with the same disagreeable military management styles, all over again.

In a society of free will, everyone has the right to choose his or her reality. Selecting jobs that do not work may involve unreasonable expectations in the selection process, or a subconscious habit. The key may lie in de-bugging the original programming. Until your programming is overwritten, you may make the kinds of choices that made sense in the military. Until you change your expectations, you may find yourself making bad choices over and over again. You may not even realize what is happening for several iterations (as in my case). Once fully transplanted into your new civilian reality, you may be puzzled to find the same problematic situations that you left behind in the military. There is no evil conspiracy sticking you with unsatisfying jobs or abusive bosses. Instead, you have to acknowledge that there is an active choice involved on your part, and then you have to take responsibility for those decisions. People do these things to themselves whether they are aware of it or not, and the remnants of old programming can last a lifetime.

The reason why is because of how such programming deals with uncomfortable feelings. For example, one of the ways of dealing with the inflexibilities of military life is for people to view difficult situations as an "eternal space." It is accepting the perception of being powerless and immobilized in place, with no means of extracting oneself. In other parlance, it is known as "hunkering down" and dealing with the situation.

Military people do not look forward to being trapped, but they construct mental models that help them manage situations that they cannot control. To cope with their situations, they strategize an emotional siege campaign of attrition.

A way of conceptualizing this is via analogy. In the analogy, it is like getting used to being confined in a cage. Not a physical cage, but a psychological cage. The person learns to be in the cage, and exist as if it will be their eternal space. Somewhere in this analogy the cage door is unlocked, opened, or removed from its hinges. Confused by the new circumstances, the person begins to feel anxious contemplating what to do next. As ironic as it may seem, the person actually feels too uncomfortable to leave. The outside looks too uncertain to risk disrupting the situation, even though the person is imprisoned. The reason is because people become relatively "comfortable" with functioning in their setting, regardless of its absolute discomfort. The effect of this coping mechanism is that the person is too frightened to exit the world they have gotten accustomed to, even though it is still a cage. Instead of looking at the prospects of a new life, many military members may find the unknown so intimidating that they become paralyzed in their decision making. They opt for what they know, just to be on the safe side, and miss all the other opportunities available. It becomes easier to just go with the flow, and do what everybody else is doing, instead of what they really want to do. In the end, very little change actually occurs, and displaced veterans can find themselves stuck in situations where, although expedient for paying bills, very little true change actually occurs.[1]

For all the desire to move on from the military, the person never really leaves.

The problems associated with *not* leaving when it comes time can lead to other issues. One of the more troubling is how people in a psychological cage may relate to others. Specifically, functioning in an eternal-space mindset can make people seek out others who emulate the cage environment. This makes veterans vulnerable to others who embody directive management styles. In the worst cases, they become a target for abuse by unscrupulous managers who manipulate the belief that the only way out of the cell is through hard work, regardless of misuse or mistreatment. In the civilian world, options exist that are not available in the military. Despite the options available, vestiges of indoctrination can persist in military people for *years* after separating. Never realizing that they can simply leave their current situation, veterans rationalize conditions that might legitimize their departure.

They may believe that there is some prerequisite task for them to accomplish, or need to satisfy that will allow them to feel justified in leaving. Likewise, they may feel that there is a minimum pain threshold they must experience before they can go.

Those who seem more prone to falling into this case are people in "the 20 percent." They believe that their situation will improve if they simply try harder. They believe that after superior performance their bosses will see that they truly are valuable employees and deserve better treatment. Of course this is a self-generated illusion designed to maintain their focus and optimism in difficult times. More importantly, it is a by-product of institutions that believe employees must first "pay their dues" before being treated equitably. Insert into this equation the occasionally unscrupulous manager who consciously seeks out individuals to exploit, and the likelihood of disaster skyrockets. To avoid these situations in the future requires learning how to recognize the self-limiting behavior of the cage, the defensiveness of eternal space, and the need for a sense of worth. Recognizing and controlling those kinds of reactions, will help put high-risk individuals more at ease in new environments. An even more important outcome of paying attention to these kinds of reactions is making oneself less of a target for further abuse.

Shoot the Racehorse

What happens to capable, talented individuals who find themselves unexpectedly in the confines of the cage? To describe the effects of such a situation I have created a parable I call "Shoot the Racehorse." In this parable, the owner of a racehorse is too stingy to buy a mule or hire a tractor, so he goes into his stable and enlists his prized thoroughbred racehorse for the job. The racehorse, thinking that it is going out for a run, is excited and enthusiastic. It does not know what the plow is, so it thinks nothing of it. Then when it is harnessed to the plow, suddenly feeling immobilized, the racehorse panics. After sufficient lashing by the owner, the horse finally settles down into numb submission.

It is likely that the field will be plowed (eventually), but at the end of that season it is also likely that the racehorse will have to be put down. Broken and humiliated, it will never pull a plow again, and certainly can never race again. Confining and coercing a thoroughbred to perform in a capacity that is contrary to its natural talent eventually renders that racehorse all used up, and useless for future work.

The parable demonstrates that living creatures have a basic requirement to pursue their nature, and misusing that nature can be catastrophic. People leaving the military, especially those in "the 20 percent," can feel this way if their new civilian jobs clash with their nature. For example, if you left the military because of all the paperwork, why transplant yourself into a purely administrative job? You might as well clench a bridle in your teeth at your interview. Human beings have infinitely more choices at their disposal than they know, certainly more than the horse in the parable. People can determine their own fate, but to make it work they must be true to their nature. Denying people the ability to pursue their innate talents can have devastating implications on their well-being in the long-term. It kills both their spirit, and the drive to take advantage of opportunities when they do arise. Bridling employees makes them more malleable to managers, but ultimately less effective to the organization.

Military people separating from the service, especially "the 20 percent," may be at risk of this in their new jobs. Employers know they are willing to work hard and bosses with military experience may see this as an opportunity to re-apply inflexible military management approaches for a profit. Managers may coax employees with promises of being "part of an elite team," and "once you prove your stuff in your first job, then you will move right up the line." Be careful of sales pitches like these, especially from former military people who have been exposed to the same kind of indoctrination. This is not the military anymore. It is only a job. The imperative is not to "support and defend the Constitution" anymore; it is to maximize profit. Overworking and undercompensating employees is an expedient means to that end.

Talented individuals are among us, but their talents may never be realized if they are denied opportunities for discovery and growth. This is at odds with the demands on management to achieve results and an immediate return on investments. This pressure can sometimes cause managers to disregard opportunities for employee growth, seeing such prospects as frivolous or wasteful. These managers have forgotten that the return on any investment is in the future and forcing the return can jeopardize the outcome. Ironically, the success of a manager's people means success for the organization. In the simplest terms, management exists *because* of their people, and no organization can survive without either.

Ideally, if someone truly has a recognized talent, it only makes sense that management would want to cultivate it, if only to capitalize on its benefits.

Remember being the round peg in the square hole? Do you want to find your placement in the civilian world because you can walk and chew gum at the same time? Managers who come from the institution of "warm-body management" might not care about your ultimate growth potential. Some managers simply view people as assets, pieces on a game board that are moved around at will to support larger decisions. In truth, these managers are not all former military. The business world is ruthless enough. What should concern separating military members, though, is when these kinds of managers use their military background as a means of luring new hires. Be extremely cautious when "rejoining the team" becomes a negotiating point. The military is over for you, but clearly not for these people. They will never let you leave the cage. In intelligence parlance, these are kinds of people you must "spot and assess" early. It could make a big difference later. Since you must buy into a new corporate culture when you transition out of the military, consider the following ancient Roman warning: *caveat emptor* (let the buyer beware).

Caring for Yourself

When change finally does come, all that you once knew transforms into something completely different. It can be disconcerting as you begin to question everything that you thought you understood. This level of anxiety is completely understandable and normal. As the transition progresses, it could take months, even years, to finally settle into a comfort zone. Try to remember that comfort is not necessarily the goal of this transformation. Comfort is good, but what is happening now is *growth*. You are growing into a new skin, and if you are feeling anxiety and discomfort it may be a good thing. It means you are shedding the old emotional limits, and expanding into new limits. In this case, a little pain is good medicine.

Anyone who is uncomfortable with being out of control may feel a particular challenge during their transition. The military system that you are leaving behind has boundaries that were known. The boundaries of the place where you are going are unknown. All you can expect is that the environment will be very different from what you once knew. Of course, there will be some similarities, here and there, in your new life. But remember the point of this transition is to move on, not cling to remnants of the system you are leaving behind. You must let go of the old to understand the logic of the new civilian system. The pecking orders will be different, the privileges and rewards will be based on different criteria. Like a freshman, you will have to start all over again and learn as you go. No matter what you mastered before, the simple truth is that you are leaving. All that control must

be relinquished for the promise of something better. The whole world is
changing, and you are changing with it.

A natural reaction is to project these frightening emotions. If you project them outward, they can manifest as blame, rage, or aggression. If you
project them inward, they can manifest as depression or fearful vulnerability. Shame may emerge just because you feel vulnerability. This is completely
reasonable under the circumstances. Life change like leaving the service is a
major source of stress. You may be unable to manage the changes the way
you managed the certainties before leaving, and that creates many projected
emotions. Watch them, try to notice yourself acting, reacting, and behaving.
Taking note of the problems you are having, as they are occurring, may be
the way of heading off even more problematic circumstances that may arise
by ignoring your feelings.

At times when you are calm and relaxed, disquieting racing thoughts
might suddenly erupt. These are internalized anxieties bubbling to the
surface when you are not under any external stress. Racing thoughts tend
to overanalyze and question your plans, undermining your tranquility.
Expect this to occur when you are in a twilight state of nearing sleep, or
early in the morning nearing consciousness. Try not to listen. These fearful thoughts are only distracting static. Try not to engage these racing
thoughts with rational arguments because they are irrational in nature.
They have emotional, not logical, origins. A way to handle this noise is to
shut it down with a disciplined campaign of diversion. When it starts, try
something calming, like reading or meditating. If that does not work, it
might be time for a run. Divert your attention elsewhere and have room
built in your life to pursue things that you enjoy and things that bring you
peace of mind.

While all this is going on, try to be mindful of reoccurring themes in
your behavior. Classic overachievers tend to deal with stress by immersing
themselves further in their work. All the psychological energy churned up
by impending change needs to go somewhere, and usually it goes into what
is a "known." For overachievers, that means work. Instead of limiting their
involvement, they take on a plethora of projects to keep them busy. It suc-
ceeds in diverting attention away from anxiety or racing thoughts, but it is
also exhausting to the overachiever and everyone around them. More work
is not the answer. It may make you feel better, but your new responsibility
is to yourself and getting ready for the big life change ahead. The office is
not the place to make that happen. The military gives you terminal leave for
a reason. Use it.

The recommendation for coping with everything going on is to slow down. "Cool out," as Dr. Jane Flax suggests, and try not to react to everything. Notice what is happening (around you and inside of you), but do not respond. It is time to take all that psychological energy and channel it into productive endeavors that assist in your job search, and into time off. Focus on nurturing yourself first, and the needs of your transition. Attend to the needs in the here and now, and orient yourself in the present moment. Your challenge is to make it from Point A, to Point B, at the other side of the transition. That requires (a) owning up to what needs to be done and (b) doing it. Difficult choices must be made, and avoiding the decision does not help the situation.

Resist the temptation to simply take the easiest options that only skirt or delay future obligations. The longer-term consequences may only limit you achieving more desirable results. That means if you always dreamed of getting an advanced degree at a prestigious school with your GI Bill, do not waste it going to a lesser institution because it will be easier. Push yourself for more. You deserve it, because you have earned it. Do not sell yourself short. It is time to leave the past behind and move forward.

Manic Defense and Other Inappropriate Diversions

Throughout your transition, you may find yourself challenged by your worst enemy—yourself. No one knows how to beat up on you quite like yourself. Change can bring out the best in people, but it also can bring out aspects we do not like to acknowledge. It is your responsibility to watch for both. Those are the times when you might resort to counterproductive behavior. A common behavior for energetic military people is "manic defense," or pouring inordinate energy into pursuits that only serve the purpose of taking your mind off the real issues at hand. These types of behavior may relieve stress, but in the long run can distract your ability to think, plan out actions, and make progress.

By contrast to the previous section advocating you to "pursue things that you enjoy and things that bring you peace of mind," manic defense is when you take those things to an extreme. So, for example, if running clears your mind, but now you are running more, and more, and more, something may be wrong. The stress might be great for your running, but it also risks the possibility of injury. If you do get injured, you will not have your old stand-by stress reduction mechanism handy, and all the good stress reduction may

turn into a tailspin. If in the middle of your transition you go extreme moun-
tain-biking on Saturday, and Class V white-water rafting on Sunday, there
may be a bigger problem than the rapids. If every weekend is an exhausting
paintball marathon and motocross followed by a keg, so-called "stress reduction" may not be your intended goal. You may be hip deep into manic
defense.

People have interesting ways of generating their own "noise" to drown
out stress. This noise is also effective at dealing with fear of the unknown,
emptiness, and silence. The important thing to remember is that this noise
is *self-generated*. No matter how disagreeable their situation they will still
avoid the possibility of change because it means confronting uncomfortable
unknowns. Anxiety may arise in the gaps between all the exciting activities.
It may range from subtle lapses in confidence about one's own abilities, all
the way up to imagining irrationally implausible catastrophes. It is important to analyze this fear, because underlying its irrationality is a rational message. In the case of the irrational fear, the message may be grief. A profound
sadness accompanies leaving a former home, the military, and feeling as if
there is no new home to go to.

The irony is that as people leave the service they will have more opportunities for starting over, redefining themselves, and achieving more success
than they may ever have had before. While still in transition, it just *feels* like
there is nothing to go to. On the brink of a completely new life, and in a
world of possibilities, the challenge is to trust in your abilities and discover
aspects of your personality that you may not have taken seriously before.
You will have unrestricted authorization to completely unleash yourself. This
is it, the time in your life you have been waiting for. This country was built
on the premise of "opportunity," specifically so that people would have the
freedom to pursue their unlimited potential. Start thinking of it that way.
Do not let this get in the way of you taking the first step.

1. The Distractions

This is the time to create your own new life, not run away from it. You served
your country, now commit to serving yourself for a change.

As you shed the old skin of the military, you may find that those old
behaviors might not fit the way they did. This is normal because all the
rules are changing, and you are redefining new ones. Resign yourself to the
fact that the old comfort level is gone, and you are building a new comfort

level day by day. Part of you is holding onto the old, despite knowing that you need to move on to the new. The part holding on is afraid of change, afraid that you will not be able to make it in your new situation. And in a way you know that if you take this step your life really never will be the same.

Some years ago I went to an island resort that featured, of all things, a pair of trapezes. Having never played with them before, I thought it would be fun to try. What I learned was shocking. You cannot grab the second trapeze until you have fully let go of the first with *both* hands. My natural tendency was to hold onto the first trapeze with one hand and reach out with other hand until I had the second trapeze firmly in my grasp. Although sound in theory, it always failed in practice. In fact, onlooking holidaygoers reveled in watching with glee as newbie trapeze artists attempted this maneuver, only to end flopping wildly into the safety net. It was good fun for all, but the lesson learned was even more profound. To reach the other trapeze means completely letting go, sailing helplessly through the air, and trusting that the other trapeze will be there. In the context of transitioning out of the military, it means trusting that you will be able to grab onto an opportunity when it comes. You must have faith that you can. Success means letting go of what was behind you, and focusing on what is in front of you.

2. Feeling Alone in Your Decision

Unfortunately, a decision about your life is a decision that can only be made, and should only be made, by *you*. No one else can make that decision, because no one else can understand your motivations and feelings. In addition, no winning answer, or breakthrough moment of revelation will guide you on your path. If there is, count your blessings. For the rest of us, the process of discovering outcomes to our decisions will be the rule. Amid all these contemplations, people can end up feeling very alone. To a large extent, we must be alone because other people may inadvertently distract us from what we really want—no matter how well-meaning their intentions. Regardless, this does not help with the feelings of isolation that come with transition.

Some people will actually go into a kind of seclusion to come to terms with their struggle. This can put immense pressure on loved ones, who must be patient with the process. The man or woman who comes home from the military is no longer the youth that left. Much has happened during the military experience, and the disconnection he or she may have with family can border on estrangement.

If a family has never been very good about talking about feelings, now is a good time to try. First, some ground rules. Veterans probably do not need a million questions. They need time to think. They do, however, need three good meals, clean clothes, and sometimes just a hand to hold to know someone else is there. They do not want to feel probed. If they have something to say, they will say it. They just need others to pay attention to what they are saying. They may blurt out a feeling that makes no sense, and it may be just so they can hear it themselves to know they are feeling it, feeling anything. This is a hard time for them, made harder by knowing that only *they* can unlock the riddle of their life's new direction. All the suggestions in the world may only confuse them, and to avoid being overwhelmed they may seek the quiet of isolation. Let them.

This may be especially difficult for type-A personalities accustomed to making decisions, and this might fool them into believing that they can easily decide what is best for them in their new life. A problem may emerge because professional decisions have a habit of being emotionally detached from the outcomes. Making decisions that affect *other* people may be easy for them, but now the focus is on them. They may be totally unfamiliar with their own internal desires, and what is best for them outside the work context. This is especially true if they have always put their own needs second to the needs of others, or to success. After years of this, they lose touch with what is really important to them. They may feel lost without a staff meeting, negotiations, contracts, and so on. The resulting feeling of aloneness can be overwhelming.

3. An Unexpected Lack of Self-Confidence

Another struggle for type-A personalities is with their own self-confidence. Most successful people believe that they can to do anything. Issues of confidence are the least of their concerns. Unfortunately, overconfidence, especially professionally, is sometimes compensation for a lack of personal confidence. When faced with a professional challenge, they know that they can overcome any problems that arise. When posed by personal challenges, however, these same successful people may find themselves in unknown territory. These are not issues with which they are comfortable dealing, or have much successful experience. Transitioning to a new life, then, puts them outside their natural comfort zone. So, instead, they turn to work.

Venturing into the new territory of emotionally challenging topics can yield unwanted apprehension and anxiety. Without a string of past successes to fall back on, their awkward navigation through uncomfortable feelings might yield additional embarrassment or exasperation. It is a doubly difficult road for them, so they immerse themselves where they are comfortable, back at work. People who can mastermind new business processes without a second thought might be completely confounded by the task of something as simple as enjoying their off time or meaningful interpersonal relationships. They will almost certainly land a great job, but the deeper question is whether they will be happy with their new life.

4. Control Issues

A person who is accustomed to being in control of his or her life may find it particularly unnerving to relinquish that control, as the trapeze story illustrated. This is because control is more than just a means of getting things done; it may be a source of its own emotional comfort. Control equates to stability for these people, and moments during life change require a person to let go and allow other things to happen. Control-oriented people like managing uncertainty. They are accustomed to success, in part from controlling all the variables. It validates their belief that the more control over uncertainty they possess the more likely the outcomes will favor their success.

To continue the trapeze analogy, in transitioning out of the military there is a brief moment when those doing so will be helplessly between both worlds. This will be an especially uncomfortable period for them. Sailing through the air in search of the next trapeze will not be fun, to them; it will keep them awake at night. The fear generated by such a movement can be debilitating.

People want to believe that they have the power to make the correct and best decisions for themselves, but oftentimes there are just too many other things going on that they cannot control. Even if they are successful, they may find the effect of not living up to their expectations crushing. Successful people expect more, and often have unreasonable expectations of what they will achieve. Inasmuch as this fuels them to strive harder, it opens up the possibility of perceiving failure just because their expectations have not been met.

> "Be careful what you wish for. You might just get it."
>
> —The Military Assignment System in Action

It is important not to let the anxiety of letting go overwhelm our ultimate goals. It is no small feat to let go of the trapeze with both hands. Trust that another will be there. When it comes, you will find yourself full of energy to devote to settling into your new situation. Have faith in yourself. Once you have passed the point of no return in your decision, your focus will shift, and every bit of you will be poised for the new challenges ahead.

Note

1. From discussions with Dr. Jane Flax.

CHAPTER ELEVEN

Where Does Talent Go?
Others Will Put You in "Your Place,"
If You Let Them

"Bureaucracy blinds vision, deafens improvement, mutes creativity, numbs initiative, and crushes genius in its tracks."
— Mavaxiom 111

The military is *not* an evil institution, although some of my so-called superiors in the military were of questionable motive. I believe that military service is a noble profession. Liberal friends had a different view of my choice to enter the service. One described it as my "blunder into the cult of death." Regardless, I still have positive memories of my service. Supporting and defending the U.S. Constitution is not about mindless obedience, it is about defending the *idea* that a nation of individuals is stronger than the sum of its parts. More importantly, being American entitles you to object, even with things going on in your own country. After all, how else can you be objective unless you are allowed to object?

There was unity in the rebellious band of former British colonial upstarts who created our nation, and we became strong because of it. Rebellion formed America, and the dynamic tension written into the Constitution continues to make the nation great. Rebellion is in our blood. It is not, however, welcomed in military ranks, conditionally or otherwise. The need for discipline is clear in any military, and the U.S. Armed Forces is no exception. Something to consider, however, is what happens when a people rooted in the rebellious idea of self-improvement begin to see improvement as threatening to the establishment?

Great leaders realize that talented subordinates are not threatening, but rather a benefit to the larger institution. It takes a great leader not to misuse that gift and, instead, urge it to its own greatness. Ordinarily, the threatening power of talent, especially natural talent, produces a managerial imperative to control or shun such individuals as nonconformists. When institutions fail to cultivate "the odd-ball," they run the risk of eliminating the person who might have the solution to a vexing problem, or the person with the ability to think outside the limits of conventional perception.

Look back through history and consider those who were great and did not "fit in," and by not fitting in possessed the perspective to see things that others could not. Militaries today do not provide a safe place for the next Leonardo Da Vinci. In fact, some would argue that Leonardo would have no place in the military or even the Intelligence Community. For that matter, if we were to consider great leaders from just the World War II era, many of them would struggle to fit into today's defense and intelligence infrastructures. People like CIA founder William "Wild Bill" Donovan, Army General George S. Patton, Jr., Air Force General Curtis E. LeMay, and others would likely be branded as frenzied, insubordinate, or dangerous misfits by today's standards. Legendary founder of the "Flying Tigers," Claire Lee Chennault, and champion of air power William "Billy" Mitchell had difficulties even in their *own* times. Throughout history, visionary leaders faced more problems from within their own ranks than they did from their adversaries,

So where is a visionary to go? This is perhaps a topic for (yet) another book. In the meantime, such individuals might try the military industrial complex, the world of defense contracting. Having worked in the military, Intelligence Community, and in defense contracting, myself, I would submit that Leonardo would probably have difficulty there as well. The reason why has to do with how people who do not "fit in" are treated by the defense establishment. These people, who command tomorrow's technology, collide with institutions that make them feel unwanted and that they do not belong. But the military and Intelligence Community need such individuals because of their technological know-how. Such is the conundrum. Despite the fact that these talented people are devoted to protecting the nation, they run a gauntlet between those who naturally fit in because of their toughness, strength, or aggressiveness, and those who hold on to bureaucratic power. When a "young Leonardo" does not embody alpha-male qualities that the traditional military respects, or tout the party line, they risk immediate ostracizing. The result is that very talented people with potentially incredible contributions find themselves being pushed out of the defense establishment.

The Techno-Anthropology of Talent

When people do not quite fit into established institutions, it may be difficult for them to categorize their talents. My experience exemplified this challenge. In the 1990s the military underwent wide-scale downsizing. Across the services, the valued skills of the Cold War came under scrutiny for relevance in the twenty-first century. It was clear that technology would play a vital role in combat of the future. As an aerospace engineer, and an intelligence officer, I regarded it a foregone conclusion that the military would maintain and foster these skills. In fact, the opposite was true.

The new demand on the military was to spread its employees thinly across a range of worldwide operations. An "inch deep and a mile wide," as we used to call it. The new demand was for people with more so-called fungible skills. What this meant was that individuals in particular jobs could replace or be replaced by other service members in identical specialties. The idea made sense, on paper, but required a military that was composed of mutually interchangeable members. Specialization would, therefore, get in the way of this new plug-and-play philosophy of the military generalist. Service members with rare, in-depth skills that took years to cultivate became a liability. Such was the case in the intelligence field, which already had a notorious reputation for eating its young. There seemed to be a push in intelligence fields to unload anyone who was not:

1. A shooter
2. A bureaucrat, or
3. Subservient to shooters or bureaucrats

I was doomed. Worse, I was faced with the task of quantifying and qualifying my skills to the outside world. I tried numerous ways to describe my specialty in civilian terms. When I could not find adequate titles to describe what I was really good at, I had to create new terms.

Sometimes, talent is not obvious to those outside (or inside) the military. It may require reinventing yourself in terms that the outside world can understand—so you can find your place in an otherwise alien civilian environment. In my case, my military skills (and new professional aspirations) were somewhere in the nexus of technology, people, and behavioral sciences. Seeing that my skills were understood became essential when trying to communicate to employers the value that I added to their organization. They needed a rationale for paying me, and an understanding of what they were getting for their money.

I had to not only quantify my skills so that civilian employers could employ me, but also create terms that they could understand. I had to translate from military- and intelligence-speak to English, and communicate my post-separation anxiety. The word I invented to describe this uniquely individual talent was "techno-anthropology." So what is techno-anthropology? The way I defined it was as a branch of knowledge dealing with the interaction between humans and technology. For example, a computer engineer could install hardware or software, but a techno-anthropologist would realize that the problems with the new system were due instead to poor staffing procedures. Rather than focusing solely on issues with the technology, itself, the techno-anthropologist aspires to understand how users interact with technology.

Then I took the definition one step further. I reasoned that a need existed to trailblaze comparative studies between different cultures and the technologies they adopted. Specifically, noticeable distinctions existed before, during, and after the application of information derived from advanced technology. I was struck by how organizations shuddered from the introduction of radical new technologies, because their management structures, internal bureaucracies, and/or means of compartmentalizing ideas could not support the expanded capabilities from the information technology (IT) world.

Then I realized something even more profound. What I was doing in virtually all my military and post-military jobs was developing a new kind of appreciation for explaining organizational behavior and business change process. These processes seemed tied *more* to factors such as corporate culture, demographics, and conditioning, than to mere technology. Even though much of my military experience was in technical applications, the solutions to these new challenges required me to fall back on basic leadership training. I tried instead to target basic cultural and management aspects of organizational problems, without appealing to technological solutions.

> "When you make it look easy, people believe that it is easy, and then they take you for granted."
> "There is no substitute for talent, nor does a process make it fungible."
> —Mavaxiom 112

In a sense, I came to understand that altering human behavior and patterns of expectations that these organizations had about technology were the best way of treating internal disorders that new technologies had created.

My civilian career became figuring out new ways (as well as employing good old-fashioned techniques) of making people and technology play nicely together. In other words, I was developing my own marketing plan.

Just having talent is not enough. As with a résumé, packaging and selling can make all the difference. Either you will convince an employer that your skills are worth paying for, or you will not. It might sound petty or superficial, but talent without good sponsorship can end up going nowhere, no matter how valuable. Even Leonardo Da Vinci needed what was known as a "patron." The practical truth is that employers must believe that they can profit from you before they will pay for you. It is one of the tests of one's dignity in the job search: having to prove your worth.

I am sure that all who have served in the military can recall a time when they felt categorized, pigeonholed, grouped, classified, characterized, stereotyped, labeled, branded, sorted, ranked, and rated. The civilian sector is different in that economic imperatives to answer consumer demand facilitate the creation of new categories, groups, brands, labels, and so on. These new categories are known as niches. If your niche is not readily apparent in the array of available titles, it may mean creating a new one. Sometimes this is a way of answering the important question of knowing what you really want.

In this way, having to sell yourself is not always a disadvantage. The upshot of defining yourself in the civil sector is that if you do not fit neatly into the prevailing boxes you can create a whole new niche for your skill set. If there is a demand for what's in that niche, then you are in business. That is the power of creativity. Creativity saves you by opening up opportunities that people have not even thought of before. It also makes room for you to finally explore those aspects of yourself that you could not before—providing you can get outside the limiting military mindset.

Origins of the Bureaucratic Species

So where do talented individuals go to feel safe? What does it take to feel professionally engaged, fulfilled, and accepted? How will they know the right institution to go to, with the kind of environment that will take care of their particular needs that make them distinctive? Where does genius go when it is time to move on? It seems obvious that such people would *not* want to take their chances on yet another bureaucracy. Who could blame them?

Intimidated by real talent, and desperate to protect their precious positions, the masters of organizational bureaucracies are the real threat to gifted individuals. From an intelligence perspective, then, it is important to identify the characteristic traits of the bureaucratic threat. Before being able to detect, locate, track, identify, and characterize this formidable system of intellectual destruction, it is perhaps important to first understand how it functions.

Let us examine this threat, up close and personal. Where does it come from? Who are its agents, and how do they organize, train, and equip themselves? How does their command and control function? Last, but certainly not least, why are bureaucracies such a threat to justice, domestic tranquility, the common defense, the general welfare, and the blessings of liberty?

In their defense, perhaps bureaucracies do not represent a completely toxic threat to human creativity. My apologies; I erred. What was I thinking? Let me rephrase that so that there is no misunderstanding as to my intent. *Bureaucracy is the scourge of all mankind.* If bureaucracy is a necessary evil, then let us agree that it is, in fact, evil. So where did this contemptible instrument of malevolence come from? Or more precisely, who let it in?

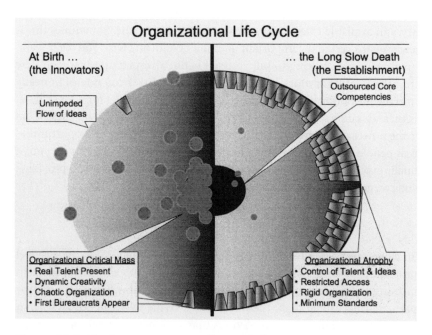

Figure 11.1. The Bureaucratic Atrophy Model[1]

In what I call my "bureaucratic atrophy model," I hold the view that every great organization is born virtually devoid of any bureaucratic influences. The first people who come together are the ideological founders. These people are doers, the subject-matter experts in their fields. These are the kinds of people with the rare qualities of inspiration, energy, and often intimidating creativity. These founders do not necessarily all get along because they are people of great passion and even stronger opinions. The energy between them feeds the process of creative development and eventually the organization achieves critical mass, and takes on a self-sustaining quality. With a life of its own, it is able to draw ever-increasing commitment and devotion from its members. The founders seek new talent to answer the pressing need for decisions, requirements, and tasks. A new organization has been born.

At this stage in its evolution, the fledgling organization is tiny, a loose alliance of a few individuals who gave life and gestation to the concept and delivered it to the world. In the philosophical view of a sage intelligence consultant and coworker of mine, the number of founders is perhaps as many as, but never more than, five people.

This is a time of great enthusiasm and high aspirations in the organization. Creativity flourishes with new life, vitality, and hope for the future. As the concept for an organization forms, so too must the membership grow. The euphoria soon morphs into pressures to confine the organization to reality, to record activities, and track progress. Documentation, once a virtual afterthought, was ignored lest it get in the way of creativity in full flight. Initially, there is little need to document the steps because all the steps were in a continuous process of change, experimentation, and refinement. Keeping track of this dynamism would waste time and energy that might otherwise go into creation. Once the organization starts consuming inventories and resources at frightful speed, keeping track of all aspects becomes an overwhelming concern. This is when the organization becomes most vulnerable to infection by "the first bureaucrat."

> "Every project comes down to *only* five people—who actually make it happen."
>
> —The Sage Consultant, 2006

The First Bureaucrat

The first bureaucrat does not appear infectious, or even a threat, at the time of its introduction. In fact, the arrival of the first bureaucrat is actually seen as a godsend. This is someone who can attend to all the necessary details, and leave the founders to focus on their precious new baby. No one sees the arrival of a pathogenic vector or harmful toxin, but rather of the means for developing order from the chaos. What few realize is that at this moment, the first bureaucrat will herald either sweeping success for the organization, or its descent into mediocrity and eventual demise.

The first bureaucrat is usually an accountant, a chronicler, or secretarial assistant. This person will try desperately to track all the elements of the organization as it achieves critical mass and chain-reacts. If the organization were an astronomical feature at this stage, it would be a formless cloud of gas and stardust collapsing in on itself through the tug of gravity within each atom. In the instant a once-nebulous cloud ignites with the light of a new star, a self-sustaining organization is born. The job of the first bureaucrat is to catalog every grain of cosmic stardust, account for every gram of collapsing matter, and measure the before, during, and after of the creation of a sun. No easy task, and not a task for just anyone. Only a person built for that much attention to detail will suffice, so picking the correct first bureaucrat is crucial.

Every aspect of the organization will undergo inspection. The bureaucrat will not necessarily contribute to the life of the organization so much as observe it and keep track of its operation. In this sense, the first bureaucrat is not a source of income for the organization, and in fact, they may represent the first overhead cost, a salary expense for the cost of conducting business. This is also when the first bureaucrat will face his or her great temptation. In confronting the monumental challenges of all the tasks at hand, the first bureaucrat will face seduction by pride. This dark emissary of malignant narcissism will set into motion the initial cause of doom for the organization. The pact will focus around a single emotion: resentment. The more the bureaucrat resents the amount and types of work he or she must do for the founders, the deeper the bond with future bureaucrats will be forged.

The deluge of organizational detail will be overwhelming, but the first bureaucrat will succeed in making documented sense of a swirling milieu. The bureaucrat's worth to the new organization will be incalculable. But, as the organization lurches forward in growth and operation, the first bureaucrat will not be enough. The organization will require an additional person, adding another overhead cost to be subtracted from total income. It is time for the first bureaucrat to divide into two. If the first bureaucrat has already submitted to the will of self-interest, the organization could be in exceptionally grave danger.

This is a critical time in the organization's development for four reasons. First, the number of bureaucrats will increase by 100 percent in the mitosis that will yield the second bureaucrat. If left unchecked by the founders, the number of bureaucrats could increase 100 percent more in each subsequent cell division of the number of hired bureaucrats, if left unchecked by the founders. Second, the founders may be so busy building up the organization that they mistakenly shift decision making for hiring future employees to the first bureaucrat. Third, no matter how well-meaning, the first bureaucrat will very likely hire new employees with whom they feel "safe." Fourth, the first bureaucrat may be unaware of detrimental traits inherent in a new hire, traits that may not appear immediately, but may manifest themselves in determining future hires. Traits present in the first few bureaucrats tend to self-replicate in a growing crop of new employees.

There is no getting around this progression. It happens in every organization's birth and growth. Even if the selection of the first bureaucrat is flawlessly made, the risk reappears with *every* subsequent selection of a bureaucrat. This invariably challenges an organization's ability to retain its original character and energy. The four cited steps (hiring more bureaucrats, hiring delegated to bureaucrats, expression of bureaucratic need to feel safe, and replication of undesirable bureaucratic traits) are critical because they will ultimately determine the lifespan of an organization. In addition, if the first bureaucrat lacks the capacity for humility, warmth, and nurturing in the face of chaos, or does not revel in the performance of his or her work, the shortcomings in his or her character will afford the forces of evil recesses from which to establish a perpetual grip on the organization. This translates into the single most precarious moment of organizational development.

All organizations come to decision forks along their developmental paths. A potentially disastrous milestone marks each fork if inattentive leadership permits modification of the original character of the organization. As said, it is in the organization's infancy that its lifespan will be determined. The genius and energy of the founders must be involved in these early decisions; otherwise they risk deferring their responsibilities to a conveniently positioned, but unqualified, bureaucrat. There is a possibility that founders will choose their first bureaucrat wisely, and he or she will faithfully preserve the organization's core ideals. That the first bureaucrat understands those ideals, and believes in those ideals, should be the immutable prerequisite.

The Insurgency Begins

Like a young living organism, an organization grows to accommodate its success. When founders are off conquering the world, they leave a growing numbers of bureaucrats behind as caretakers who, in the worst possible outcome, take charge of vital leadership decisions. If they take the helm in the absence of the founders, their actions will almost certainly veer in a direction without the vision, creativity, and daring that led to the point of success. The strengths of bureaucrat are financial accounting, process, and chaos control, not vision.

Bureaucrats seek out and enlist more of their own kind when they find a need to control corporate entropy. If anything, their motivation shifts ever so slightly to enhance the security of their growing numbers. To buttress their fortress, they invite in others sharing their mindset, and unfortunately inclusion often fosters a senses of elitism, privilege, and status. The psychology of power can take hold, and the organization may never be the same again.

To protect themselves, bureaucrats create walls of other bureaucrats around them. Each controls new administrative functions and approval gates. The organization becomes a castle or walled city built for safety, security, and self-preservation. As they assume more senior posts, bureaucrats also harbor the discomfort of knowing that they do not *own* the fortress. Their insecurities emerge and, without humility, the most well-meaning bureaucrat tends to compensate by attempting to mold the organization in his or her own image.

Before the walls rose, only a semipermeable membrane separated the organization and the world, and energy and information flowed freely between the two. New people and new ideas entered and exited the organization freely, and as needed. This was the very process of dynamic creativity in action, building momentum and vectoring in unexpected directions.

In their growing numbers, bureaucrats impose a new order to an organization. They attach themselves like parasites to the inside of the organization. Bureaucrats embed themselves in the inner workings of an organization, siphoning its life and energy. As they link with other bureaucrats, their colonies grow biggest around the entry and exit points of an organization. In this way, they position themselves as gatekeepers, regulating the flow of resources, people, information, and, eventually, ideas. Their goal of protecting themselves is reached by controlling all sources of organizational collateral entering or leaving the organization.

The semipermeable membrane that once carried the free flow of organization creativity becomes clogged with layers of bureaucrats who micromanage the flow of information. Bureaucrats can now modify the tone and rhythms of the organization to their liking. Creativity is now kept in check, managed, and bridled. Territorial boundaries emerge, bureaucratic fiefdoms consolidate themselves, and the once vibrant organization is no more.

Overwhelmed By Sectarian Violence

When its long, slow death begins, the organization has evolved far beyond its original formation from intellectual stardust, and now resembles the landscape of medieval Europe. Barons, duchesses, earls, countesses, viceroys, and all other manner of victors emerge from the battlefields of interoffice nation-states. Staff meetings, once forums for sharing information, now make daily pronouncements on matters of organizational hierarchy and regality, and stage vacuous pantomimes bestowing honorifics upon the undeserving. Across artificially drawn borders, e-mails pound entrenched areas of resistance with heavy-caliber memoranda of agreements. Returning volleys rain down with incendiary track changes and cannon balls of staff summary sheets. Standardized templates and approved formats lay siege to pockets of individual originality. Task-force committees in the chapel officially validate the new dogma and issue it in website proclamations. Hyperlinks herald initiatives to "synergize," "integrate," "facilitate transformation," with "network-centric processes," "enterprise collaboration," "reorganizing," "realigning," and "reprioritizing" "interoperability," while "mapping a path for closure and victory."

Pointless buzz-phrases and managerial jargon choke the real power of language to exchange ideas. This Orwellian "new speak" lethally usurps creativity and stifles open debate. In their place come a barrage of slogans and managerial mantras that are precisely what the organization soon seeks in the résumés of its employee candidates. What was once an enlightened organizational renaissance has entered a dark age of institutionalized bureaucracy, and a malignantly parasitic life form has effectively taken over. Eventually, nothing happens without the regulating influence of bureaucratic oversight and control. Nothing moves, nothing changes, and nothing really *new* pushes the organization forward. It is as if an administrative weir has been intentionally constructed for the express purpose of checking the flow of progress. The organization has become a fortress of servitude, a medieval castle complete with towers, walls, moats, and bureaucratic dragons. In fact, one of the terms often used to describe such individuals when I worked at the National Reconnaissance Office (NRO) was "moat dragons."

The organization atrophies. Where there was once energy and vitality, now a stonework system prohibits risk, experimentation, and failure. A formidable outer wall of regulations protects the now-ravenous bureaucrats as they multiply. They are safe, and their job security is assured. Life is good for the bureaucrats: they are confident that they will pay off their mortgages and kids' college tuitions.

In sociological terms, the organization appears to be another shining example of capitalistic success. What has really happened, though, is that the once-great organization has passed its apex. The genius that sired its creation is now gone. Gone are the requirements for core competency. *Loyalty and obedience trump ability.* To protect those less than competent, minimum performance standards are established and rigorously enforced. Excelling at endeavors, exceeding expectations, and new ideas become threatening to the establishment, upsetting its now cherished goals of stability and predictability.

The organization no longer functions as a profitable answer to a business need. Instead, the organization now serves to house and employ its minions, and to fiercely defend its self-preservation. Cumbersome processes have made introducing new talent or new ideas prohibitive. Only lateral changes are possible from incestuously trusted inner circles. The organization embodies a stifling atmosphere, evident in subtle indicators: drab-grey carpeting, endless white walls, and bland decor. Employees with dull looks and shadows under their eyes shuffle through hallways, eager for each day and the week to end.

Persona Non Grata

The founders are long gone, forced out by a gradual, methodical, bureaucratically instigated overthrow. Control has been transferred, and talented individuals go into exile. All become *persona non grata* (PNG), outcast from the organization that they helped create.

One of the worst fates to befall intelligence professionals overseas is to be declared PNG by the nation where they are stationed. It means that a foreign government has found your behavior disquieting enough to require you to depart its borders, and never return. Sometimes, if a government finds your shenanigans particularly distasteful, they will have you "rolled up." That means you are arrested, roughed up a bit, asked uncomfortably probing questions (perhaps related to even more uncomfortably revealing photographs of you and others), and *then* assisted in your departure. Nobody really wants to be rolled-up. It is just bad form.

It takes a special level of tactlessness, or outright hubris, to achieve PNG status, and it is especially troublesome if you have a fondness for the country, its people, the food, or the lifestyle. I liked traveling abroad, so whenever I did I kept my head down.

The same could not be said for my organizational travels in the Intelligence Community. I came into the community with the foolish idea of "making a difference." I expected to engage in critical thinking and informed debate. Unfortunately, when a person becomes "smart enough to be dangerous," bureaucrats can smell him or her from miles away. Like so many others in "the twenty percent," I just wanted to do my job, take pride in my work, and defend the nation. Over time, this won me PNG status from organizations throughout the community. That translated into fewer choices for future assignments. I was rapidly running out of agencies that I could work for. As I discovered, PNG status applies not only to organization founders, but also to those perceived as possessing similar energies that would threaten the bureaucratic species.

Ultimately, those in "the twenty percent" recognize that there may be no personal or professional profit to be gained from their efforts to stay on under such constraints. In fact, by overachieving or employing their special talents, they increase the risk of being viewed as threatening to stability. Again, that is where good management makes all the difference, and without which the disillusioning balancing act of "the twenty percent" is long and unapplauded.

The Illusion of Technological Dominance

Modern western society is convinced that technology is the answer to everything, especially to the atrophy and eventual demise of organizations at the hands of bureaucracy. Bureaucrats fail to remember that technology is only as good as those who use it, and, if users fail to take into account their own flaws, technology will only speed the replication of those flaws. As some were fond of telling me in the high-technology side of the intelligence business, "There are some things in life that you do *not* want to automate." Now, when we make mistakes, we can send them to the other side of the planet at the speed of light.

These concepts are, themselves, not new. In his, "Complexity and Counterterrorism: Thinking about Biometrics," Patrick O'Neil outlines how societal needs almost demand technological solutions for what might otherwise be interpersonal and organizational management challenges,

"Technology is a beautiful thing—when it works."

—Mavaxiom 113

> "[A]dvanced democracies often prefer high-technology solutions over low-technology ones. High-technology solutions play an important symbolic role in society, providing the sense that the absolute utmost is being done to protect the public. Schneier terms this 'security theater,' creating the visual and dramatic perception of security to reinforce public confidence in risky institutions. Rosen similarly captures this with the term 'technopositivism,' or a sense that existing organizational problems can be solved by escaping forward through dramatic technological innovation. At the policymaking level, too, there is what Philip Selznick spoke of decades ago as the 'retreat to technology,' which he described as 'the belief that the solution of technical problems will solve institutional problems.' … In addition, by focusing on a technological solution the public is not only treated to an important ritual of security at work, but one that appears to shift responsibility away from fallible humans (security employees) to objective, rational, cutting-edge technologies that are imagined to be infallible.[2]

Perhaps as disconcerting is our near-blind dependence on technology in day-to-day life. When it was realized that computer systems might crash if software programs failed to register the date shift from 1999 to 2000, the Y2K scare quick-changed from an obscure concern of computer geeks into a headlined threat to all of western civilization. Much to my chagrin, ATM machines did *not* spit out all their cash, as had been feared, and I had hoped. Beyond its opportunity for programmers to cash in on the chronological glitch, Y2K illustrated how highly dependent modern society is on its technology.

While we have forgotten the widespread fear raised by Y2K, it is entirely possible for similar technological crises—as potentially devastating or worse—to arise at any time. For example, if all electrical power were to fail for a week or more across any large area of the country, state, local, and federal governments would find maintaining public order their single most important concern. So, despite all our technology, when the essentials of comfortable life and stability are temporarily interrupted, the ugly side of human nature quickly emerges. We like to think that technology has somehow transformed humanity beyond its barbaric nature, and the allure of that belief plagues us today. It is an illusion that technology has transformed us into something "better." After his successes in Iraq, Army Colonel H.R. McMaster warned, "military forces must abandon the dangerous and seductive illusion that technology can solve the problem of future conflict."[3]

Technology protects modern societies, but it also isolates them. It isolates militaries from their adversaries by providing a safe distance from which to operate. Cruise missiles and smart bombs can be launched from afar, and the operator launching the weapon may never see its effects. In fact, targeting as a military career now exists out of our necessity to understand and predict the effects of such weapons. In doing so, technology functions as social armor, shielding the protected society while inflaming the populations that are its targets. An unintended consequence is that technological armor provokes outrage. In other words, *armor invites attack.*

In my view, our dependence on technology, in addition to distancing us from others, may actually create threats that would not develop in the presence of direct human interaction. Talking to a person over tea is easy. Negotiating with heavily armed soldiers is more difficult. Communicating with a column of tanks is virtually impossible. The underlying correlation is that the greater the social distancing, the greater the perceived threat. It consequently becomes easier to destroy things, rather than people. The tank becomes an easier target than the crew inside it, with whom you might otherwise speak face-to-face over tea. Giving armor a human face would make attacks more difficult because, despite their differences, most humans have a great deal in common with one another. Hiding behind technology almost makes war easier because it dehumanizes the human beings on the receiving end of weapon systems.

So can individual human beings transcend technology? Consider the incredibly brave young man who stood alone before a column of tanks to bring them to a halt in Tiananmen Square in 1989. He did not possess impregnable armor or some new technology. What he possessed was the raw human courage to engage the human beings buried behind the armor of the tanks. His belief in humanity impelled him to engage military might and, for a moment, his courage transcended technological firepower. His humanness prevailed and, perhaps, the mere mortals inside the tanks recognized his strength. What daring and bravery. One incredible act stole technological superiority from the powerful and gave inspiration to the poor. China needs other similar acts of bravery and inspiration. Who was that young man? Was he a university student? Or perhaps he was a sort-of Chinese Robin Hood, stealing from the oligarchs and inspiring the downtrodden?[4] I wonder. Whatever the case, he certainly had guts. I was so moved by his courage that I adapted a motivational poster from the despair.com web page in his honor.[5]

So what does this have to do with bureaucracy and, more importantly, job search? The answer is in the opportunity it affords certain individuals. We seem to habitually use technology to address problems that are best solved by better managing people. We are a techno-centric culture that believes precision guidance, satellite navigation, network connectivity, and sufficient horsepower can solve all our problems. In the process, we forget that at the heart of the matter are people. Technology is only a tool, and the tool is ultimately dependent on the people who use it. If the technology works, there is no guarantee that the people will use it correctly, or at all.

Figure 11.2. *Guts* Inspirational Poster

Part of the contradiction of our dependence on technology is that we may eventually grow to resent it as much as we are dependent on it.

The techno-anthropologist in me struggled with this love-hate relationship every day. Ironically, I was *never* the first person in my office with the latest, greatest high-tech gadget, the next-year's model, or the newest-generation software. In fact, I never owned a computer until I was satisfied that one would work as well as this Mac. Perhaps this inherent distrust of technology is what sensitized me to its interrelation with people. I think I was effective as a techno-anthropologist precisely because I did not implicitly view technology as a cure-all. Behind every so-called technological shortfall that I worked on in the Intelligence Community, there were also a slew of managerial deficiencies that were real contributors to the problem.

For decades, intelligence trends showed both promise and disappointment in the use of cutting-edge technologies. Although nontraditional technologies offer some of the most innovative collection and analysis capabilities, they are disciplines that still face difficulty gaining acceptance and use against the threats of the twenty-first century. Few intelligence professionals actually realize that such powerful tools are even at their disposal. Fewer still seem to understand or employ them in their daily work. The causes of, and solutions to, this dilemma still confound the Intelligence Community, even in an age of unprecedented security challenges and reforms. My own experiences convinced me that the "failure of imagination" described by the 9/11 Commission report is *not* a technology issue at all. It is a people issue. Specifically, the way military and intelligence professionals are managed stymies their talents. Poor leadership and widespread mismanagement prevent the best employment of new and more effective sources and methods against twenty-first-century challenges. It is here that the savvy, up-and-coming techno-anthropologist can find a profitable transition out of the military. As long as such mismanagement exists there will be a corresponding need for those who can troubleshoot the nebulous divide between technology and management.

In my dealings with those customers, any time intelligence professionals needed some kind of new tool to solve an intelligence challenge, a territorial or technophobic bureaucrat would be standing in our way. The tool might be a new technology, or just a data line to connect Point A to Point B. In many cases, the so-called advanced technology would actually be old technology not yet integrated into the greater system. Typically, we had the solution within reach all along. We just could not use it because some manager would get in the way. As my role evolved from technologist to salesman and lobbyist, my team would have to hit the "campaign trail" just to convince the chain of bureaucrats that our proposal would not present any threat to their organizational control. We had to make peace with all the mission partners, develop their "buy-in," and *then* we could begin discussing the proposal. These were programs that would prove a huge benefit for all involved, and an improvement to the security of the

> "Don't be too proud of this technological terror you've constructed. The ability to destroy a planet is insignificant next to the power of the Force."
>
> —Darth Vader, 1977

nation—and still, just getting started required going begging for a major marketing effort. As my colleagues sometimes said, echoing the immortal observation of the late Walt Kelly's long-gone cartoon character, Pogo: "We have met the enemy, and he is us."

Notes

1. The analogy of bureaucracy to a viral life form was inspired by the author's discussions with defense consultant and rock-star guitarist Jeff "Skunk" Baxter in 2005.

2. Patrick H. O'Neil, "Complexity and Counterterrorism: Thinking about Biometrics," *Studies in Conflict & Terrorism* 28, Issue 6, http://www.informaworld.com/smpp/title~content=g725841289~db=all (November 2005): 559.

3. H. R. McMaster, "On War: Lessons to be Learned," *Survival: Global Politics and Strategy* 50, no. 1, http://dx.doi.org/10.1080/00396330801899439 (01 February 2008): 26.

4. Growing numbers of pro-democracy thinkers are envisioning the notion of a Chinese Robin Hood. As is commonly understood, the original Robin Hood was an individual who stood up to the authority of his day. Part of his mission was to "steal from the rich and give to the poor." Perhaps such a noble individual will arise in China, and come to the aid and comfort of its downtrodden masses? We can only hope so.

5. The design for the *Guts* inspirational poster was, itself, inspired by the Despair, Inc. web page of de-motivational posters, http://www.despair.com, (30 Mar 2008). My many thanks to despair.com for their perspective, humor, and wisdom. This single image was also the inspiration for the documentary, "Tank Man" on *FRONTLINE*, http://www.pbs.org/wgbh/pages/frontline/tankman/view/#morelink, which investigated the event and its worldwide repercussions:

"On June 5, 1989, one day after the Chinese army's deadly crushing of the 1989 Tiananmen Square protests in Beijing, a single, unarmed young man stood his ground before a column of tanks on the Avenue of Eternal Peace. Captured on film and video by Western journalists, this extraordinary confrontation became an icon of the struggle for freedom around the world, http://www.pbs.org/wgbh/pages/front-line/tankman/cron/icon.html. Seventeen years later, veteran filmmaker Anthony Thomas goes to China in search of 'The Tank Man,' http://www.pbs.org/wgbh/pages/frontline/tankman/etc/thomas.html. Who was he? What was his fate? And what does he mean for a China that today has become a global economic power-house? Drawing on interviews with Chinese and Western eyewitnesses, Thomas recounts the amazing events on the spring of 1989, when a student protest that began in Tiananmen Square, the symbolic central space of the nation, spread throughout much of the rest of China, http://www.pbs.org/wgbh/pages/frontline/tankman/cron/."

CHAPTER TWELVE

Creativity and the Bottom Line
We Are All Created Equal, but Not All Employed Equally

"Not only does he march to the beat of a different drummer, he has a whole percussion section."

— John Wiant, 2006

The Problem with Process

For much of my early life I did not like modern art. Aside from works of minimalist simplicity, most modern art disturbed my longing for structure and order. When I left the military, that all changed. I found myself strangely compelled by modern art. Any previous mental blocks had crumbled in the face of inspiration, and this was the key. Always the intelligence analyst, I tried to decipher the hidden meaning in this new trend. At one point I reasoned that a code awaited my decryption in my new fascination with inspiration. I eventually found myself intensely contemplating a piece of art that could best be described as looking like the aftermath of a tornado. Appropriately enough, it was called, *Black Hole*,[1] This compelling work was a mishmash of wooden beams, fluorescent lighting, and everyday objects seemingly thrown together (as if by gale force winds) into a dandelion-like sphere, more than thirty feet across. I sat down in front of it and tried to draw it in a pocket journal. My first rendering of this imposing structure looked awful. Without any context from which to draw, my initial impression struggled for form. I flipped the page and drew it again, trying to deconstruct the object in my second rendering. As I flipped the page for a third attempt I realized that I was hooked.

In trying to understand this intriguing piece of art, I had *allowed* it to captivate me. I let its message in, and I tried to put it into a context I could conceptualize. As I studied it from casual points of observation, a figurative line snapped taut, and I was reeled in by the work's raw complexity. The intelligence officer in me had crossed over onto the other side of the intellectual battlefield to better know his target. I was extending beyond the ordinary and accepted. Suddenly I realized that I was alone and in unfamiliar territory, but it was in a way that was personally satisfying.

All those years in the military had perfected my spit-and-polish and ability to hone the simplest thing to the smoothest state of presentation. But this work was catastrophic; it was like watching a train wreck, and I could not pull away. I realized the beauty of its raw, unrefined presentation, so unlike anything military. It was totally open to interpretation by anyone. I was stunned. The freedom to interpret the work, at will, encouraged my imagination to conceptualize, to think in new ways, all in an effort to understand the artwork. Every time I was sure that I understood all aspects of the form, I discovered yet another completely unanticipated feature. Inspiration was coming directly from the act of self-discovery. In a sense, the artwork was teaching me its language. It was communicating in a way I did not yet understand, and it compelled me to untangle its mysteries.

> "The grand irony of humanity's greatest discoveries is that many were accidental."
>
> —Mavaxiom 121

As anyone who has been in the military or government can tell you, nothing, and I mean nothing, can go forward in raw, unfinished form that is in any way open to interpretation. There are usually so many "chop chains" for comments, outside opinions, and approvals that nothing can move forward until the original submission is mutilated into something that everyone approves.[2] Somewhere in this process, the essence of the work, the one thing that might make it unique, is forcibly amputated. It then goes before the group for acceptance, grotesquely deformed from its original, inspired, state. Often, anything new, original, challenging, or otherwise worthwhile about it has been replaced by an old, predictable, submissive, and ineffective expression of the status quo.

Groupthink failures are not a problem with "the system," they are problems with the people who are part of the system. In other words, groupthink is a failure of leadership. When managers fail to trust the creativity of their own people, new ideas submitted without sponsorship or protection are consequently torn to shreds by default bureaucratic processes. By that train of logic one might ask if bureaucracies are *that* dangerous to creativity. The answer, of course, is absolutely. Instead of exploring possibilities, creativity runs a gauntlet for approval, and anyone in that process becomes a threat to the solution. One chop of dissenting opinion in the chain can render the best of new ideas inert. Instead of seeing potential, or inviting collaboration, chop chains seek reasons for disapproval and protecting positions of security. Ideas not couched in the approved language of bureaucracy are viewed as uncooperative. Any hint of genius is considered threatening to this language of submission. This is where leaders must function as advocates, restraining petty politics, and demonstrating that risk yields change and revolutionary improvement.

In intelligence circles, we describe individuals who coagulate the lifeblood of change as "moat dragons." These nefarious bureaucrats usually represent middle management in organizations, with little legitimate authority to make change, but a consuming need to take credit for any organizational success that comes into their sphere of influence. In short, they are the people who get in the way of anything for which they cannot take credit. Moat dragons do not look for new ideas, inspiration, progress, or profit. They look for stability. Dragon-filled bureaucratic moats are clearly the *last* thing military veterans want (or need) to encounter after leaving the military. Sadly, the reality is that organizations that profit from military contracts are generally composed of military veterans themselves. With their former service, many veterans bring with them many of the same management approaches and philosophies resident in the military. Although the potential for profit exists, something to strongly consider is whether a veteran is looking for "more of the same" when he or she transitions. Ultimately, one of the casualties of such an environment is creativity itself. Moreover, an environment like this can ultimately cause employees to think that "this is the way things work around here," and just give up trying to make it any better.

"How could an algorithm know that a rain-drenched window screen flaps in a breeze like a ship sail?"

—Mavaxiom 122

The Code Breakers

Visual art conveys its own language. People who do not speak a second language might find the idea of communicating, or even thinking, in another language difficult to comprehend. For those who can speak other languages, the language of visual art is challenging in a way similar to understanding nouns, verbs, and the structures of grammar. Art employs symbols, iconic forms, and imagery that reaches in and stirs our emotions. It encourages our senses to understand its language and decipher its meaning. In essence, the intended message of art is encrypted in a cipher whose key is not universally known. Like intelligence professionals working at their craft, those who experience visual art must unlock the cipher to read its message. They must undertake their own translations of the symbols into the colloquial speech of their own minds. That process may involve thoughtful analysis, emotional connection, divine inspiration, or a combination of all three. An entire intelligence field, known as imagery intelligence (IMINT), encompasses the study of photographs. When these images are captured, the target can inhabit all manner of orientation in three-dimensional space, and four-dimensional time. Exploiting and analyzing their meaning therefore requires thinking in multidimensional ways. Those in the field would submit that the moment of recognition in any photographic interpretation or imagery analysis is nothing short of an emotional event. As a matter of profession, inspirational breakthrough is an occupational hazard. For appreciators of art, it is entirely a pleasure. Art generates creativity, inducing viewers to become participants in the pleasures of deciphering its secret meanings.

Perhaps it is this hidden aspect of art that makes the very idea of creativity challenging. Sun Tzu did not entitle his classic work *The Science of War*, or *The Bureaucracy of War*. It is *The Art of War*, for a reason. Art is power. It transcends the human experience. Wars are waged with art painted on shields and on war machines. The iconic symbols of our beliefs follow us on to the battlefields, under which soldiers die by the thousands. How could this be, unless creative expression had the power to inspire people to fight for a cause? It is therefore ironic that so few who fight in wars understand its language.

For those leaving the military, art has an equally important function. In the civilian world, business lives and dies by new ideas. Many of those new ideas come from the mind of artistic creativity, seeing old problems in new ways and inspiring people in new directions. "Move fast, hit hard, and get the new idea on the street!" is the rallying cry of commercial armies outmaneuvering competitors to exploit new ideas first. New ideas, the immeasurable commodity of inspiration, give capitalism its unstoppable horsepower.

I think that art and creativity confound bureaucrats by requiring them to think beyond the nouns and verbs of their own language. Art forces observers to perceive from a different vantage point. Art carries messages of emotional content that teach others how to discover expression. Those who internalize the messages of art grow in experience until conversant themselves. In this way, art teaches us about our own ability to perceive. We are compelled to learn more because art reaches out to us with conviction and power. The more art teaches, the longer it lives, and the more likely its immortality.

So why is such an important language so difficult for so many in the military and government to understand? More importantly, how can understanding help those returning to the civilian sector?

Why Stay in a System that Limits Your Potential?

When you find a civilian job that employs you for your military specialties, take notice of its environment. If no one else with your specialty holds supervisory positions, it may be an important indicator. Likewise, if your supervisor knows less in that specialty than you do, you may have a second point on the trend curve. As in the military, those in supervisory positions may not be experts in your field. They may be in supervisory positions for purely managerial reasons, or business development purposes. This, in itself, should not generate immediate changes in your threat condition (THREATCON), but it should put you on alert to other possible indicators.

> "Managers who fear the unknown, use it to justify the status quo."
> —Mavaxiom 123

In my experiences, both in the military and as a civilian contractor, management skates upon a precarious precipice of distinction. Their inexperience in your specialty can become a source of trust in your opinion and contribution. Do not hold your breath long for this option, as it is reserved only for true leaders. The other, seemingly more likely, path is to see your expertise as a difficult-to-manage cause for stress. If they do not trust you, they are likely to skate off the cliff's edge and spiral your contribution into an assembly line approach. As more of these indicators unfold, you should respond in kind with a higher THREATCON and increased tasking, collection, and analysis of information about your new employer. If subject matter experts are restrained at lower levels of employment, and management is an amorphous generalist skill set, you may find yourself returning to the system you left behind in the military.

It is difficult to imagine that unique skills and talent would prove a hindrance to career advancement, but they can be depending on the company. In the military, the skills required to accomplish tasks are identified, isolated, and simplified so that certified personnel are readily interchangeable with one another. This approach creates a force composed of members who are a "jack-of-all-trades, and master-of-none." They become elements of organizational machinery that can replace one another in the event of emergencies. This makes sense in a resource-constrained military, and it makes sense in a civilian firm whose personnel philosophy was crafted by former military managers. If you left the military because you did not agree with its approaches, it makes little sense to return to a civilian version of the same.

The next question you may ask yourself, are there that many companies with former military managers? The answer is a reflection of history. As military services downsized during the 1990s, the "more-with-less" mantra took on a particularly problematic manifestation. The unintended consequence was a crop of generalists with no great depth of experience in any one area. As a consequence, when expert opinions *were* needed, finding in-depth expertise became a challenge unto itself. With fewer and fewer experts, a need to "outsource" necessitated hiring civilian contractors. As more service members with expertise grew disenchanted by management devaluing their skills, more expertise left the military. The vicious cycle that emerged fed the outsourcing bonanza for those who could capitalize on highly marketable skills.

Another, subtler, side effect of "more-with-less" was that military members who stayed in the service found themselves on endlessly frustrating learning curves. Those seeking to develop an expertise in a field of interest, beyond those to which they were assigned, were confronted with a difficult choice: submit to developing breadth or look outside the military for more challenging activities. Inquisitive and eager individuals feeling root-bound by such limits, found little job satisfaction in professionally underachieving. The best and brightest can submit to this for only so long before succumbing to distraction. Large *quantities* of work can keep people busy, but the likelihood of being intellectually satisfied will plummet over time. Overachievers, in particular, felt unfulfilled and unsatisfied by these demands, and the outsourcing conflagration was further stoked.

Not only did skilled personnel benefit from partaking in this brain drain from the military, but so too did managers who conceived and perpetuated its necessity. This is why service members seeking jobs in the civilian sector can find themselves in the peculiar position of once again being supervised by former military generalists.

When the Writing is on the Wall

Just after Operation DESERT STORM in 1991, I noticed a strange shift in Air Force intelligence career development, and perhaps in military intelligence in general. Originally a highly introverted community, concealed behind what was called the "green door," the military intelligence profession underwent upheaval. It had been the practice to protect sensitive and perishable intelligence sources and methods, always an intrinsically difficult task. The challenge of managing this information grew dramatically more difficult after the realization that intelligence information was amazingly useful to tactical military users. Remember, many of these sources and methods were designed to support senior decision makers and weapons designers. The Information Age allowed intelligence to be received by a much wider audience of tactical consumers, all eager for more usable information. Operational commanders, accustomed to seamless control of their assets, bridled under the constraint of not having intelligence sources and methods under their direct command.

Fueled by their victories in Operation DESERT STORM, they sought ways to make invaluable targeting intelligence more readily available for their operations, and the result was a post-war influx of nonintelligence personnel into intelligence ranks. Proponents argued that the presence of operationally focused war fighters would widen the awareness of intelligence analysts to the needs of their customer base, and that the cross-fertilization would benefit both communities in the military. Over the next decade, however, what I perceived was wholesale dilution of the core expertise of personnel in the intelligence field. When young intelligence professionals, such as myself, looked to our senior staff for guidance, what we saw looking down on us were superiors with little functional expertise or experience in intelligence.

This was the period when I began to seriously contemplate leaving the artificial limits of what I saw as a glass ceiling in the military intelligence field. By 1999, when I left active duty, the trend had reached troubling levels. The obvious concern is that this diminished appreciation for intelligence as a profession would have inherent implications

> "There are two kinds of people in the U.S. Air Force: pilots, and everybody else."
>
> —An unpopular perception in the U.S. Air Force

for national security. September 11th and the Iraq War were apparent illustrations. For the separating service member, though, it also has implications for finding a new job and establishing a new career. Taking my intelligence skills and applying them to the business world was not easy. The nature of my profession had necessitated secrecy. Now I had to evolve into a business model. I had to learn in a hurry how to become an entrepreneur and venture capitalist.

Immersion in Life

One of the underappreciated things about intelligence gathering is that it requires its practitioners to extend themselves beyond the limits or bounds of their own cultures. Like informational ambassadors, intelligence professionals acquire their insights deep within the cultural realms of others, and to some extent to do so they must appreciate (if not embrace) certain aspects of other cultures. In foreign-language instruction, the most expedient means for acquiring fluency is immersion. Likewise, and in some cases, some intelligence requires working or living abroad, immersed in other cultures. The more open-minded the intelligence professionals, often the more readily they uptake the information in this new cultural context. Suffice to say, this takes a special kind of person.

In the process of intelligence immersion, as if for a new language, the deeper the background and learning, the more the target culture becomes a part of them. When philosophers and strategists quote Sun Tzu's counsel to "know your enemy and know yourself," this sort of absorptive immersion is what they are talking about. As such the intelligence officer could also be described as liminal. In anthropological terms, liminal refers to a trait that certain members of a village, tribe, or culture possessed allowing them to "crossover" into other realms. Those other realms could be spiritual, gender-related, or just cross-cultural in nature. It was the duty of liminal beings to perform this function, acting as information gatherers, ambassadors, or (in the spiritual case) shamans. Modern society has people who perform these tasks as well. Having said this, however, not every institution is effective at utilizing such unique skills.

As an intelligence officer, the more I came to understand the viewpoints of other cultures, the more difficult it became for me to overlook the shortcomings repeatedly pointed out to me by non-Americans. My expanding worldview was getting in the way of my blindly accepting views. For example, while traveling abroad I was once accused of being an employee of the CIA. This is ironic, because I have never been a CIA employee. It was so strange for someone to see an American in such a far-flung locale that other travelers joked that I must be on some kind of "mission." Even more amusing was that after my return, my own organization began to immediately question my reasons for traveling to such a far-flung location. In both cases, the prevailing opinion was that "Americans do not travel like that."

As my viewpoints seemed to shift further away from comfortable American norms, I found myself living in an in-between world. I had become a liminal being in my own culture.

Desperately Seeking Culture

Every culture comes with its own language. When no one can speak that language, culture dies. With a culture's demise, creativity, imagination, and innovation depart in company with the courage, daring, and initiative that made the culture uniquely possible. Today, this issue is especially important because failing to imagine the possibilities and outcomes of actions can have grave implications. When a culture ceases to evaluate the creative energies of adversaries, the end results can be cataclysmic. Not so long ago it would have seemed farfetched that nineteen men, armed only with an extremist ideology and box-cutters, could change the world. In the events ensuing September 11, Americans struggled to understand how the Intelligence Community could have overlooked such possibilities, and why these instruments of national security failed to thwart the attack. Numerous causes were blamed for the failure, but the most important was one of imagination:

> Across the government, there were failures of imagination, policy, capabilities, and management. . . . The most important failure was one of

imagination. We do not believe leaders understood the gravity of the threat. The terrorist danger from bin Laden and al-Qaeda was not a major topic for policy debate among the public, the media, or in the Congress. Indeed, it barely came up during the 2000 presidential campaign.[3]

For some in the military, especially those who had endured the personnel reductions of the 1990s, that conclusion was not at all surprising. In fact, it seemed to *validate* a trend that they had seen developing over the decade since the fall of the Soviet Union: the culture of the military and Intelligence Community was increasingly unable to creatively anticipate threats. This was not because threats could not be conceptualized, but rather because their proposition often flew in the face of the more comfortable status quo. Career intelligence professionals knew it had been a failure of leadership's own ability to inspire and encourage creative approaches by their people.

Imagination is a quality not easily measured. There are no metrics for creativity that are easily definable or measurable for managers trapped in status quo mindsets. The outcomes of imagination do not necessarily yield predictable results, improve scheduling, or save costs. In short, imagination does not necessarily make a manager's job easier, and many managers suffer from already being overwhelmed by their responsibilities. In addition, imagination does not conveniently come from a box in a form that is always useable. By its very nature, imagination transcends the bounds of everyday boxes, and requires a different kind of handling. In short, those with the responsibility and authority to lead, advocate, and cultivate imaginative solutions must themselves be creative.

The reason why is because for imagination to flourish, management must create an encouraging and helpful environment. Imagination also requires leaders not afraid to fail, who can look beyond the immediate appearance of loss with confidence and withstand establishment disapproval and ridicule. Most importantly, in my view, imagination requires leaders who will cultivate imaginative employees, and sequester them from others unappreciative of their contributions. That will require an uncommon combination of leadership and talented people whose efforts will still meet almost certain resistance.

Truly creative people do not grow on trees, and some people would contend that it is impossible for creativity to be grown at all if not inherent in the individual. Holders of this opinion would submit that creative people are only *born* that way. If that is true, then, like any other rare commodity, creative people must be especially valued. Failure to do so is not just costly but, as we have seen, can have far-reaching impacts on world affairs. For those creative people leaving the military or government service, your creativity can have real economic impacts on your future career—if you are able to fully apply it to your next job. Contrary to the born-that-way skeptics, to make the most of your talent will require finding a work environment that allows your imagination to blossom and help it grow. That means go somewhere where you will be valued for your talent, or create a safe place to grow your talent.

The Soul of an Artist

Your departure from the military way of life will require a transformational approach. After you discard the uniform, get inside yourself and find what the military might have stifled: your opinions, your feelings, and your heart's calling. Those intangible elements will tell you where you want to go next in life. Some people claim to already know, or think they know. Others, perhaps, have known their civilian calling throughout their military careers. I envy the people who always wanted to, say, be a chef, or run an espresso bar, or be a florist. Pursuits that diverge from the military provide a source of direction once the military is behind you.

For others, who always wanted a military life, the task to figure out what to do next is a little more challenging. It is probably important to first understand why other directions and desires became dormant. When their service ends, however, unfulfilled feelings will continue unabated unless something fundamentally changes.

Therein lies the conundrum for veterans. You have sworn to uphold the well-being of the nation through service and commitment. You pride yourself on being ready, willing, and able to put your needs aside for the needs of our defense and security. Over time, you forget how to do the same for yourself. In essence, you lose yourself in a profession that demands so much of your service. You forget how to "be." You become accustomed to allowing others to make decisions on your behalf and determine the direction of your life. Eventually, you might not be able to function without others directing you, and this makes you vulnerable to influence when finally pursuing your new civilian career.

Figure 12.1. Opening Up Space (Intentionally Left Blank for Contemplation)

When you leave the military, you may not know how to open up space in your life to cultivate your specific talent. The important thing to remember is that the right job is the one that cultivates your specific and individual creativity. It has to feel like a safe place that does not damage your sense of self or intrude upon your limits. You may find yourself in a job that fits but provides no room for growth.

The Artist-Capitalist

After leaving the service, few reasons seem worthwhile for further impeding the rest of your life's happiness. For this reason, you must be willing to sacrifice the financial benefits of a great job if the psychological costs are too high. Your ability to produce via your talents should have a definable capitalist metric: *compensation.* In fact, a recent historical study by Chicago economist David Galenson shows that there is a traceable relationship between creativity and the bottom line.[4] In Galenson's *Old Masters and Young Geniuses: The Two Life Cycles of Artistic Creativity,* he describes two kinds of creative personalities. In both he shows that, in "almost all cases, the largest number of [creations were produced] at the same age that [their] works brought the highest prices at auction." That means both kinds of artists, those who had perfected their skills over a lifetime (the old masters), and those who demonstrated incredible skill early in their careers (the young geniuses), made the most money when they were the most creative.

However, I noticed that firms were prepared to pay whatever it took to put the right person in the right position, and especially at the right time. If a person's timing was right, impressive compensations could be acquired by enterprising old masters and young geniuses alike. The trick was to penetrate a market with sufficient skills to yield a company's desired impact.

An example of this is demonstrated by how overarching, or "prime," contractors delegate subcontractors to supply the skills that do not exist in their own personnel pool. In some cases, landing a subcontract to fill the coveted position of subject-matter expert can be extremely lucrative. In other cases, it might require working in a stifling bureaucracy. To make this endeavor succeed, timing and contacts are critical.

Maintaining contact with prime contractors, clients, employees, competing subs, and potential clients make contracting a perpetual game, with variables in constant motion. Contractors will generally "float" résumés of highly sought people to their clients to elicit hiring opportunities. It is in everyone's best interest to do so aggressively. The process can move quickly, as in *days*. Sometimes it takes an election for contract dollars to finally materialize. In either case, your ability to readily market your creative talents may make the difference in getting the rewarding job you want.

Alpha Crew

Not long ago, while rummaging through a box of my old military-uniform items, I came across a patch for my first intelligence watch crew. As a second lieutenant I was assigned to NORAD-SPACECOM, the North American Aerospace Defense Command and U.S. Space Command Combined Intelligence Watch Center in Colorado Springs. Each of the round-the-clock nuclear-attack warning crews had their own patch. Mine was "Alpha Crew." As I mused over the name and its connotations, I came to see it in a different light from my vantage point outside of the service. I wondered where I would find another alpha crew in civilian life? I could no longer rely on a seemingly random military personnel assignment system to place me in my new alpha crew; I would have to bring about the necessary conditions on my own. What began as a moment of nostalgia soon led to my asking myself a handful of important questions that you might want to ask yourself.

Alpha-Crew Questions

Q_1: What is my new alpha crew?
Q_2: Where will I find its members?
Q_3: How do I get there?
Q_4: Will they value what matters to me?
Q_5: How will I occupy my space and time?
Q_6: How will I overcome recurrent old themes, and move on to this new crew?

In contemplating an alpha crew for yourself, consider what kind of life you really want after you leave the service. Where your pursuits will lead will depend on the requirements you establish for yourself now, and the directions you choose downrange. This is why knowing what you really want matters so much before you ever leave. The personal discipline you learned in the service will now come in handy. You will need to navigate around the usual distractions along the way if you want to make any progress. There is no need to feel guilty about no longer being interested in the old pursuits. Regard these experiences like a class reunion where people want to think of you as who you *were*, instead of who you are now. So much has happened to you since that you may have changed beyond recognition. It may be uncomfortable for others to accept, but it is a necessary aspect of growth. Decide how you want to take care of your new self in a way that ultimately leads to your own alpha crew.

Knowing Your Calling, Versus Your Job

In my view, there is a fundamental difference between what a person does for a living (a job), and what prompts them to feel alive (a calling). "Why do you work" is a different question, altogether, from "why are you here?" Some people might think those kinds of questions are too philosophical to worry about as they are transitioning out of the military. If the purpose and meaning of the rest of a person's life are not important after they leave the military, may want to consider the following exercise that arose from discussions with Dr. Jane Flax. It explores the distinctions between job and calling. [5] Take some time to think about the following lists:

JOB	CALLING
Your professional employment	Your personal vocation
Your means of earning a living	Your passion (what you love)
Paying the bills	Your life's work
The place you labor for money	The place where you belong
What you do from 9 a.m. to 5 p.m.	Who you are as a person

Becoming the Unintended Leader

People who enter the slipstream of change, particularly from the military, become of considerable interest to others. If my case is typical, then people in the throes of transition attract crowds of onlookers tactically eying your every move. Many a naysayer contended that I was lost on an endless trail to nowhere. To some extent I would agree with them. Others constantly wanted updates on my every course change. I sent them all e-mails describing my encounters with strange people called "civilians," and provided intelligence on their capitalist ways. I would analyze odd civilian tactics, techniques, and procedures (TTP), and disseminate my findings in situation reports (SITREP) to those still safely in the military. I was eager to furnish my friends with all the intelligence I could.

I had not yet found my fortune, but it was clear that I was trailblazing for others. Each new SITREP was another exciting installment in the ongoing campaign to establish a civilian beachhead and expand deeper into uncharted territory. I was leading the way for friends, coworkers, comrades, and even supervisors who would soon confront the same daunting journey. This gave my journey added purpose, and so I was happy to lend my assistance. More importantly, I had taken on a new role as an unintended leader.

Whether you like it or not, when you leave the service you will become an advance scout, leading the way for others. Like me, you might be an intelligence professional providing SITREPs on the capabilities and intentions of potential civilian employers. Any way you look at it, however, is an opportunity to lead simply because you are leaving where others remained. In that capacity, aspire to be an example for others. Inspire them to pursue *their own* personal growth, to risk, and to challenge their own limits.

Finally, pay attention to what is going on all around you. Your situational awareness now can be important for reasons you may not yet appreciate. Sharing your successes and failures with those left behind will not always be

Figure 12.2. Peenemünde Athletic Club T-Shirt

easy as leading means risking and failing in front of others, and having the guts to tell them so. It is time to confront these issues, because you are the leader now.

Notes

1. Dahlem mixed-media work, *Schwarzes Loch (Black Hole)*.

2. I am not completely sure of the origin of the phrase "chop chain," but I am sure that in the context of military and government jargon it has a cruel and/or violent connotation. Like so many other military phrases, though, someone, somewhere along the path of obedience must have observed military decision making and made the connection. The phrase seems to capitalize on the convergence between an assembly line and a slaughterhouse. The visual image that comes to mind is a long line of new and original ideas, running the gauntlet of bureaucrats who are determined to claim some ownership (and hence credit) for their passage through the

system. As each new idea comes across their desk, like a piece of meat on an assembly line, the bureaucrat assesses whether this work will enable them to receive approval or generate negative judgment from peers and superiors, alike. They consequently slice away any variations from the norm and other uncertainties that could cause disapproval. The visual metaphor of this process is apt, as the final outcome of such "chop chains" rarely resembles the original submission, much the way a hamburger bears no resemblance to a cow.

3. National Commission on Terrorist Attacks, *The 9/11 Report*, xci–xcii.

4. Starkweather interview with Galenson, *Smithsonian*, 18.

5. The philosophical exercise of comparing and contrasting one's job and their calling arose from discussions with Dr. Jane Flax.

CHAPTER THIRTEEN

Great Pay Expectations
The Specter of Creating a Metric for Self-Worth

"Gain is joy . . . welcome gain."[1]
— Pompeii wall inscription, August, A.D. 79

Your boss is not supposed to be your adversary, but chances are that you can acknowledge having had an adversarial relationship with an employer at some point in your career. The relationship starts off on the right foot, but then an issue arises, often on the subject of salary. The manner in which negotiations over salary unfold can set the tone for the rest of the relationship. The employee wants to be gracious and grateful for being offered the job, but also wants to feel sufficiently compensated. The employer is under pressure to turn a profit, which means getting the most out of the employee at the least possible cost. In many situations, underpaying employees is easy, especially when employees are uncertain of their worth. If, and when, employees come to this realization, gratitude can turn quickly to indignation.

Your Adversary's Strategy

Such are the hazards to veterans reentering civilian life. Compensation issues derive directly from the needs of business and indirectly from the naiveté of new employees. To understand potential employers, you might cast them initially, as intelligence analysts would, in a somewhat suspicious light. At their best, they may become your allies, and a partner inclined to compensate you fairly for the gain they reap from your efforts. At their worst, they will become ruthless and cunning adversaries, skilled in every tactic and technique to increase company earnings at your expense. Somewhere between those extremes, your employer will be a coalition partner that you are not sure you can trust entirely, but you are able to work with closely.

It might appear pessimistic to begin with combative viewpoints, but in the intelligence business we tend to use worst-case scenarios as helpful starting points from which to deal with the unknown. It is a measured approach, bracketing the extremes in an unclear situation. It is also a way to frame expectations should anything go horribly wrong. Sometimes we are wrong, and our intelligence assessments overestimate the threat. When we look at why, we realize that something misdirected our perception. We take special note of the shortfall, readjust perceptions, and make sure that the telling indicators are not missed again. In this sense, it seems easy to understand how adversaries become demonized, and viewed as the cause for all our ills. What we seem less inclined to do is to look at our own team, our mission partners, allies, and (perhaps most importantly) ourselves, because this is where misperception will often have the greatest impact to our assessments. With so much at stake, a second look at our decision-making process is always warranted. This is true in the intelligence world and the business world, alike. Where business is concerned, that means applying special scrutiny to our salaries.

Employers must make a profit with their businesses. Breaking even or losing money will not do in the highly competitive world of capitalism. Breaking even does not even work for non-profits and charities, which must keep up with the effects of inflation. For everyone else, profit is the bottom line. Profit allows growth, and growth fuels more business.

For example, China has been able to sustain its amazingly high domestic-product growth rate it part because it pays its workers so little. Some of my most lasting memories of a personal trip I made to China in 1999 came from shopping in its markets. Wherever possible, I would do my analyst thing and wander off the beaten path into areas not normally frequented by Westerners. I could always claim that my

"Profit is the lifeblood of any business"

—Mavaxiom 131

intrusions had been accidental because I could not read Chinese. Untutored in the language, I became especially proficient at referring to myself to puzzled Chinese as "laow-why." Technically translated into English "laow-why" means "non-Han," or non-Chinese. The Chinese found this most amusing because the phrase has a different connotation to the common person. In the colloquial of their language "laow-why" refers to "foreign devil," or the racially different people with big noses. I just worked it for all it was worth. This foreign devil wandered through factories and saw young children, not even teenagers, trying to sleep during breaks in their work shifts. Ever wonder why seemingly everything we buy these days is made in China? It is simply cheaper to make items in China than in the United States. Chinese workers' wages from our perspective, but not theirs, are criminally low.

Businesses are unyielding in their efforts to minimize costs. If it is cheaper to send work to other countries, then businesses will do so to make a profit. Businesses will do this even if the country disregards American child labor, worker-safety, or union standards. *There are no labor unions in China.* China's economic success story has come from its wholesale exploitation of the single largest population on the planet. It is their age of robber barons. Often high-ranking military and Communist party officials, these new industrialists are profiting from what we would consider the mistreatment of their own people. China has entered the twenty-first century outwardly more capitalist *than* capitalist. Like proud parents in the West, we admire China's phenomenal economic growth and chalk it up as a victory for "the western way." What we fail to see amid all this celebration of capitalism's apparent success is that China exemplifies the worst of take-no-prisoners market economics. Their success is an inconvenient mirror that reflects the ugly side of ruthless economics, the "zero sum" game where winning can only occur at the expense of others. The relevance of this to the separating military veteran is that whether in Shanghai or Chantilly, employers find it easy to minimize costs is by paying employees less than they deserve.

> "Pay negotiations only work *down* from the salary you first ask for from an employer."
>
> —Mavaxiom 132

For those leaving the military or government, achieving the best salary possible won't be a matter of vanity as much as a matter of necessity. No matter what you think you should be making, your employer will want to pay you less. No matter what happens, if you do not account for a few basics, you may end up earning *less* in civilian life. Pay attention to getting paid correctly.

At a minimum, you must account for the following things that will bite you if you do not factor them into your minimum "hard deck" for pay:

1. Federal and state tax, which were not deducted from your base pay before,
2. Retirement fund (401K), into which you now must put your own money. In 2007, the limit was $15,500 of income not subject to tax, and each year it typically increases. Your goal for the rest of your life is to contribute the absolute limit that you can reach, and every year. No exceptions.
3. Living standard, which could cost you at least 10 percent more now that you are not benefiting from military subsidies. To maintain the same standard, even if just to eat, will require you making that much more than at your last duty station.

To recap, maintaining the quality of life that you enjoyed in the military requires adding federal tax + state tax + 401K contribution + medical + dental + cost-of-living increases = a total that you must know to realistically determine your civilian pay. Not factoring in these costs will leave you with less money than expected, further complicating your transition.

Marc's Completely Oversimplified Formula for Calculating Pay[2]

If you are going to work someplace, you have to be able to live there. I am talking about living with a reasonable level of dignity. This means just being able to pay your mortgage. If your biggest fixed cost is your mortgage, then your income should probably take it into strict account. In this sense, I devised a completely oversimplified formula for calculating your pay. The beauty of it is that this formula was actually based on a concept I learned in the military. When I entered the service, all the young-buck lieutenants were repeatedly warned not to sign leases or mortgages taking more than 25 percent of their base pay.

That was a good rule, and it served me well for my years in the service. My civilian approach to salary assumes a new career at a company of your choosing of approximately twenty years. The trend is that fewer people stay at one company that long, but use this assumption for the math, nonethe-

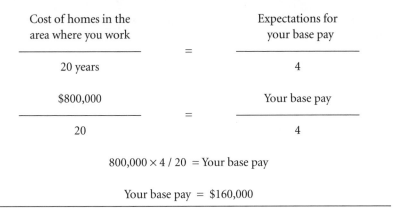

Figure 13.1. Marc's Completely Oversimplified Formula for Calculating Pay

less. The formula is based principally on the real estate prices of the area in which you will be working and living. If you are single, and looking for a job in Washington, D.C., for example, your base pay will have little buying (i.e., living) power, unless it is on par with the stratospheric housing prices. If you intend to buy a multi-bedroom house on Capitol Hill that goes for, say, $800,000, then your pay to afford it will have to be commensorate.

The reason that this model is completely oversimplified is because one-quarter of your annual salary ($40,000) over 20 years will only pay the part of the mortgage known as the "principal." It does not take into account any of the interest accrued over time—which will likely be much more than the sum of money on which interest is paid. That means that $160,000 should be at the low end of your pay scale if you work in an area where the housing prices average $800,000. It also means that $160,000 annually should be your after-tax income, otherwise you simply will not have the money to afford a mortgage. This formula came some years too late to prevent the mortgage meltdown—not that it would have deterred Americans from buying homes they could not afford anyway.

The next time a prospective employer shirks from such a rationale, or tells you that the company is a "not-for-profit" or that you "will not get rich in this profession," ask for the rental cost of its office space, or the cost of residential real estate nearby. Better yet, find out for yourself first. Shop around and find real-estate flyers for housing within a five-mile radius of the new office *before* you discuss salary. If they could not afford the rent, the company would not be there. It would only make good business sense for a company to locate itself in an area whose rent it was able to comfortably pay. Likewise, it makes just as much business sense that the company would be located in an area readily reachable by the caliber of employees it needs. Housing costs within a reasonable distance then suggest a reasonable salary that is affordable by the company. If local rental costs for the company head-quarters were an issue, then there might be an even bigger problem with the firm's ability to responsibly manage its own fiscal well-being. This would be an important indicator for a job seeker. If the decision-making apparatus of a company cannot pay its own rent, then it might not be the kind of company that you want to work for.

Vacation and Work

So many questions plague people when they consider the number of days off they need a year. It is an important issue because employers often use vacation and sick time as a counterbalance to salaried compensation. Think about all the different aspects of this issue carefully. For example, how much vacation time do you want to take annually in civilian life? Do you need a lot of time off to recharge, or would you rather take fewer days off and make more money? Do you take a lot of time off while sick? If you like to travel, would you accept a lower salary with a higher number of paid vacation days? Consider the latter when your interviewer winces and says, "I am sorry, we will not be able to compensate you with that many days off at *that* salary."

> "The only trip I ever regretted was the one I never took."
>
> —Mavaxiom 133

It is standard practice to give new company employees a set number of vacation days. Most big American companies offer about two weeks, which is to say ten days (or eighty hours) of paid time off per year. This does not include federal holidays, which you may (or may not) receive. In fact, it is quite common *not* to get all federal holidays. Right about now you are per-haps beginning to realize how cushy the military and government really were when it came to paid time off. With thirty annual leave days (which, in civil-ian terms, translates to six weeks of work days) plus nine federal holidays, and generally the day off after Thanksgiving as well, federal employees become accustomed to working only ten months out of the year. This does not include virtually unlimited sick time in the military. From a purely pragmatic standpoint, do not expect anything similar after your departure from military or government service.

In the business world, vacation varies from two to four weeks. That means time when you are being paid for not working. I reiterate this because in the American business mindset, nothing is free. That time off costs the company the same as your salary. That is why it becomes a hot negotiating point. Civilian firms also have options for sick time and unpaid time off from work. All of these numbers must be factored into the bottom line before an offer can be extended to you. It is therefore vital that *you* consider them before you ever get to that point in the process. You will not get everything you want, so start thinking now what you can live with. Employees usually get roughly eight paid days off related to federal holidays, and some companies allow employees to shift these days about. If you did not want to take Veteran's Day in November, you might use that day after Thanksgiving to make a four day-weekend. As for sick time, employees usually get five paid days to be at home or to attend to health issues. One week of fighting off the flu, though, and you had better remain healthy for the remainder of the year, because any additional sick time will cost you vacation days.

I had a job with a company that gave its employees *unlimited* sick days. That would be a dream come true for some, but in this case the company was a high-end engineering firm anxious to see its employees take *any* time away from work. Its engineers might have been technological savants, but were inept when it came to their own health and wellness needs. Having nothing resembling a life, most employees would just work: day, night, weekends, Christmas. You name it, they never went home. The company actually had to lure them away with free sick days. When a giant corporation absorbed that engineering firm, guess what was the first benefit to go? Of course, the unlimited sick days, followed promptly by all the engineers who were looking for kinder, gentler employers.

When you go to a job interview, make sure you discuss the company policy on vacation days, federal holidays, and sick days. Draw a chart. Compare on one side of the paper what you were accustomed to in the military, and on the other side what the company is offering you now. Then think about your own lifestyle, and do the math. You may want to take more time off in your new job, especially if you have not done so in the past. Now that you are a civilian, maybe you are looking for a change in lifestyle? From my own experiences abroad, vacation days spent on trips are highly undervalued in the United States. Overseas, especially in Europe, it is common for companies to provide three *times* as much vacation as American companies.

Six weeks of paid time off is not unheard of in Europe. While vacationing there, I found that Europeans are much more at ease about their jobs because they know that they will have plenty of holiday time to fulfill family obligations, as well as unwind on their own personal vacations. So much time also affords them longer stretches for travel; two- to four-week treks across countries are fairly common. I once joined a small group of British travelers in Djibouti who had just come from two *weeks* in Ethiopia. Such trips give people the opportunity to mentally release the increasing pressures of modern life. Americans seem content to work themselves to death in their race to an elusive early retirement.

It is your choice: more money, more time off, whatever you want. For the moment, America is a free country, so the choice is yours. In my case after separating from the military, I just did not know any better. My clumsy process of finding out that I had so many options when it came to vacation came the hard way, via trial and error. Mostly error. While in the military, I could afford to waste days capriciously, but as a civilian my days off became precious. The reason why was because I looked at work from a different perspective as a civilian, namely that my civilian job was unlike my military profession. The reason becomes clear when you realize that your civilian job is only a job. Consequently, the mental engagement is different, because you are not employed 24/7 as a civilian the way you were in the military. You do not "live" and "breathe" your civilian job, it just pays the bills. Without that level of intensity and focus, civilian jobs have a tendency to wear on you in ways that necessitate more frequent breaks.

So, if you do *not* vacation, you ultimately affect your own productivity, and your work performance drops. That probably needs to be one of your chief justifications for negotiating vacation time. Vacation is not time to goof-off; it is vital for good mental health. It always was, even in the military, but now its significance centers around you being at the top of your game. Vacation is time to center, refocus, and get your mind *off* work, so you can come back to your job prepared to work harder and more effectively. In addition to ensuring that their workers are not operating at marginal efficiency, vacation time also benefits firms by reducing stress-related illnesses among employees. If a company is stingy about granting vacation time it may be an important indicator, a warning sign that the health and well-being of their employees is not a priority. Learn to pick up on these queues; they will serve as telltale signs of your next employer's real underlying philosophies. As you will soon see, if you ignore these valuable sources of intelligence it may come at your own peril.

The Scams

Some of the approaches that companies take to manipulate employee vacation time border on the shameful. The unscrupulous will sometimes offer what sounds like the highest possible number of vacation days available by any firm in that business. The underhanded strategy that allows them to make such claims is by advertising the total of all other paid days off *combined*. For example, some companies will advertise four total weeks of leave for employees. It sounds great; just like the military. Upon inspection, however, and sharp questioning, you will discover that the four weeks is a conglomeration of different kinds of paid days off. That total includes annual leave, federal holidays, emergency days, and sick days all rolled together. Now become the intelligence analyst for a moment, and do the numbers. Deducting five sick days (one week), plus eight or nine statute holidays (one and a half weeks) from the touted total of four weeks, leaves less than two weeks of true vacation time. Pardon me, comrade, but can I please have some more boiled cabbage with my borscht? Unwitting new employees accepting such a vacation package quickly find themselves in a bind. With the usual family obligations at times like Thanksgiving and Christmas, and only a week of actual vacation days at your disposal, you will be left with no extended free time at all for yourself.

Slick managers also sell an equally dangerous combined pool of sick days and leave days. On paper it sounds great. The rationalization that they expect you to accept is that a payoff of more leave time comes to employees who do not get sick during the year. Sure, in a perfect universe. The idea of converting unused sick days to vacation time sounds tempting, but how many people have *that* much control over their health? The military service member might not remember the last time they were sick, and out of sheer pride accept a leave package deal expecting to profit from more paid time off. Maybe in the military, but in the civilian world no one is chasing you around ordering you to get your annual flu shot, medical, and dental exams. They are easy to forget the first few years as a civilian, and some military veterans might see such necessities as superfluous. But without the demands to exercise daily, the more sedentary nature of civilian office work, and being surrounded by a higher population of adults who are less healthy than their military counterparts, the probability of you succumbing to the common cold and/or flu increases. In the grand, random scheme of life, there are no guarantees. Just one bout with the flu or an unforeseen accident can easily gobble up all your sick days. Then, when you have run out, the process eats into leave days. If you try to "tough it out," and make it in to work, you only risk infecting all of your new civilian coworkers – none of whom will appreciate your contribution to the office. The bottom line: keep Murphy's Law in mind, and do not gamble with sick days.

The whole point of holidays, leave, and sick time is to give people the freedom to recover and refresh. Putting all those days together to create the illusion of a larger grand total is a scam. It is unnecessary for management to fabricate unreasonable expectations for their employees, and it undermines to the trust that managers should be trying to build. Policies such as these reflect poor company values in caring for their people.

Workload

When I left the military I became a one-man subcontracting team for a defense-industry company trying to establish a foothold at a new client site. Being a hard-charging veteran, I was quick to take on work as it was assigned and to do my best to keep my customer happy. Soon, however, there were simply too many tasks for me alone to sensibly handle. My sense of duty and commitment to the mission began to undermine my quality of life and job satisfaction. I perceived that the problem was the sheer *quantity* of work assigned to me. I was drowning in it, and needed help. The job did not necessarily require another person with my qualifications, but it did require somebody who could assist me. An administrative assistant or graphic technician would have saved the day by producing the many briefing slides needed by my client. The number and quality of slides could not be significantly reduced, and a little math revealed a troubling problem. The number required, divided by the hours required to create them in a work week, plus all the other tasks assigned me, equaled another full-time employee. But no such person was hired, or sought, while I was there. The reason would become obvious only later. My own perception was that "the team" would naturally grow around my lead, that others would see that my dedication justified building a greater presence at the client location. Perhaps on a military beachhead, but not necessarily at a defense contracting firm. After all, why pay for two people when one person was willingly taking on twice a normal workload? Now can you see how business really works? Meanwhile, all I could do was keep my head above water.

My tragic mistake was my loyalty to the mission. In going the extra mile daily I had established a high performance standard that I could not sustain indefinitely without assistance. The company was at fault as well, because it had not grown a business opportunity with additional personnel in the contract with its client. Although I was effectively working, I was neither being aided in effort nor reward for superior outcomes. In fact, the company did not want to acknowledge my success at all because that would validate the need for additional compensation. My monthly activity reports constantly reiterated potential growth opportunities, but no one heeded them. In the 18 months I worked there, my corporate manager made two visits to my location. In the intelligence business, we call that a flashing red indicator. All that mattered was that the customer was getting the value of two workers for the price of one. The client paid less money for my company's services, and my company saved money by not giving me a bonus or help. I eventually left that position with a heavy heart. I truly enjoyed the work, but "the business" was entirely too draining.

When I left, I was astonished by the amount of work I had done. I was disappointed by how the company had allowed a business growth opportunity to slip through its fingers, simply because it did not want to invest additional people, or reward quality work. I also realized how drastically my new civilian pay had fallen short of my military expectations. When I was stationed in Washington, D.C., three years earlier as an Air Force captain, I took home more pay than as a civilian. This just added insult to injury. My compensation had been below what even one person deserved, and my employers had been getting more than a bargain at my expense. No one aside from me saw anything wrong with that. Belatedly, I learned that only I could take care of me. See to that upfront in your new civilian job. Know exactly what your salary, vacation, and work specifics are before drowning at your new job.

Negotiations

When you take a civilian job, you need to secure the highest salary you can from the start. My own misperception was if I took a lower starting salary to get my foot in the door, I could always work up to correction later when my skills were recognized. In theory, that sounds right, but on the planning ledger at money-making civilian businesses, it maps out a little differently. Management is not too keen on sudden spikes in employee salaries, especially unforeseen spikes because of miscalculations on their part. Salary may also reflect corporate cultural expectations. For example, and from my own experience in defense contracting, those in managerial positions originate from—guess where? That's right, from government service, especially the military.

As those in the military already know, salary increases follow a stair-stepped approach. After promotion to a particular pay grade, you gradually, ever so gradually, step up within that same grade. The increments are often too small to build any incentive, drive, or dedication in the ambitious, and hence why many are eager to make a transition to the civilian sector. Unfortunately, because of the cultural expectations of former military management, defense contracting works much the same way. If you come in at a pay grade, say $75,000, it will be a while before you make much more money very quickly. Raises are generally only 3 to 5 per cent—yes, 3 to 5 percent—and then only annually. That means that after a year of working you will probably be bumped up 5 percent, or $3,750, for a total of $78,750—a monthly increase of $312 (before taxes). Now, if you project forward just a bit, and discover that you are a year behind where you would like to be, there is no way of speeding up the process. It may be forever before you make significantly more money. You can break your back working more hours a week, make your customer really happy, and, despite a relatively large raise, you may be left feeling overworked, undervalued, and unhappy.

The moral of the story is "sell high." Sell yourself as high as possible upfront. Come in at the highest possible salary because, once you are in, you will find yourself on a slow-moving escalator to incremental raises that barely pace inflation. If you want to make *any* more, more quickly, you will likely have to leave your company and join another, at a higher starting level, on another slow escalator. That is why people jump between companies. They are seeking their real worth level, because no one is going to tell them what it is.

Employers know that former military people will work to death and never realize their true salary worth. They know that $60,000 or $70,000 thrown at a former military person will be perceived as "big bucks." So you are probably not asking for too much until they *tell* you that you are asking for too much. If they accept your offer, no questions asked, then you have just undersold yourself. It is not that you are greedy; it is just that everyone in business is cheap when it comes to compen-

> "The most closely guarded secrets have nothing to do with national security—they are the salaries of all employees."
>
> —Mavaxiom 134

sation. And quite honestly, they have to be because their financial success is at stake.

More Negotiations

If, in the process of negotiating your salary, you have flashbacks to haggling over details with a car salesperson, you are in the right place. It will be a series of highball-lowball exchanges until one of you flinches. Some people love these standoff games. One of the best moves is to just pause after you hear the offer. Do it for two reasons. First, employers want you to react so they can see where you stand. Do not give them that advantage. Second, employers always want to bid low. They do so because their *job* as managers is to minimize costs. Do not assist them. Allow them to stew in their guilt for lowballing your worth. Let them to react to the silence. Let them think that they may have insulted you with their offer. You almost certainly deserve more, and they know it. No one else but you in that room is looking out for your best interests, so be your own best negotiator. A good way to do so is to appear devoid of need, and only a desire to work with a superior institution.

Are most companies straightforward about their offers? In my experience, companies are not straightforward at all with prospective employees. They have no obligation to be up front with you. They want you to mistakenly

The Power of the Pause

When a prospective employer gives you a salary figure directly or by phone:

1. Do not react in *any* way by expression, voice, or gesture.
2. Immediately stop what you are doing or saying or thinking.
3. Clear your mind and very slowly, silently begin to count to 15.
4. As you do, remain peaceful, devoid of thoughts or feelings.
5. Allow the interviewer's conscience the time to awaken.
6. Let the awkward silence continue until you reach the count of 15.
7. Return to the conversation as if absolutely nothing has happened.
8. Respond *only* with, "Let me think about your offer. Thank you."
9. Do not reveal *any* emotions, or react to the offer in any way.
10. Move on in the interview, and do not bring up salary again.

expect less money than they might be prepared to pay. Remember, all companies survive and thrive on a bottom line defined by revenues exceeding costs by the highest possible margin. You are just part of that equation. If your salary is $20,000 lower than it should be, then the company can invest $20,000 elsewhere, with some of it going to shareholder dividends. To stiffen your resolve to obtain the pay you deserve, you might imagine that $20,000 going directly into your boss's pocket, although in reality it probably will not add a penny to his pay.

So now you need to sit down on a big, warm flat rock at the end of a sunny day, watch the sunset, and the stars come out, and *then* decide the answers to a few questions. The obvious one has already been discussed,

What do you really want?

That question essentially asks you to *qualify* your purchasing power. It is another way of asking yourself how much you think buying things will please and comfort you in life. It is a way of gauging the expensiveness of your satiation, the money it will take to keep you materialistically happy. The second, more prudent question asks you to *quantify* your living requirements,

What do you really *need*?

I do not regard it as a foregone conclusion that people necessarily want more money. Instead, the question asks how much is enough, *really*? Lots of money is great, unless it makes you miserable in the earning of it. So you need to ask yourself, and often. Sit still and think through the hard task of finally, finally, attending to your own needs as part of a long-range strategic plan. This process demands answers like, "I want to take two trips a year, at least one needs to be international and for at least two weeks." That is a legitimate answer. It might sound selfish, but if that is what you need for stimulation and sanity, then that is what you need. The only problem is that you have to be painfully honest with yourself about it. It may mean taking a lower salary just to get that much vacation time. It may also mean taking leave without pay to get away when you need to.

You Must Decide What Is Important to You

If you do not know what is important to you, then you start your new life at a disadvantage. In fact it is in everyone else's best interest that you do *not* know because then they can act freely in their own best interest. This may mean paying you less, working you harder, or both. Your worth to a prospective employer depends on what you have to offer, what they need, and the timing of the hiring process. Different companies have different profit margins based on the current fair asking price of their products and services. In the defense contracting industry, that margin can be gigantic. For example, if a person is hired at $100,000 per year, chances are that they are billing the government $200,000 for that position. The additional monies are used to pay for things like overhead, benefits, and severances packages.

I had first-hand experience with realizing the full scope of possible salary ranges when I overhead my vice president discussing a job opening with one of his friends who was still in the military. This friend was apparently balking at the offer, to which the vice president replied, "look, don't worry, we'll start you out as a Senior Engineer." That got my attention because I was hired as a senior engineer. I then heard the vice president say to his friend, "no,…I can pay you $127, 000 at that grade." That really floored me because it was *fifty* percent more than what I had been offered, and I had an engineering degree. At that moment, it was clear how drastically someone could be underpaid. It also led me to wonder what my *real* worth actually was.

> "Greed and fear drive the engines of economy, powering progress."
>
> —Mavaxiom 135

Notes

1. Cunliffe, *Rome and Her Empire*, 142.
2. This formula is intended to spur thinking about unanticipated living costs that even a terrific-sounding salary might not cover. Critics, I expect, will see this formula as filling veterans' heads with false expectations. My loudest critics—managers who derive much of their own salary from the ignorance of their employees—will have the most to lose from veterans taking this formula seriously.

CHAPTER FOURTEEN

Compensation Shortfalls
Once it Happens, You Hope it Never Happens Again

"That relationship was like Death."

— Mavaxiom 141

Money pays the bills, and when you do no have enough of it in our capitalist society, even simple things become challenging. The struggle creates a shift in your priorities, and having "enough" becomes a hub around which all other conditions revolve. One of the most difficult things for me to endure after leaving the service was being underpaid because it took my attention away from my goals of accomplishment and focused it instead on ways of simply making more money. For years I was underpaid, and, as a Type-A personality, I allowed my frustration to gnaw at me until it seemed to be consuming my very sense of worth and self-confidence. I despised that feeling. I resented those whom I perceived to be undervaluing me, and, worst of all, I hated myself for letting it happen.

The next hurdle to get over was waiting any longer to change my situation. Procrastination has a way of consuming your efforts and expending intense amounts of personal energy. It allows the deafening cacophony of daily distractions to get in the way, eventually mortgaging your ability to accomplish goals. You know you need to make change but subtle, almost subconscious, task avoidance tendencies push back the act of "doing" from ever happening. This not only prolongs your self-hate, it allows it to metastasize into full-blown poison.

Let the Numbers Do the Talking

In my case, when a company gave me a raise long after it was due, it felt as if I was only being thrown a morsel. They already knew that I was worth considerably more. A company once offered me a job at an unbelievable 50 percent higher salary than the one I was earning at the time. The shock was twofold. I was neither looking for a job at the time, nor was I prepared to believe that I was worth so much more. Few military people realize how much their training, experiences, values, and security clearances are worth to civilian employers. This would-be employer certainly understood the value of my contribution, and pushed me hard to leave my job. Despite the eventual outcomes of that experience, and all the experiences that followed, that one employer was the *only* person to ever offer me more than I asked for. The temptation was huge, for obvious reasons. In a field of employers headstrong to underpay their employees, only one man recognized how closely tied earnings could be linked to validating feelings of self-worth and confidence. Unfortunately, I was completely devoted at the time to a project that, once finished, I believed would make a long-lasting difference. I did not want to abandon it midway in its development. After the longest twenty-four hours of employment contemplation I declined the offer, much to the shock of this prospective employer.

Years later, I documented all the pay levels on my civilian job curve at that time. I looked at the results as an intelligence analysis problem, and interesting trends emerged. They revealed not only my employment successes but also my compensation shortfalls.

The diagram shows how my pay increased (and decreased) after leaving the military. Unlike in the military, where the pay intervals are clockwork regular, pay periods in the civilian world vary according to corporate practice in ways that appear unrelated to the calendar milestones. These were, instead, internal corporate accounting milestones tied to company policies and practices. To the untrained participant, like myself at the time, they appeared confusing to the point of irrational. For the purposes of the table, and to account for these seemingly haphazard divisions in time, I have calculated the pay changes as fractions of the year, including percentage changes, as well as percentages reflecting cost-of-living increases estimated at 4 percent annually.

Table 14.1. Compensation History

Period	Time Span	Change Reason	Percent Change	Actual Change	Performance Rating
G	8 mo. (.66 yr)	Out-of-cycle adjustment	12.9↑	10.23↓	Commendable
F	2 mo. (.16 yr)	In-cycle award	6.8↑	6.13↑	Commendable
E	7 mo. (.58 yr)	Regrouping	0.0↑	2.33↓	—
D	3 mo. (.25 yr)	Retitling	0.0↑	1.0↓	—
C	4 mo. (.33 yr)	In-cycle award	1.0↑	0.3↑	Good
B	10 mo. (.83 yr)	In-cycle award	1.5↑	1.83↓	Good
A	—	Begin employment	0.0 ↑	4% / yr Cost of Living↑	—

On the positive side, civilian pay changes and rewards do not have to wait for a calendar year-end to take effect. This responsiveness was evident when I received yet another offer from a company, prompting my current employer to quickly boost my pay by 12.9 percent. They were trying to hold on to me, which worked, but only for a time. As part of the deal, I asked to be moved to another location. I needed a change, and a break with past work. I was burned out, and the reassignment really helped. To the company's credit, and my own peace of mind, I really loved my new job and did well to make a difference. After only a short time, though, the contract dollars began to dwindle. It marked the end of the honeymoon and, this time, I had to rescue myself.

In my pay-history table, note the ten-month span from D to E. Right in the middle was when I received the job offer for 50 percent more pay. After declining, I had another look at the offer letter. It stared back at me and said, "Marc, you are worth at least 50 percent more than what you are making right now." That was hard to hear, and even harder to internalize. If you look at the chart, you will see something else in that ten-month period. Changes in that time are listed as "Regrouping," and "Retitling." In that period a larger firm had just bought my company, and in the process of the takeover the company's accounting system changed to align with that of the larger parent company. It was an awkward process, and over the months much of the old company's culture, management style, perks and benefits, and identity were modified to fit the new, larger corporate model. In some cases, it was not pleasant. In others, it was outright intolerable. Many of the old guard decided that it was time to cash in and leave before they grew resentful of the changes. Young bucks were thinking the same thing, but optimistically waiting to see if the situation would somehow "get better." Ah, naiveté.

Here I was, in the middle of a personally important project, and for the first time realizing how mistaken I had been to procrastinate. Now, with its new accounting realignments underway, my disappointments began to exacerbate. In those ten months, my pay increased not a penny. Considering that the cost of living increases by about 4 percent a year, my real pay had actually dropped by more than 3 percent. That might not seem like much, but consider that another company had just offered me *50 percent* more.

Shortly after receiving that offer letter, I went to discuss my compensation with my management chain. I was diplomatic, and not confrontational, but paid close attention to every word and nuance. I wanted to know how they evaluated my pay, and why, since my hire twenty-one months prior, it had only gone up slightly, and then only on paper. My sole increase in that time, of 2.5 percent, had actually left me with less real buying power than I had when hired. In the back of my mind (and tucked in my back pocket), was the offer letter for 50 percent more, and I was in full collection mode to gather every bit of data possible to decipher my employer's decision-making processes. Their pay policy was like a nuclear war-fighting strategy, and I wanted the launch codes.

I should mention that many of the people in my management chain were former military officers who had been hired after their retirements for their management abilities. If you have left the military to get away from it, as I had, do not place yourself back into an environment full of ex-military types employing their old management techniques. In my case, I was negotiating with retired guys who were part of a *new* good-old-boy network. They were at the helm of contracting firms booming from the post-9/11 defense expansion. When I began to talk money, they all went into denial, asserting to me that I should feel lucky to be employed. So persuasive were they that I walked out of that meeting almost feeling undeserving of what I was already being paid. And yet, there was that huge offer letter in my pocket.

It is one thing to be marginalized. It is quite another to leave a meeting with your managers feeling like they are laughing behind your back at your attempts to negotiate your miserable pay. Not one of them had been interested in responding to me, and saying, "Gee, Marc, we gotta do something to straighten this out." Certainly not one admitted that I was not being paid enough. They dug themselves in to wage a battle of attrition.

Ironically, what does history teach us about entrenchment? If you build a fortified position, a successful adversary will simply leave that battlefield. Why attack a stronghold? Go around it. Fly over and bomb it from the air. Adapt, and create a new battlefield attacking the weak points of the old. In this case, their ideology was rooted in their old military mindset. They believed that I had to engage them on their terms, on their battlefield from which I could not leave. The flaw in this strategy was that none of us were in the military anymore, "Sir / Ma'am." We were all civilians, and at any time I could take my toys and go to some other sandbox. They gambled that I would not. They were wrong, and it left me feeling confused.

The possible explanations for my pay problems that came to mind were more disturbing than the circumstances. My managers would not admit that my pay was too low. If they did, I reasoned, then it would reveal that they also had very little respect for me, or my skills. I felt terrible being underpaid, especially knowing that another company wanted to pay me much more. That struck me as a lose-lose relationship, and there seemed nothing for me to gain by staying. When you put your trust in a company, you expect to be treated with some dignity. This is not, however, a foregone conclusion. Managers are only people, and people have a habit of making mistakes. If managers fail to show you respect, then it is becomes easy to distrust your management. When managers misplace your trust, you will quickly feel that it is not worth your effort to continue working in that environment. You must leave; begin envisioning yourself elsewhere.

Alternatives to Pay

Amid all this drama, and in classic compensatory fashion, I tried detailing all the possible alternatives available. I wrote down all the financial incentives I could think of for a person to stay in a job aside from a paycheck, and actually provided them to my management for negotiation possibilities. They brought up not *one* in any of the discussions.

Salary is not the only form of fiscal compensation. Other benefits have merit and worth as supplementary income that may, in some cases, actually out-weigh salary. The different types of com-

"What good is money if you have to spend it all on therapy?"

—Mavaxiom 142

pensation include annuities, one-time incentives, and nonmonetary benefits. From the list it becomes readily apparent that a large variety of job enhance-ments have evolved over the years to attract and keep employees. As you will see, the greater advantages of some will often offset the shortfalls of others. The degree to which some outweigh others depends on your own values and circumstances.

---

1. Annuities (pay that builds on itself, year after year)
   A. Base salary?
   B. Vacation (four weeks = 20 days = 160 paid hours)
      1- Paid *extra* while on vacation?
      2- Earned time for a sabbatical?
      3- Maximum accruable (10 weeks)?
      4- Use or lose at year's end?
   C. All federal holidays? In addition to vacation days?
   D. Stock options?
   E. Days allowed absent annually
      1- Two weeks of sick days?
      2- One week for a family emergency?
      3- One day for personal emergency?
      4- One day for moving?
   F. Interim raise first review (percentage range expected)?
   G. Shorter timelines for promotions and raises?
2. One-time incentives (for current year)
   A. Spot-awards (out-of-cycle; performance, or new-business)?
   B. Lump-sum / year-end bonuses, dividends?
   C. Paid extended time off (sabbatical earned in how many years?)
   D. Hiring bonus?

E. Travel benefits
    1- Travel reservations / tickets?
    2- Expenses covered and processed?
    3- Expense limits?
    4- Administrative assistance?

F. Free information-technology (IT) equipment and tools
    1- Home computer?
    2- External memory / drives?
    3- Laptop?
    4- Software?
    5- Cell phone?
    6- Cables and add-ons?
    7- PDA?
    8- Accessory equipment?
    9- Printer / scanner / fax?
    10- Disk / CD / DVD supplies?

G. Vehicle lease / purchase?

3. Equipment/support
  A. IT help desk
    1- Annual IT tune-up, trouble-shooting?
    2- Software upgrades / updates?
    3- Maintenance and repairs, turnaround time?
    4- Security software?

  B. Home service
    1- Internet service provider (ISP) fees?
    2- Cell phone bills?
    3- Equipment warranties?
    4- Company vehicle use?

4. Employee services
  A. Transit fare cards / garage parking / tolls / mileage?
  B. Health-club memberships (or reciprocal access)
    1- Lockers in building / nearby?
    2- Nurse on site?
    3- Access to multiple facilities?
    4- Annual flu shots?
    5- Good equipment / quick repair?
    6- Free health screening?

C. Educational benefits (local universities, tuition assistance)?
D. Personal travel consulting services?
E. Administrative services, help for shared-office issues
   1- Scheduling / room availability?
   2- Bulk typing services?
   3- Trouble calls on equipment?
   4- Mailing services?
   5- Time cards (on-line?)
   6- Social events / greeting cards?
   7- Spreadsheets / reports?
   8- Expense Reports?
F. Executive assistant services
   1- Call-forwarding reception?
   2- Liaison for other departments?
   3- Tailored / individual support?
5. Work Environment
   A. High-end offices
      1- Private office / window/view?
      2- Cafeteria / vending machines?
      3- Appealing desks / work spaces?
      4- No cubicles / rat maze?
      5- Warm / welcoming decor?
      6- No kiosks / shared workstations?
   B. High-end equipment
      1- Well-stocked office supplies?
      2- Easy / fast Internet access?
      3- Easy / fast intranet access?
      4- Robust phone service?
   C. Office building location
      1- Easy accessibility outside the building?
      2- Nice outdoor areas / parks?
      3- Safe area / safe part of town?
      4- Running trails?
      5- Services nearby?
      6- Ease of access (by walking)?
6. Quality of Lifestyle
   A. No more exhausting/mind-numbing work?

B. Commuting
    1- Car / public transit / taxi / bus?
    2- Distance each way?
    3- Time to travel each way?
    4- Tolls each way?
    5- Stressfulness / ease of travel?
    6- Safety / threats of travel?

7. Leadership Values
  A. Cultivating expertise
    1- Creative license to explore?
    2- Consulting of opinions?
    3- Individual talents capitalized?
    4- Sharing / communication?
  B. Objectivity in profession
    1- Excessive handholding for clients?
    2- Outside opinions solicited?
    3- Strategic focus?
  C. Management Issues
    1- Poor prioritizing?
    2- Emergency-mode management?
    3- Micromanaging?
    4- Hands-off / trust of employees?

8. Sustainability
  A. The future of this work
    1- How long is the contract?
    2- Does work require justification?
    3- Is funding reviewed each year?
    4- Is the work tied to elections?
  B. Is promotion tied to bringing in new work/ new contracts?

Staffer to the Rescue

As was mentioned, I compiled alternatives to pay when it became apparent that my management was not going to budge on the issue of monetary compensation. For much of my time in the military, and later in the defense contracting business, my focus was on identifying shortfalls and suggesting options for solutions. That is what staff officers do. In short, staff officers do a lot of the thinking *for* their bosses.

In my case I believed that I was doing everything that I could for my employers. They had their rules, and in their minds the rules were absolute. They followed those rules to prevent all order in the universe from breaking down and chaos prevailing. Some firms follow rules similar to those of the military, and they follow them with similarly draconian zeal. This is primarily a reflection of management. People bring their management styles with them, sometimes from the military. That was certainly the case with some whom I have dealt with. I found myself challenged by corporate managers obstinately reluctant to explore alternatives. With forms of compensation painfully limited, and few alternative incentives, a creative solution was needed. I tried to assert solutions, but in the process discovered something else far more important.

Just because a supervisor does not know what to pay an employee does not mean that they are necessarily a bad manager. Some supervisors simply do not know what options are available. Others would be content to have their "psychic" staff person anticipate all these kinds of issues, and develop alternatives before problems ever arise. That might be fine for an assignment or two, but if a staff person ever managed to develop psychic abilities that were that good, why waste such skills on underpaying managers? Take that kind of talent to the Stock Market, and retire early.

Back in the real world, having such expectations puts a staffer in a precarious philosophical bind. On one hand, the competent employee wants to act in the best interests of their client. On the other hand, they are subordinate to their management who may not function with the client's or their employee's interests in mind. Absolute subservience is sometimes required of employees, twisting the limits of loyalty to a frustrating degree. The full extent of managerial incompetence may never become apparent to the customer or senior managers because of how hard the staffer is constantly working to solve problems on both sides. The dysfunctional manager-staffer relationship, then, is almost symbiotic. It relies on its participants to willingly accept their roles in performance of the job.

My experiences in the military and civilian sectors have taught me that there is an intangible, but undeniable, value to one's self-esteem and dignity that even salary cannot compensate. The rewards of subservience may include access and advanced promotion potential, but the costs to one's dignity are generally higher. Demanding individuals take a toll on their subordinates' lives, no matter how you look at it. My hope is to show that after leaving the service veterans should not give the same degree of unconditional self-sacrifice to employers that they gave in service to their country. The two worlds are separate and unequal. By its very design, capitalism is conditional on the ebbs and flows of the market. The market determines directions to which every firm ultimately submits. More importantly, as a veteran in this marketplace you do not need to forfeit your self-determination. A job is not worth sacrificing your self-respect. If you do, it will let you know in the worst ways possible.

Some people will suggest that they have few alternatives because of the situations in their lives. They have families and debt, and they must do what they can to tend to these obligations. I do not debate the need to uphold one's personal responsibilities. In such cases, it is necessary to adjust one's expectations on what they can and cannot do as far as a job is concerned. The new expectations must be reasonably established and reinforced by management. If something is outside a manager's control then managers need to say so, and keep employees from building up their expectations. That requires a great deal of communication. As the superior, management must lead that dialogue. This is because there may structural organizational issues that only a manager can possibly know. In other words, no matter how good the staffer, or how "psychic" they are of their bosses needs, the company in which they all work may simply not be structured to provide big incentives for some employees. All employees are not treated equally when it comes to pay. For example, some firms measure the value of employees based on the revenue that employees generate through contracts. This is especially true of government contractors, that live and die on the basis of direct contact with their client base. In these cases, corporate pay structures give preference to those in a small cadre of employees who generate new contracts. Despite all the good work that other employees do, those who create new business become the most rewarded employees. Their prime metric for promotion or salary increase will read, "personally responsible for $2.1 million contract award." Naturally, that skews the metric for evaluating the worth of other employees whose talents and skills contribute significantly to *maintaining* contracts. This is the market at work. Since I was not in business development, it was important for me to know that I would never be recognized financially for merely a job well done. I would have to bring new business for a big raise, but nobody ever told me. The entire situation was dependent on management developing the proper expectations as to what would, or would not, improve an employee's position. As the staffer, stuck in the middle, this left me feeling little consolation.

Glad to Hear that You Talked with Your Supervisor . . .

Not too long ago, I received an e-mail from a friend. She is an absolutely beautiful woman, but does not think of herself in that way. She wants to be thought of in terms that do not focus on her physical beauty, or the warmth of her personality. In fact, if you were to ask her to describe her life in five minutes or less, you would immediately sense that this single mom works absolutely way too much. Her work had been a noble pursuit, but the harder she wrestled with its blessings the more she had to contend with its unintended curses. She was one of "the 20," and her job was throwing her more off balance with each passing day.

In speaking with her, I had the sense that she had not been taken seriously by her employers for some time. They are good people for the most part, but the uncomfortable atmosphere at her job was wearing her down. In her case, her steadfast focus on overcoming the drawbacks of her attractiveness simply *added* to the more pressing issues of her increasing workload and failure to receive adequate compensation. Every minute that she preoccupied herself with trying to be taken seriously, and not for being beautiful, her management manipulated her to take on more tasks that others were not doing. In a sense, she found herself fighting two battles; one that all employees face when demanding fair treatment by management, and the other one a shadow cast by her feminine attractiveness in a male-dominated profession. In many ways, her workplace atmosphere was one that many people in the military and government deal with daily.

We all know that managers press people to work harder. We also know that work is done for money; that money pays for life, and the more we work, the more money we can expect. As we know even better, when managers get people to do more work without an increase in pay, they are seeking more profit. And this friend of mine was very profitable for her company.

To her credit, she was not blind to the amount of work she carried for others. She routinely took up the slack when others did not show up to work, or failed to produce when they needed to deliver. She had become a savior-figure in her company. But she was blind as to why, which was: As long as she kept up the work, she would never have to deal with the possibility that she had been successful *because* of her looks. This prospect terrified her, and her means of suppressing her fear had proven a godsend to her slacker coworkers and to her management. While she compelled herself to seek what she thought would be legitimate recognition for doing inhuman amounts of work, her management sat back and watched productivity in action.

This could not go on forever, and, as her health began to falter, she became plagued by one chronic ailment after another that affected not only her work but also her ability to handle her demands as a mother. When I became aware of her plight, and learned that her view of herself had worsened, I suggested the outrageous: *Ask for a pay raise!* If her management could not deliver on more money, perhaps it could do something about lowering her workload and the incessant demands upon her to rescue delinquent coworkers.

— Original Message ————————
From: A concerned friend
Sent: Tuesday, 8:01 AM
To: Marc Viola
Subject: Just had a talk with my supervisor

Marc,
Work has been a lot better. I had a serious talk with my business lead last week and got a lot of issues off my chest. I think that things are really going to be improving even more.

My response to her began as a cautionary letter, a warning that her business lead might tell her what she wanted to hear and then do something completely different. A page later, I realized that my reply had become a particularly strong message that I would only give to her directly, if at all. I eventually decided not to hit the "send" button, realizing that her situation would not, perhaps could not, change because of the enormously high standards that she had demanded of *herself* for so long. This is the e-mail reply that I never sent:

—— Reply Message ————————————
From: Marc Viola
Sent: Tuesday, 8:01 AM
To: A concerned friend
Subject: RE: Just had a talk with my supervisor

Hey there,
Don't be surprised if the guy listened to every word
you said, but then does nothing substantive. Don't get me
wrong, "some" things *will* happen at first, but it will be
the things he can afford to let happen without directly
impacting his situation. Just observe. Watch what happens. See what it is, exactly, that he gives you. Make
sure they are not merely "good faith" gestures. If you
are not careful, everything may be exactly the same a
year from now. Some managers master the art of shaping
everything into a rut that never changes. Change is
impossible, because it upsets the comfort-level for
everyone else. Any change, anywhere, runs the risk of
disrupting all that these managers have worked so hard to
create: safety, security, and comfortable profits. They
just want you to work. If an employee is appealing to the
eye *and* works like a machine, then it's a bonus for them.
  Call me pessimistic, but resistance to change has been
my experience when it comes to problematic managers. They
are like young children you have to keep reminding, and
they pretend to keep forgetting. When you catch them,
they laugh and tell you, "You are right," and "I've gotta
be better about remembering things." If you get tired of
reminding them, and give up trying, then it is one less
thing they need to worry about. This is what makes bad
bosses "bad," they do not want to take responsibility.
If they stay in denial long enough, they win.
  People with control over a lot of money and influence,
who are not held accountable, seem to regress into irresponsible, mischievous children. The problem is that they
cannot possibly be innocent ever again because they have
already been exposed to the real grown-up world. Watch
how innocent they act. Watch how much they eat, and play,

and pretend everything is going great, especially at the "all hands" get-togethers and holiday parties.

Listen to them laugh aloud, and tell you about the new SUV they bought, or the great colleges their kids are going to. If you play along with them, and seem interested in their stories, you might be surprised by what they tell you. Without their spouses there to slow them down, they might tell you a little more than they should. So much so, that the following day they might suddenly appear at your office and tell you that they just "happened to be in the neighborhood." Then they'll back-peddle and clarify all the drunken details they divulged. The truth is that they just don't want you to realize how much they are profiting from your efforts.

When you start to find out how much these people are really making it will make you sick. They get you to work overtime for free, and then buy mansions out in horse country. Anything that upsets that fantasy, or asks for a little more in *your* pocket, is a threat to them. They need people like you. Their entire skill-set is based on how much they can get other people to do things for them. They are adept at making other people live with less. That is the ugly truth behind the grown-up world. Seen any of your programs completed on time

"One of the first casualties of civilization is civility. With so many laws protecting them, and few disincentives for bad behavior, some of the more callous citizens find few reasons to be civil to one another."

"When we reward our members for their cunning and ruthless treatment of others, instead of for their intelligence and goodness, there remains little reason to be intelligent or good."

"Legislation becomes the moral minimum standard."

—Mavaxiom 143

```
or under budget lately? That did not keep them from get-
ting a raise.
```

Perhaps one of the unfortunate things about work, as I've experienced it, is that those who excel at making employees feel truly valued are the minority. The opposite is so common that people simply expect to inherently distrust their management. It may be that the measures of success in business encourage this adversarial relationship.

As humans, we want to believe that survival of the fittest is no longer a savage evolutionary necessity. At the same time, however, we are torn as thinking, thoughtful, and feeling creatures. We are capable of living beyond, and perhaps above, the brutality of natural selection. As a species, have we not progressed to a state where some reward is given for intelligence and goodness? We want to believe so, but indications are that we still have far to go. After all, is it the kindest, most knowledgeable people who are promoted? Or do "nice guys (still) finish last?" We promote and reward those who succeed, and those who succeed in the trenches of the Capitalist Theater of Operations (CTO) seem to be fairly ruthless. They only become philanthropists *after* their success.

For now, it seems that legislation helps quell the more nefarious tendencies of human (and animal) nature. Inasmuch as not all citizens are law-abiding, there will remain some determined to live by the loopholes. For them, the temptation of gain is simply too strong to resist.

CHAPTER FIFTEEN

The Ethics of Generalists
How Mismanagement Undermines Job Security

"Idiot-proof systems have a habit of putting idiots in charge."

— Mavaxiom 151

S pying is an interesting business; it teaches its practitioners how to see things that others tend to overlook or disregard. Some years ago, I was working as a civilian contractor for an intelligence organization, putting new technologies into the hands of field operatives. Although our office advocated using some of the most cutting-edge technologies, few in positions of authority understood them, and fewer opted to employ them. Instead, the focus for the organization was the "crisis du jour," pouring effort, funding, and personnel into the latest headline issue. In an age of unprecedented security challenges, I was dumbfounded by organizations scrambling to be part of whatever hot topic grabbed the attention of political leaders. For years I had watched that sort of behavior in the military, and now I was watching it again as a civilian. I realized that our sophisticated and challenging new technology was not a problem. Instead, the problem was the *people*.

This "people problem" remains a fundamental flaw in how managers prioritize issues, and how organizations mindlessly follow them. The same conclusion was expressed by a senior U.S. intelligence leader at a meeting in

Denver in 2006 as part of efforts "to fix the nation's ailing intelligence system," according to a *Denver Post* writer, who paraphrased the official this way: "One leader compared the sixteen-agency U.S. Intelligence Community to eight-year-old soccer players bunching around the ball with much of the field uncovered. That could mean potential deadly misreads on terrorism, Iraq, Iran, China, and North Korea."[1] My term for that behavior is "fog ball," and I am not nearly as generous as the unnamed official in suggesting that eight-year-olds play that way. No, that kind of behavior is more characteristic of five-year-olds, and the fact that this kind of behavior is characteristic of managers in positions of responsibility and public trust is all the more disturbing.

On an individual level, when someone leaves behind their military or government service it is usually because they want to move on with their lives. Transition requires leaving the past behind, and seeking out new beliefs, norms, and expectations. If "fog ball" is an acknowledged managerial behavior in your military past, then you should probably try to avoid reinserting yourself into yet another culture that espouses it as an accepted institutional approach. For better or worse, veterans have an underlying understanding of, and respect for, hierarchical structure. As subordinates, they trust that their managers will employ them in ways that will take advantage of their talents, and abilities. In organizational cultures that condone "fog-ball" something else happens that is both wasteful and irreparably damaging to the spirits of employees. In its worst manifestation, entire organizations cater to the reckless pursuit of managerial ambition, and allow managerial success to frequently come at the expense of employee dignity and value. This is no place for a veteran. As a public service to those who serve their country the following is an intelligence assessment of that adversarial doctrine; a doctrine better avoided than engaged.

Terrorists and Bureaucrats

An indicator of how these behavioral issues impact staff people at the lowest levels can be seen in how management reacts to unanticipated events. Here is one illustration. Today's public security environment is fertile ground for terrorists seeking to provoke costly reactions to their random attacks. These acts are costly to free societies because they instigate the intended target to enact measures that ultimately make them less free. Terrorist acts need not be large events, just enough to result in basic stimulus responses. In the summer of 2006, with the security decision to regard any and all fluids in carry-on airline luggage as suspect, decision makers all but submitted to terrorist tactics, techniques, and procedures (TTP) for disrupting our way of life. With one action, an attempt to sneak explosive-related chemicals aboard a plane, terrorists were able to elicit exactly the desired outcome: fear instilled in entire populations. The act itself was not fear inspiring, but rather the *reaction* by security forces. The response by western security officials, a classic knee-jerk to the slightest tap, was draconian in measure and widespread in its effects—ultimately disrupting millions of airline passengers. With inadequate staff and inspection stations to deal with the threat of hair gel, lotions, and perfume, aircraft boarding in the entire U.S. came to a screeching halt, and remains hampered to this day.

Beyond the obvious impact on flight schedules, the less obvious effect was in abruptly shifting accountability from those responsible for air travel onto airline passengers. Suddenly, citizens came under attack from their own uniformed protectors for overlooking shampoo bottles in their bags. Like an autoimmune response, protective cells turned on their own body. Terrorists realized that they did not need to wage follow-on attacks because free societies would carry out the attacks for them. The overly reactive backlash adversely impacted the very thing that our security organizations are sworn to protect—what the preamble to the U.S. Constitution aptly describes as our "domestic Tranquility." There is no question that safety takes precedence in such matters. That is not the point of this discussion. What is at question is the *method* under which security must be employed so as not to impact the very principles it was designed to protect.

At what point should security management balance discretion against impinging on the freedoms of enormous numbers of the citizens they are entrusted to protect? In failing to act with tactful restraint, prudence, and judicious caution, the reaction yielded a two-fold outcome. First, it exposed the apparent lack of consideration by security organizations on the public's inherent freedom of movement. In this way, our country's trusted decision makers risked alienating their own constituencies and fellow citizens. Second, a minor event was all that was needed to tip our hand. Successfully exposing the hair-trigger nature of Western security organizations will only invite follow-on attacks. Terrorists have at their disposal what intelligence professionals can only aspire to; readily available, real-time, multisource confirmations of effectiveness—also known in intelligence circles as battle damage assessment (BDA). Armed with this invaluable intelligence source, terrorists will continue their assaults at will. Terrorists also know that for each one of their attacks a cascade of second- and third-order autoimmune aftershocks will follow, amplifying their intended signal to wider populations.

In effect, we *encourage* the terrorist by power-boosting every attack over a globally interconnected society that panders to fearful reaction at the speed of light. Until our security policies embody the confidence, competence, and maturity to balance discretion with superior situational awareness, we will likely continue to play into future baiting by terrorists tactics. If those in positions of Western authority continue to wildly react to every such issue in the future, we citizens become potential victims of not only terrorists, but also of the very decision makers we entrust to protect us.

The Sports Analogy

All organizations, as with sports teams, are composed of members with varied skills and talents. Organization missions, like team games, follow assortments of rules and logistics. In either case, the mentalities of the participants, their intelligence and modes of thought, will directly influence how they play, and ultimately how effectively they will achieve their goals. To illustrate the detrimental consequences of unfocused and reactive forms of management, I have adapted and expanded the following analogy. Imagine two soccer games occurring simultaneously on the same field, as depicted in figure 15.1, "Team Positions Versus Fog Ball." One game is played by twenty-five-year-olds, the other by five-year-olds. The two games exhibit wholly different approaches to playing, and both convey important lessons about the management of bureaucracies.

The first game, in this analogy of managerial approaches, is played by twenty-five-year-olds, and employs operational tactics, techniques, and procedures (TTP) best described as "position playing." Position playing means that the players dedicate themselves to the positions that they have been assigned. Why a player is assigned to a position directly relates to that player's expertise. If the coach has any sense of strategy, the person with the highest demonstrated aptitude plays that position, and is exhorted to focus all effort on that position for the duration of the game.

The second game in this analogy, played by five-year-olds, is fog ball. Five-year-olds, upon hearing the starting whistle, typically abandon the positions they are assigned. Instead, they allow where the ball happens to be at any moment to drive their actions and reactions, rather than follow a strategy. Any previously agreed upon TTP subsumes into a single motivation: self-interest. As a result, in their dashes for the ball, the players forget to

Team Positions Versus "Fog Ball"

Figure 15.1. Team Positions Versus Fog Ball

employ any specialization or expertise they may have been taught. Everyone becomes a generalist, operating all over the field, where the self-interests of all players preclude a coordinated approach. In fog ball, as players leave their designated positions, any semblance of team harmony disintegrates into disunity and chaos.

It is worth noting that 5-year olds are neither completely entropic, nor are they uniformly self-driven and autonomous as suggested. Their behavior is more likely somewhere in the middle. More importantly, however, is that their formative ideas of self are still prone to puppet the will and wishes of their parents and authority figures. Their drive is to ensure that those to whom they are tied are pleased with their behavior and, as such, they need constant reinforcement of what they are supposed to be doing. Some would suggest that this is not far removed from the behavior of some managers and their superiors.

All of us can agree that a certain degree of self-sacrifice is required as a prerequisite for a team to function effectively. Understandably, five-year-olds are fueled largely by "me, me, me" motivation, and do not restrain their actions for the benefit of the team. In a positive sense, the chaotic, random progress of a moving ball stimulates five-year-olds in making up their own rules as they go. The ball is both the center of their attention and their single means of obtaining credit for involvement in its movement. As a consequence, none of the players contribute their talents to the greater goal (ignore the pun). With no structured contribution or communication, teammates become adversaries, and some of their energies are wasted in combating one another. At their level of confusion, the most that they can ever achieve is simply *reaction* to the ball. And, one would hope, score the occasional goal. Figure 15.2 depicts the kinds of motivations found in fog-ball players.

In the managerial decision making of bureaucracies, the "ball" in this analogy is whatever concern happens to draws everyone's attention. In some cases, this focus is carried to the point of overlooking any other logical concerns. For example, in addressing concerns about terrorism after September 11, focus shifted from carry-on luggage to knives and box-cutters, and a bit later to anything metal that could possibly inflict harm (except, of course, first-class cabin cutlery), then to sneakers and boots, then *all* footwear, and on to belts, and then finally to unspecified fluids in 2006. Taken together,

5-Year-Olds Playing "Fog Ball"

Figure 15.2 Fog Ball: Soccer Played by Five-Year-Olds

those concerns became a bouncing fog ball of potential harm, and travelers stood patiently on the sidelines of every airport waiting room, struggling to follow the constant changes in the game. Likewise, the attention of entire government organizations shifted overnight from what they were doing to combating terrorism, despite lacking trained personnel, institutional knowledge, and practical experience. Although noble in purpose, such dramatic shifts in focus were potentially at the expense of the organization's original critical mission areas. In effect, an entire federal security community began to function like a group of five-year-olds playing fog ball.

By contrast, to continue with our sports analogy, twenty-five-year-olds, while playing the best they possibly can in their assigned positions, trust and rely on each other to concentrate on their own positions as well. Adult players restrain themselves from running far from where they should be. Professional players do not manicure the turf, or sell tickets, or guide cars into the parking lot. If a drunken brawl breaks out during a game, their job is not to break up the fight, or clean up the mess, or repair the grandstands, or provide security for the rest of the season. Professional players are paid to play their position as best as possible. Even if the ball never comes to them in an entire game, their team can still win, and they will be recognized for their season-long contributions. They are professionals. They understand their roles and stick to them, and their coaches would rarely ask them to do anything else. And it is only reasonable for coaches to expect their players to do their best at nothing else.

A powerful Zen underscores this concept: Athletes play their game. Foremost in the wisdom of that notion is the realization that expertise is finite, so there is no point in expending talent anywhere other than where it will do the most good. Likewise, there is also no reason to waste energy running the ball all over the field. When all players on a team have unity of purpose, then all can work together toward a greater goal. When all players communicate with one another, their team builds *cohesion*, which leads to proactive planning, coordinated action, and the ability to respond dynamically throughout the course of a game.

The motivation of players of fog ball is simple and self-centered. Their intent is not to play efficiently, or to win, but rather to *gain attention* from those above them. In the simplest terms, the intent of bureaucratic fog ball is to (a) seek praise and (b) avoid negative judgment. Player behavior is fueled by a belief that praise will bolster standing in the group, or improve self-image. Ultimately, success generally comes at the expense of others; striving for recognition is more important than contributing to the greater cause.

This behavior undermines morale, and eventually erodes the integrity of entire organizations.

A ground rule for self-centered play is the idea of "perceived scarcity." The perception that success is derived from a finite resource applies to most bureaucratic fog-ball games. Fog-ball managers rarely believe in the sufficiency of their situations. Since they perceive that there is never enough to go around, rarely do they find enough. So they hoard, strictly controlling resources, and even the effort-levels, of their people. Most notably, fog-ball managers incessantly reallocate resources and people in hopes of achieving results that will win favor from superiors. Superiors who rely on decisions from fog-ball managers are in constant jeopardy of being misinformed, misused, or misled. Subordinates are at even greater peril; they face being internally reassigned endlessly, randomly, and spread too widely across too many functions, their careers blunted because they are never left in one job long enough to build expertise.

Onlookers are not blind to this game playing. They see self-promoting and egotistical fog-ball strategies crushing the confidence and dedication in an organization, and betraying those who rely on its output. Eventually, the needless confusion and lost productivity of constant emergencies, reorganizations, and crisis-actions demoralizes all but the most slavish subordinates to the point of realizing that their own management is the real problem.

No rational adult would comfortably entrust his or her credit card, bank account, or car keys to a five-year-old. Likewise, no rational adult should comfortably entrust their well-being to government bureaucrats who behave like five-year-olds. In our complex world, there are simply too many issues for any one organization to cover with any reasonable facsimile of credibility. Any single agency attempting to react to *all* the most pressing issues simultaneously does so at the expense of giving due diligence to their position. In the case of terrorism, the fog-ball management approach of security organizations comes at the expense of the liberties of all of us as citizens, the very people these organizations are supposed to protect. In trying to make meaningful contributions to every issue that matters, a fog-ball approach yields meaningless results.

Nowhere in this analogy has the idea of a referee been introduced, and perhaps because no real parallel exists in the real world. In a soccer game, of either variety, overseers are ever-present in enduring that the game play moves in a forward direction. Some would suggest that the Intelligence Community (IC) parallel of this entity should be the Office of the Director of National Intelligence (ODNI). That would, of course, also assume that the ODNI has the authority directly affect game play, possessing the equivalent of penalty power and sanction to eject unruly players. In loose confederation of stove-piped institutions dominated by bureaucratic agencies, the main objective is keeping up with the demands of the "inbox." It is a daily challenge just to keep track of what is going on, let alone moving game play in meaningful forward directions. With managers vying in the interests of their own stovepipes, and without a detached entity above the playing field effectively laying down the law, the end result is neither meaningful nor forward. The importance to separating military members should be clear. If you are leaving the military or government *because* of bureaucratic nonsense, do not re-immerse yourself into yet another chaotic fray. Watch for the signs, and avoid further drama.

Lord of the Flies

Most people would agree that all members of a group are as much to blame as its leaders for any unpleasant group outcomes if they enabled self-centered and potentially unscrupulous individuals to seize control and produce those outcomes. Typically, such group members are followers: people who seek security in *belonging*, a need that may be unrelated to what is best for them, or best for their work. All that matters for them is the stability of knowing what to expect. Herd mentalities like theirs make organizations vulnerable to groupthink. Following the group norm becomes more important than legitimate outcomes. Any dissent is dealt with harshly, because dissenting opinions attack group beliefs, norms, and expectations. Dissent particularly threatens systems that rely on chaotic behavior, as is the case with fog ball. If unchallenged, individuals seizing control of such systems can command the herd in any way desired, according to any whim.

> "Sufficient ambition to lead does not imply sufficient morality to trust."
>
> —Mavaxiom 152

In groups with a herd mentality, the temptation of fog ball is ever present. What is important today will change tomorrow. Management will constantly change priorities to better position itself for praise and advancement. In such groups, docile members, even docile leaders, relinquish responsibility for the actions instigated by stronger leaders. At the same time, accountability is diffused throughout the group, since few individuals are eager to skirt any direct liability. Bureaucratic fog ball is therefore as much a consequence of individuals unconditionally submitting to the group will, as it is a consequence of individual mismanagement.

In *Lord of the Flies*, the novel by Nobel Prize-winning author William Golding, disciplined young schoolboys undergo a transformation illustrative of fog ball when stranded without adults in a plane crash on a deserted island. Without the continued influence of mature societal guidance, their civilized behavior rapidly breaks down and is replaced by vicious new beliefs, norms, and expectations. Their challenges in coping with an unanticipated new environment become overwhelming. Soon, their attempts to remain calm and organized are replaced by fears and ambition, and in the end the children revert to savagery. Similarly, without sound leadership, organizational managers sometimes find themselves reacting brusquely and negatively, if not savagely, to unanticipated challenges, putting incredible strains on their personnel and resources. For some managers, the lure of prestige and advancement is all too great for their ambition to resist. The urge of its managements to react to the most popular issues, and take credit for participating, can plunge the most highly disciplined organizations into a downward spiral.

My own experiences with fog ball were central to my desire to end my military active duty. I hoped that I would find that economic imperatives would necessitate the institution of better management techniques in the civilian world. In where I looked I would be proven wrong, but not without a realization of great intelligence value: *beneath every banner exists human nature.* Everywhere, the rewards won by the basic human drive of ambition may be more highly regarded than those for the continued well-being of all the group's individual members. Such is the human condition. The challenge for all veterans, then, is finding an institution-management model, a better rulebook, that can more fairly govern the competition between those two fundamental drives at a game level tolerable to all people, players and spectators.

The Institutionalized Waste of Fog Ball

Managers are supposed to be decisive, and are given authority accordingly. They are expected to make decisions that yield the best return from limited resources. Members of their groups are expected to trust management and willingly relinquish their autonomy. Since those who control the resources do so either to the benefit of their organizations, or to their cost, their management results reflect their values. Plainly, with limited resources a standard feature of government agencies, their managements prioritize what they value.

A clear reflection of organizational values can be seen, typically, in the treatment of in-house expertise. Experts do not grow on trees, and the cost of misusing the experts available is enormous. To truly master an exceptional skill requires years of study. Few can become an expert without investing the necessary time. No level of short-term effort can produce the same competence that comes with time, exposure, and working experience. In my own intelligence field, depth and expertise were probably the exception rather than the rule. The reason for this goes back to management decisions. The value of human talents and skills is difficult to quantify, and equally difficult to manage. When managers pull experts away from their specialties, they do so at a loss, potentially, to the organization and the expert employees. When such misjudgments are an institutional norm, practical common sense has lost the game to fog ball.

I found as a military officer that some senior managers desperately needed to feel that they were not "left out of the fight." Wangling to involve their organizations in new mission areas that had nothing to do with their assigned responsibility, they were able to artificially achieve a sense of belonging and contribution. The nature of such shifts in priority put huge burdens on already thinly spread staffs. Enough time or manpower was never available to fully grasp a new priority with the same level of competence as the original, institutional mission. I watched as formerly motivated team experts struggled to provide the appropriate level of competence, depth, or understanding to the new mission. The net effect was that it made team members feel as if they were being asked to underachieve. Over time, their inability to function at their accustomed levels of proficiency became demoralizing, and the organization suffered.

What prompts managers to play fog ball? To understand this kind of managerial behavior also requires understanding the thinking processes and mentality that lead fog ball. Figure 15.3 depicts what might be termed the shotgun approach to prioritizing. In the figure, each dot represents an issue, threat, concern, or possible outcome. A random sampling of today's national-security headlines might yield such topics as: North Korean missile or nuclear tests, Hezbollah attacks on Israel, the looming hurricane season, the possibility of civil war between Sunnis and Shiites, Iraq, fluctuations in oil prices, Iran, the latest terrorist bombing plots, and so on. With limited resources, which of these issues would be the focal point for any single gov-

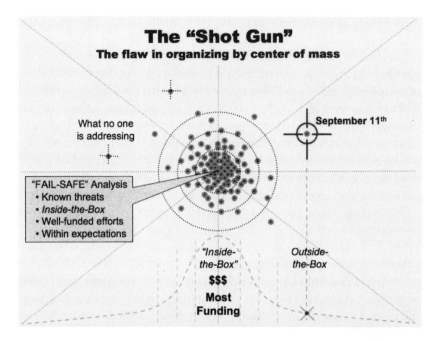

Figure 15.3 The Shotgun: The Flaw in Organizing by Center of Mass

ernment organization? The most common answer where fog ball is the strategy of choice: *All of them.*

Most hot issues cool with time. When they do, it becomes an opportunity for organizations to pull back from the brink, reevaluate their resources and strategies, and regroup in a way that might prevent surprise in the future. Logically, militarily, that makes sense. In Cold War intelligence studies it was the modus operandi for indefinitely forestalling nuclear Armageddon. With fog ball management approaches, however, that cooling period is not an opportunity to evaluate lessons-learned, but rather to move on to the next emergency. When cooling issues fall off the hot list, they often also fall to second-rate attention because only by remaining hot and glamorous do issues ensure further funding and close attention. Examples of enduring and difficult issues that routinely fall off the hot list include: weapons of mass destruction (WMD), starvation in Africa, strife in Africa, Africa in general, slave and prostitute trafficking, the Kurds, economic upheaval in South America, natural disaster relief, human-rights concerns in China, and organized crime. On Figure 15.3 any of these issues would be on the outer fringes of the shotgun distribution. Without a mechanism to ensure they remain focused on relevant areas, organizations invariably attempt to seek acclaim by gravitating toward the hotter issues at the "center of mass." Managers take care to notice when peer organizations focus on topics rapidly drawing popular interest. Those that reach critical mass trigger epidemics of interest. As more and more organizations find it in their best interest to focus on one burning issue, their re-prioritizations become fixations, and soon they are diverting resources and efforts, and new fog-ball behavior ensues.

How Process Trumps World Cup Soccer

If the shotgun fixation on issues with the highest popularity leads to fog-ball playing, then what approach can managers use to address evolving issues more effectively? Given the sports analogy, one possible solution to the unseemly fog-ball pursuit of self-interest is to have organizations behave like a team. *What a concept!* Professionals playing World Cup soccer are easy to imagine, but very difficult to put into practice as human nature consistently interferes. The team concept requires managers (and entire organizations) to (a) focus on their areas of responsibility, and (b) put aside the drive for an immediate return on investment. Such a team approach would require managers to dutifully focus on their areas of expertise, cultivating their people, and committing them to the highest possible standards. In essence, managers, like sport coaches, would prepare and position their employees and organizations to be the most capable in their field. The power of this approach would lie in professionalizing each employee and expecting performance at the fullest extent of his or her expertise. Employees would be challenged to hone their skills and contribute to the ultimate team goal of winning—even if it meant not contributing to the fashionably popular crisis du jour.

This approach would not be without its difficulties. The demands of self-sacrifice would require significant discipline on the part of employees and managers alike. It would require integrity to resist the urge for personal advantage. Not everyone would score the goal. All would contribute in their way, and exceptional individuals would get credit as part of a team. The result would be an organization (even a community) that is greater than the sum of its individual parts. I know; I am not holding my breath either. Rational arguments, no matter how sound, can not shake the specter of human nature.

Throwing caution to the wind, what rational argument might make this case? To start with, without expertise, professionals would never have credibility in the eyes of their customers. Fog ball behavior marginalizes expertise until all trust in management is finally gone. At that point in an organization, checklists supplant the depth of knowledge of seasoned experts, and quality of output is supplanted by quota requirements. An example of how far this trend can spiral out of control was demonstrated in the efforts to protect airline flights to and from Las Vegas in 2006. As a CQ Weekly staff writer noted at the

> "No country, however rich, can afford the waste of its human resources.... Morally, it is the greatest menace to our social order."
>
> —Franklin Delano Roosevelt Memorial Inscription

time: "Federal air marshals . . . must meet a monthly quota for surveillance detection reports that document suspicious terrorist-related activities—regardless of any actual evidence of suspicious activity . . . marshals say their supervisors tied promotions, raises and bonuses to meeting the quota."[2] Quotas, forms, and processes soon replace what was once an in-depth grasp of subject matter.

Career human-intelligence (HUMINT) professional Bill Halpin described it thusly back in 2002: "form is permitted to trump substance, and managers fail to recognize that strict adherence to any process without a vision or strategy can be treacherous."[3] To prevent this form of self-destructive management from taking root, intelligence professionals must once again be enabled to cultivate in-depth understanding of issues, with freedom to deliver dissenting opinions based on their understanding. The trap of groupthink is ever-present in an environment of "yes men" and "yes women," and ignoring it opens organizations to potential catastrophe. When professionals are barred from saying, "I disagree because . . ." honesty and integrity become impossible. Reasoned disagreement is not a sign of disrespect to senior officials, but rather a staple of any team that embraces open communication. One can be loyal *and* be in opposition to management.

If a job cannot be done, or *should not* be done, then management should be able to debate the task and find more effective approaches. Expending limited resources on such pursuits is simply inappropriate. Those who allocate resources must realize that people's skills and talents are expensive commodities, and that they are only as good as their upkeep and maintenance. Poorly maintained skills become a prescription for inferior and insufficient professional performance.

These challenges come back to professionalism, and the leadership in its ranks. Professionals must decide what kind of profession they truly want for themselves. Young and eager professionals must have senior leaders they can look up to and respect. That requires the seniors to exhibit a worthy sense of their own confidence in maintaining a commanding position in the field. Leadership requires integrity and a steadfast determination to nurture excellence in a field of specialty, *especially* during uncertain times. Prioritizing issues, instead of using shotgun approaches, may mean doing less for fewer customers, but doing it in a way that ensures a higher-quality final product. It may mean receiving less acclaim, but in the end it will earn more trust and respect from subordinates. Cultivating the talents of subordinates is what makes organizations great, and great leaders protect their subordinates from counterproductive practices, like fog ball. In the realm of national security, there is simply too much at stake for our country to cater to individual ambition. It is no small irony that those who have dedicated themselves to the military and government should call it "service." It *is* service, serving the nation, not serving personal gain.

"Why does the military need to look outside for new ideas? It already has novel ideas being generated inside its own ranks, by those who are not listened to or taken seriously. Why do great thinkers need to leave the military just to be taken seriously?

Is its distrust of insiders worse than its distrust of outsiders?"

—Mavaxiom 153

Notes

1. Finley, "Intelligence Fixes Floated."
2. Johnson, "A Flawed Marshal Plan," 2084.
3. Halpin, "Where is Defense HUMINT?" 81–89.

Finding an "In"

"Access is expensive."

— Mavaxiom 161

In job-hunting, as with intelligence work, opportunities are what you make of them. There are a number of sources and methods available for gathering information about potentially good employers. Among the best sources are people who already work for them. During your military or government service, you will have met, worked for, interacted with, spoken to or e-mailed hundreds (if not thousands) of people. When their time came to leave the service, they all went somewhere, likely to a civilian employer.

Keeping track of others who had separated would have been no easy task then, but should carry a somewhat higher priority, as now it is your turn. This is more than catching up on holiday cards; it is about constructing an up-to-date contact list. This is an easier project if you have their business cards. Unfortunately, you are likely to have very few business cards because the military is not in the business of using business cards. It is the military, after all. Whether in or out of the military, having your own cards is not a frivolous expense. In fact it is an essential part of getting in touch, and staying in touch, with people. Go out, buy card stock, and print your own personal and/or professional business cards. The potential benefits easily outweigh the costs.

Part of the reason why business cards are essential is because people are constantly on the move, both during and after government and military service. An e-mail address might be nice, but real contact requires more information. Phone numbers are important. Even technology as old as facsimile (FAX) machines can be useful to someone on the receiving end of the line. Likewise, addresses are vital for everything from GPS directions to the postal service, allowing us to keep in touch despite geographic distance. And now, with mobile phones, text messaging, blogs, and personal web pages, we can reach one another in ways unimaginable only 10 years ago. All are terrific ways for us to network with potential employers.

Once you have established connections, the next step is to develop them as sources of information. As you cultivate these connections over time your own awareness of what civilian employers are looking for will develop. You will see patterns between different firms, especially if they are in the same line of work. You will also spot distinctions between the corporate cultures in particular industries. All of these will be important for constructing a baseline understanding of the playing field. You are now immersed in what is known as IPB, or intelligence preparation of the battlespace.

The next step is to employ intelligence-tradecraft in your pursuit of deeper "access." You will home in on specific aspects of companies that are important to you. Try to understand their corporate ideology, identify any peculiarities in their policies that may be problematic for you, and isolate any leverage points that you can use for negotiation purposes later in your interviews. You are going on the business offensive now, employing techniques the intelligence business refers to as "spotting and assessing," "exploiting assets," and even "recruiting" individuals as a means of penetrating potential employers. This chapter will put some power tools in your toolbox, all for targeting potential employers. This is where job search enters a new level of interesting.

The Mole

When looking for a job, in my experience, nothing is better than already knowing someone *inside* a company. Those that you know can most readily flag job openings suitable to you if they know you well, or fully understand your desires. If they do, they can also look for the kinds of information that would help you with an application, giving you a leg-up on the competition. If they have a vested interest in "bringing you on board," they could become your advocate in hiring deliberations. Many business people try to surround themselves with people they already know and trust, rather than chancing newcomers. Decreasing the number of unknowns makes personnel changes feel more manageable. Camaraderie and spirit also appear higher in offices where many of the people know one another—their strengths, limitations, moods, personal styles, and situations. There may be another, stronger incentive, as well, for someone to refer you: money.

Many companies offer hiring bonuses to current employees for bringing in new employees. A company I once worked for paid a finder's reward of $3,000 for new employee hires. That is a pretty powerful incentive for employees to take part in the hiring process. It can almost turn into a sideline business. I was able to augment my salary fairly well with hires. These bonuses can prompt employees to accumulate résumés of friends, regardless of whether the friends are currently looking for a job. It may just happen that a sudden availability affords both people the opportunity to profit. Generally, the company employee will do all the legwork leading up to the interview. For the friend, it becomes an opportunity to evaluate new possibilities. Sometimes these interviews also afford people the opportunity to really see how much they are worth. They have nothing to lose in pushing for a higher salary.

Having what intelligence professionals call "close-in access" to other companies is key. Literally. It is your access key to deep inside an institution. Deep assets such as these are so important that often an investment to cultivate them will begin months, perhaps even *years*, in advance. Because the process of trust building can take so long, enterprising business people need to be constantly networking, and constantly cultivating existing contacts. This is why always having business cards and updated résumés handy becomes a mission priority. These kinds of tools allow you to quickly, professionally, reach out to new sources of business intelligence. Whenever you move to a new home or business location, make sure to mail out change of address notices (with updated business cards inserted) to friends, coworkers, colleagues, and potential business contacts, alike. The more people who you are connected with, the more likely you will have an "in" if a demand arises for your skills.

Listening to the Complainer

Sometimes the best information about a prospective employer comes from those who are less-than-satisfied with their own experience. The truth is that everybody complains about something. The disgruntled employee is a treasure trove to a savvy intelligence professional patient enough to make the most of the situation.

Generally, those who are unhappy with their employment situation are just trying to be heard. They need to vent their frustrations and this is often a big, flashing indicator that management at their firm is not completely open to listening to their employees. As employee frustrations grow, individuals seeking a voice will turn outside their environment if there is no one to listen to them inside. That is where the shrewd intelligence collector comes in and lends a listening ear. Let them talk. They need to talk to you, someone, maybe anyone. They want to be heard, and you may need to hear what they have to say.

Listening will probably involve a lot of mental filtering, and consequently will leave you feeling drained after only an hour. That is why therapy sessions cost so much; they have to put up with this kind of mental draining all day long. Like a therapist, though, there is a payoff for the discriminating intelligence collector. Buried deep in all the tangled feelings and interpersonal soap operas are data points. Analysis of trends detected from all the accumulated information, along with a few well-crafted questions here and there, will begin to paint the interior of an organization to which you do not yet currently have access. In effect, you are painting a detailed portrait of a place you have never been to or seen, and people you have never met. How well that painting emerges is up to you.

Before you take up a side office with a sofa and 60-minute timer, consider what sources you really want to listen to at length. You have to spot the right people and assess what kinds of information they have. Who do they know? What jobs do they really do? Where do they work? When is the information current as of? Why are they frustrated? These five questions are what intelligence people call the "Five W's," and are important for asking the next important question: How is this information / contact relevant? Spotting and assessing is the process of discerning up front which assets have the information you need, versus the ones whose whining will suck the life force from your soul.

In short, carefully evaluate, or vet, your prospective sources of close-in access. Their potential for contributing intelligence on a company must be weighed against their own personal need for emotional gratification. For example, they may say that they are "friends with the president of the company," but that may mean that the president correctly remembered their name at all-hands get-together. Vetting people should also take into account their motivations. Why are they trying to help you? Are they trying to get you a job because they value your skills and contribution, or is this an opportunity for them to finally create the circumstances where you can become friends? Stranger things have happened. Or maybe they want you to be hired so they can leave Purgatory behind. Knowing early in the process can make all the difference. It is therefore important for you to vet your sources; ultimately this information may shape the future of your life.

Executive Search Firms

Employment recruiters generally succeed at what they do. If someone wants a job, an executive search firm will find that person a job. A number of these firms reach out specifically to people leaving the military and government. Some of them might unapologetically call themselves headhunters and flesh peddlers, but these search firms do merit consideration.

They all provide the same kind of service: finding jobs *fast*. It is a good service to provide departing military members, with one drawback: choice. While they do provide a valuable service to people who have not had the time to develop skills for civilian work, these companies excel at putting round pegs in square holes. Their rationale is that the exactness of the fit is secondary to the rapid accomplishment of fitting. They ensure that a fit, any fit, is found—and quickly. Just like the military, these firms *will* find a fit.

Unfortunately, some of these firms seem to thrive on the desperation of their job-seeking clients. Although not exact, if the fit is "good enough," it will get the recruiter a sizeable commission from the hiring employer. Using the services of recruiters means relinquishing your own active participation and choice. This may be the way you were accustomed to doing things in the military, allowing someone else to determine your fate, but you are no longer in the military. It is time to start taking your fate into your own hands. Anything less is effectively a continuation of military service, avoiding the really difficult, grown-up job of deciding what you want, versus what *someone else* thinks you should be doing.

The service that executive search firms should provide exiting military members is assistance in rewriting résumés into readable descriptions of useful and transferable skills. This is especially true for service members who have crafted résumés formidably laden with military jargon and acronyms. Recruiters would do more good by making such résumés understandable to clients than by electronically forwarding the often-confusing originals. All things considered, and in my opinion, a sign of a really good executive search firm is one that:

1. Gets to know the candidate, at least somewhat, personally;
2. Has the time and interest to edit résumés and;
3. Writes letters of introduction.

Together, these would increase the probability of fitting applicants into jobs that best suit their needs.

So if you are committed to going down this path, and trust in an executive search firm, keep in mind that executive search firms have their own priorities as a business. That business is to match individuals with jobs. Your goal is different: To get the right job for you. Often the process should take more time, and short-term gains should not carry quite as much priority. A word of caution, then, to those choosing this technique of gaining access: If you must use a search firm, it remains your responsibility to get the *right* job out of the deal.

Taking the first available job might be a necessary and acceptable evil, but you will have to decide this for yourself. Certainly people who take less-than-desirable jobs can still work toward what they eventually want to do. That not-so-perfect job might inadvertently put them closer to their dream job, without their ever knowing. This puts a lot of weight on chance, a technique that will be discussed shortly. But while you still have an individual choice in the matter, you must balance what you really want with what you really need.

Life is too short to keep submitting to constant reassignment through a series of jobs that dissatisfy you. If you are constantly on the lookout for the next, better job, you may never accomplish a more important goal of *making* the job that is right for you. Every time you let someone else make that decision for you, you risk losing ground on ultimately reaching your goal. Again, it is vitally important, before you do anything else, to answer the fundamental question of what you really want.

The Open House

Several different versions of the open house exist for job seekers. One type is held during daylight (duty) hours, and the other is held after duty hours. The variety conducted during working hours sometimes goes by other names, like job fair or industry expo. The less-flattering term for such an open house is a cattle call. Typically, the daytime open house is an open-door invitation by a company (or group of companies) to a wide audience. Prospective employees arrive at a large auditorium to make the rounds, meeting representatives from companies, or from different directorates in a single company. The representatives answer questions, hand out company pens and water bottles, and accept résumés from attendees. It has the feel of a county fair, with prizes at every booth.

This atmosphere allows for one stop shopping and time-saving in the quest to tackle the difficult task of reaching out to numerous potential employers or offices within a single firm all at once. It is akin to carpet-bombing a target area with B-52s, except in this case the 2,000-pounders have been replaced by two-pager résumés with job-seeking warheads. Because of its open-ended nature, it is sometimes possible to assign the entire strike package to a single, surrogate delivery system. Several people can pool their résumés with one trusted friend, who flies a low altitude, high-speed stealth run, hitting every résumé drop box. In this case, no conversation will accompany your résumé, so the attendant will not be able to "fast-track" yours into higher priority piles. You will have to trust that that will happen later based purely on the content of your résumé.

Another kind of open house is conducted after dark. These nighttime open houses are radically different than the daylight cattle-call variety. The nighttime open house is really an office party thrown at corporate headquarters by a small company, or a section of a large company. Prospective employees are cordially invited and upon entry are given huge, white adhesive nametags to wear on their lapels for all current employees to see. These gatherings fall into one of the more cherished human-intelligence (HUMINT) assignment categories, the "cocktail-party circuit." To prospective employees, it seems almost too good to be true. You are given beer, wine, and cocktails. There are munchies, and people are strangely eager to talk to you. You will know this because their friendliness is matched only by their enthusiasm to refill your glass. Then the questioning begins. It is benign at first, but then builds to the point of borderline interrogation. This technique elicits information from you by means of many people who will later share their notes to create a composite picture. It is like a feeding frenzy, where you are marked (with a big name tag) as "chum." They may actually call you that by accident at some point in the evening. Running off to the restroom won't save you; they are likely to follow you there as well.

The employees know it is in their best interests to ascertain, immediately if possible, if you are "one of them." They rapidly cut to the chase to determine if you are the kind of person with whom they want to work. This can make the nighttime open house a trying event. You need to keep your wits about you at all times. The number of people asking you pointed questions only increases as the night progresses. Eventually, though, you will know exactly how well you are doing. If you can get along with a group, are able to lead discussions, and get them laughing at your jokes, you may have run the gauntlet unscathed. The ultimate indication of your success might be a light tug on your suit and a quiet whisper that the president, director, or other senior official of the company would like to speak with you privately. This private audience invitation is likely an opportunity for them to tell you they are ready to make you an offer without embarrassing other candidates. You are being informed that you have passed the informal interview process and that the formalities of negotiating administrative specifics will follow in the coming days.

The intensity of simultaneously being evaluated socially and professionally in that way leaves some people feeling drained because it requires a concerted expenditure of social energy. If the job requires a great deal of socializing, or face-to-face time with clients, companies want to know that you can handle yourself in those situations. It is generally difficult to get a sense of those skills from a résumé or an online application. Truly, the only way to find out is face-to-face, in a social setting.

Interviews are generally formal. Open houses are generally informal. During interviews, the usual objective is to present a confident, commanding presence. When at an open house, the goal is to get along socially with the other sharks. Both techniques are effective at vetting candidates. Each works best for the particular needs of each organization. More formal organizations prefer interviews. Organizations whose bread-and-butter is delivered by the social skills of its members might prefer an open-house approach.

Invitations to Projects

There is a middle ground that few readily acknowledge as advantageous to their employment search. The hybrid of the two aforementioned approaches is to invite a candidate to provide professional services. This also facilitates opportunities for employers to interact informally with the candidate. Some organizations like the idea of this kind of temporary lease agreement—

where they can kick the tires and take candidates for a trial spin, without a commitment to buy.

At first blush, this test-run relationship is worthy of caution. On the surface, it smacks of noncommitment on the part of the employer, especially if you are being invited to participate in a project without pay for your services. Optimism suggests that you instead look at it as an opportunity to do well, show your worth, and then your suitability will become evident. The one "however," however, is to be careful not to choke on the task. If you do, you probably won't have to worry about a formal interview. If, on the other hand, you *do* shine, the potential employer gets the benefits of your services at no charge. Some people see this kind of pro bono work as almost like an internship or a means of maintaining contact with potential clients.

Sometimes such potential-client contact is well worth forgoing income. Some organizations thrive on pro bono work, while others see it as giving individuals unfair advantage and undue influence to obtaining paying contracts later. Some organizations actually require those performing such work to register with their contracts office and go through the bureaucratic process of documenting every service to be provided gratis. The opportunity to gain experience and exposure in this way is wide open, but it is not a way to earn money.

If you are actively seeking a job, your priorities may be a little different. The best time to take advantage of such invitations to projects is when you are neither actively seeking employment, nor about to mind that your contribution will not produce a paycheck. Since you have not signed into any legal agreement with such a firm, it is under no legal obligation to reward any proprietary skills that you may offer. Assume, for example, that your participation in a project causes a favorable result for that organization. That bodes well for you, but, if during the course of the project you develop some kind of new process or approach, they may choose to exploit it to their advantage. If the idea makes millions, you can make no legal claim to it. More often than not, it will be enough for you to open dialogue, maintain ongoing contact, and cultivate relationships. Remember, the point is to achieve access, an "in," that will serve you later.

> It's not who you know. It's who knows *you*. After that, it's what you know."
>
> —DCV

An entirely different kind of invitation to a project is one in which a prospective employer is looking to eventually hire you in the future, but is not ready to provide you any access or incentives. Instead, they make a promise to employ you if they win the contract, but to do so will require using your résumé in the proposal process. If this is beginning to sound like a precarious proposition, you are correct. The possibility exists to collect intelligence about the job(s) in question and the clients involved, but the collection environment is not a pleasant one in which to operate.

Large firms have an advantage over smaller firms when competing for contracts because their larger pool of employees ensures that larger firms can submit proposals for contract work with the most impressive résumés. After some firms win contract bids, they may employ junior (or brand new) employees on the new contract. This allows the winning contractor to operate at much lower salary costs than with individuals whose résumés were submitted in the original bid. The motivation behind such "bait and switch" techniques is to increase net profit by paying lower-waged employees to do the work. Obviously, the original promise to use high-end employees is broken. Despite generally being prohibited, bait and switch techniques afford large companies an unfair advantage over smaller companies that have fewer employees and a narrower skills selection in their proposal résumés. A counter-tactic for smaller companies is to simply "find" superior résumés outside the ranks of their own employees. With the advent of the Internet it is not uncommon for some employers to scour the worldwide web for exceptional résumés, and then just submit them to win contract proposals. The practice has become so rampant, that clients now require competing firms to prove that the résumés submitted are from full-time employees. Otherwise, the firm must secure what is known as a "letter of intent," obligating the individual (whose résumé was used) to be work for the firm if the contract is awarded.

Not employing the résumé-holder (and effectively "tethering" them) saves a company the overhead costs associated with hiring and gainfully employing an individual prior to the outcome of the contract award decision. In effect, a letter of intent affords a company all the benefits of an individual's résumé, without the commitment of actually hiring the individual. Other risks for the individual include being closed out of other opportunities because of their apparent commitment to a firm's contract bid. This makes the letter of intent a risky proposition for a job seeker. All their skill and experience is exploited, along with their devotion, without an obligation to provide them a job. In the final analysis, such employee elicitation techniques are valuable warning indicators, and may give the job-seeker insight into questionable corporate values and principles.

The Power of Chance

Some people believe that our destiny is in our hands alone. There is an equally compelling belief that we are in control of nothing. The safest bet, in my view, is that human experience floats perhaps somewhere in the middle. The final method of developing access has nothing to do with your ability to control situations, but rather to go along with situations and see where they lead. At times, when we are ready to accept its offerings, chance has the power to materialize amazing opportunities. Our challenge is to have the strength and faith to sometimes let go of our control of a situation and allow serendipity to unfold. The ability to go along with the ebb and tide of life's situations will often lead to unexpected, but beneficial results.

Science arrives at some of its greatest discoveries by *accident*. Your job search may be very much the same. Those involved with science may also understand that for every piece of information yielded there are thousands of

> "There are no coincidences."
>
> —Mavaxiom #162

new questions. While rational discovery answers our immediate questions, every variable defined generates new variables to be answered by other sets of circumstances. Every step closer to grasping the unknown leaves us in further awe of the depths of its riddles. Accepting that you only know a limited amount of the equation or situation offers the opportunity to accept that there is much more for you to learn, and this is beneficial in the self-discovery process, as you are now open to more learning.

Of all the methods to consider for finding the right job, the one that lacks an appropriate title (and appropriate merit) is the one that simply presents itself to us as if by cosmic design. It goes by many names: luck, chance, fate, destiny, a roll of the dice, serendipity. I am uncertain how to take full advantage of completely fortuitous circumstances. Perhaps the best way is to be as ready as possible when they happen and have the courage to go where they lead. This remains no easy task, for nothing is quite as scary as the big unknown. To explore it, we must have faith in our own abilities to carry ourselves to new experiences. It may also mean trusting your gut on a cosmic level.

Uncertainty

Throughout this book the tactics, techniques, and procedures (TTP) for job search revolved around collecting and analyzing data that are rooted in practical methodologies. However, sometimes we simply do not know enough to construct approaches that take into account *all* the possibilities. Some details are, for the moment, beyond our ability to know. But what should veterans do when all the practical methodologies available to them fail to yield the desired results? The answer to that question may reside in the realm of uncertainty.

In the early years of nuclear research, scientists were perplexed by their inability to measure atomic particles as precisely as needed. They discovered that exactly determining an electron's position made its momentum uncertain, and measuring its momentum exactly made its position uncertain. There seemed no way to observe one without affecting the ability to measure the other. German mathematician and physicist Werner Heisenberg described this phenomenon in 1927. It is regarded as a fundamental physical property, and bears his name as the Heisenberg uncertainty principle.

Simply put, Heisenberg suggested that our understanding of the universe is limited by our ability to observe. As we study something, the very act of observation *alters* that being observed. In a similar way, trying too hard to understand all aspects of a potential job might backfire because our own efforts may get in the way of discovering something important that we never would have imagined. There may be certain aspects of the job, company, or industry that were in flux and were neither

On Illusions of Control

"There is no plan. We plan, the universe laughs. It's that simple. We may only prevail if we buy Murphy a beer."

—Mavaxiom #164

known to us, or the people interviewing us. When we get too focused on achieving a specific outcome, it may occur at the expense of other (potentially better) opportunities, and consequently pass us by.

The reason why opportunities are elusive may be because our attention was transfixed on an outcome that *we* predetermined, not the one the universe intended. Unfortunately, the universe works in ways that are simply beyond our ability to know. This is where faith enters the equation. Some people externalize that faith to a deity. Others internalize that faith in their ability to deal with the situation when it arises.

Still others, with an inflated sense of their ability to affect success, may believe that their strength and know-how is enough to *induce* success. If employers act early and hire the candidate before developing opportunities are realized, what appears on the surface to be success might prove inherently limiting for the overly aggressive job seeker in the long run. In any intelligence effort, the challenges of not fully knowing what to expect can be both daunting and endless. Intelligence professionals struggle with trying to fill information gaps and giving the uncertainty enough time, or enough room, to unfold on its own. Sometimes unknowns make themselves manifest when we are not trying so hard to observe. Our actions to overcome uncertainty, then, may literally alter our ability to achieve the most successful outcomes.

This discussion does not suggest that passive approaches make for more successful outcomes. Instead, it suggests that you cannot demand to have all the information for a decision when *you* want to make it. Intelligence often has a way of becoming available, when we are not trying so hard, and not trying to influence the outcomes. So when your efforts hit a roadblock it might be time to stop trying to influence the outcome of your job search. Let the transition happen. For serendipity to work, then, you have to leave it alone. Try to be comfortable with the uncertainty of not knowing how a situation might unfold. Just be ready when one does, as it might not be precisely what you expected. You have to trust that opportunities will emerge, and trust in your ability to handle whatever the universe throws at you.

CHAPTER SEVENTEEN

Body Armor
Dress to Kill, and Take No Prisoners

"It's not a $100 tie, it's a $100,000 tie."

— Mavaxiom 171

I t is surprisingly easy to outdress most people in a civilian interview. Before being hired, you must look the part. The trick is looking sharp, but with the perception that you did not try too hard. It has to look natural, a natural extension of your innate strength. After being hired, you can dress as casually as the new office culture permits, but first you have to get the job. When I sat in my military transition assistance program (TAP) classes, this was the lecture I dreaded. The reason was because I knew it was going to be an investment for me. Depending on where you are stationed, and where you are looking to work, business attire can be a considerable investment. Everyone wants to save money, but avoid the temptation in this endeavor. If you skimp now, it could be a costly strategic blunder in the long run.

Your business suit is body armor, no two ways about it. You will be treated in a completely different manner in an appropriately sharp business suit versus an adequate suit. You will draw interest, command attention, and wield authority. To wear a discount suit is to go into battle with armor wholly inferior to your adversaries'. The battle then demands that overcoming such a tactical disadvantage will require superior skills, more experience, better training, exceptional courage, and luck. Or you could just have a great suit. In addition to firepower, your suit will also have to last. Seven years after separating, my only suits to survive were those of the highest quality.

Interviewers are not necessarily looking out for you, so try not to help them take advantage of you. This is where you have to take your search for a new job very seriously, perhaps far more than you ever have before. A high-quality durable suit will help achieve interview superiority.

I apologize in advance if this section seems a bit male-centric. It is. I am writing from what I know, and what I have directly experienced. Still, although our fits and styles differ, there will probably be certain philosophical vignettes here of benefit to female readers. If nothing else, the section can help women who are helping male friends leave the military. Women know all too well that men can use all the help they can get when it comes to dressing themselves.

The Suit

The Cost of Quality

If not already apparent from the chapter title, let me reiterate the importance of the suit as your body armor. It will protect you against an interviewer (your opponent) perceiving that he or she can hire you for less. The cheapness of your suit's appearance will probably influence how cheap they think you are to hire. How much does it cost to go beyond cheap? A good, dress-to-impress business suit that will last

> "It takes money to make money."
>
> —Business proverb

will cost somewhere between $1,000 and $2,000. Let me be clear on that point. Expect to pay one thousand dollars per suit. Good suits are not cheap. Unfortunately, that is not the bad news. The bad news is that you will need a few—at least three. Their cost will be roughly equivalent to a decent one-year investment in an individual retirement account (IRA), but without the good suit, and good job, you will have nothing to contribute to your retirement account.

In the business world, your suit *is* your equipment. You will use it every day, and if you skimp on the initial purchase you will not get the job or salary you desire.

> "You get what you pay for"
>
> —Older business proverb

Mission Planning

So, if you are going to spend $1,000 of your hard-earned money, what should you buy? To begin, you need to find a store. It is not a foregone conclusion that wherever you are stationed will provide the kinds of stores that will sell high-end business suits. That means you may need to travel to a major city. Think of such a trip as a fact-finding mission—also known as an intelligence-collection operation. Before you go, get online and research different brand names, stores, and their locations. Compile basic targeting information. One caution up front: if you research overly stylish suits, recognize that styles will change and you may be left with an expensive suit you can no longer wear. In short, research classic business suit designers.

As for the actual operation, it seems fair to assume that most men are not keen on exploratory shopping. They like to get in and get out of a mall or shopping center quickly, with as few casualties as possible. Forget that; this is going to be a long-haul mission. Try to avoid places that appear to be the mother of all men's clothing stores. Volume does not necessarily bespeak quality. You will find a lot that will be affordable, but many bulk-clothing stores make their money by liquidating clothing in large numbers, sometimes with manufacturing defects or inventories that are going out of style. These are good places for odds and ends, but not your core clothing items.

Do not anticipate accomplishing your mission quickly. The best men's clothing store, also known as a haberdashery will require a full day (at least three to four hours) of your time in the selection of a couple of suits. As with the cost, invest the time. In the long run it will be worth it.

Purchase Operations Plan (OPLAN)

Suit shopping is a full-contact sport, so start the day right, with a big, hearty breakfast, wear comfortable clothing, and arrive ready for combat. The kind of clothing that you wear while on business-suit reconnaissance is important. For obvious reasons, do not wear cut-off shorts and a ratty T-shirt. The haberdashery is itself a business. Please do not go in there and give them the impression that you are not serious about buying a suit. If they do not think of you as a serious customer, they will not show you the best suits. Most importantly, though, you need to be wearing clothing that will assist the suit-selection process.

Either wear or carry with you the dress shoes you intend to wear with the suit. Do not worry unduly about this point. I assure you that better shoes will supercede whatever shoes you have today. You must wear undergarments (boxers or briefs and an undershirt). Remember, these suits do not belong to you, yet. Moreover, you should be developing a professional relationship with the man or woman who will become your haberdasher. Do not jeopardize this relationship by infuriating your haberdasher on day one. And here is why:

A haberdasher will make or break your appearance. If you take this endeavor seriously, the haberdasher will take you seriously. When you are committed to investing in good suits— and ready to spend good money—he or she will treat you like royalty. You are setting the stage for one of your most important business alliances, with a professional whose job is to ensure that your suit fits you perfectly. This is not an assembly-line approach, like military clothing sales. In this business, clients are business executives whose final tailored product communicates nothing less than superiority. When you spend top dollar, you can outfit yourself for any firefight. Since your haberdasher is your weapons supplier, you will find your relationship well worth keeping and worth keeping well.

> "It is better to be overdressed than underdressed."
>
> —Anonymous

In no uncertain terms, your business suit must convey your power, knowledge, experience, and a host of other attributes you may or may not possess to the interviewer. Within it, you must feel secure in your abilities. There must be substance to your talent for the suit to function as a means of expression. It can only channel your confidence if you believe in yourself. Like real body armor, your suit can only do so much to aid you in combat. Without confidence under fire, all the body armor in the world might not save you.

Style

With near-infinite choices at your disposal, what kind of suit should you get? Simple. Keep it classic. You cannot go wrong with a dark navy-blue classic pinstriped business suit. No matter how strong the temptation, do not buy trendy suits. You have no idea where the trends or fashions are going. Unless you plan to enter the fashion industry, do not try to predict trends. From an intelligence professional's perspective, trying to predict anything as random and chaotic as fashion trends is dangerous, especially with your hard-earned money. For the first suit or two, err on the side of safety and stick with the conservative. I do not know how many ways I can say this: start with a classic suit style. Having said that, I must qualify the assessment:

> "Style can only be created at a risk, it is a form of courage; it is an exposed and often indefensible position."
>
> —Edwin Derby

The color of your suit has a great deal to do with your own physical appearance, your complexion, hair color, and eye color. For example, if you do *not* have gray hair, you should probably not buy a gray suit, especially a light gray suit, unless you have blonde hair or blue eyes. Likewise, if you do have gray hair, or gray at the temples, you can pull off gray suits easily. I have an olive complexion, so I wear greens well. And you thought that you would not be able to personalize your suit? As I mentioned, the best color for interviewing is navy blue. Black suits can come across a little severe if you are not careful.

Julia's Suit Test

My friend Julia has a little secret. She enjoys suit-shopping with men. But there is a reason why. She has a little technique for fitting suits that she executes like a master martial artist on men's suit jackets. Just when you think that you have finished slipping on a suit jacket in a store, she swoops up behind you, grabs the tails (or the flap) and gives it a swift tug downward—just like a reverse wedgie. Then she evaluates from the center of your back by shrugging the jacket outward to your arms several times, working her way up to your shoulders. Then she flattens your shoulders from the collars to your arms in swift outward sweeps as if trying to vacuum-form the fabric to your shape. She takes a step back, crinkles her brow, and purses her lips. She is making sure that the fabric fits your body. If it does not, after all that, then it needs a lot of tailoring, or you need to move on to a different suit. As she puts it herself, "Fit is important. It can ruin an expensive suit."

The Flap

This is an exercise in noticing subtle design differences in suit construction. It is like differentiating between the original Mig-29 and the Su-27 by the boom that extends between the separated engine nozzles of the Sukhoi. The next time you look at a man's suit, discreetly observe the bottom hem of the suit jacket at the derrière. Most suit jackets have a short, single vertical slit, or vent, at the bottom center that allows the suit fabric to open out when the wearer sits down. It is an important structural "tell" for the quality of its production. If there is no center vent, but rather two vents, one on either hip, the suit is likely of much better quality. Double vents are intended to improve the drape of a jacket when either one or both hands are in trouser front pockets, as well as to ease seating. If you are prone to relaxing with your hands in your pockets, or you want to rebel against years of military regulations forbidding you from putting your hands in your uniform pockets, this is the jacket design for you. Just be prepared to pay handsomely for double vents in a handsome-looking suit.

Three-Piece Suits

Three-piece suits are almost, but not quite officially, no longer fashionable. A few people still wear vests, but they run they risk of being mistaken for time travelers with faulty coordinates. If that is your intention, go for it. It is your money, and potentially your job.

Double-Breasted Suits

Double-breasted suits are entirely too much like military uniforms. The mechanics of the jacket-fastening—two buttons, one in, one out—render it a bit more difficult to wear on a hot day, or relax in and get a little more casual if circumstances require. Stylistically, the suit jacket should be either completely buttoned up or *taken off.* You cannot just unbutton the jacket, and let it flap open as you wander about. Come to think of it, I almost never wear single-breasted suits buttoned either. I spend too much of my time reaching into my jacket pockets for business cards, a pen, or my day-timer to leave it fully buttoned. Besides, I was trained to be an intelligence briefer, so, if my suit jacket is buttoned, I cannot wave my hands in the air for effect, or point to the surface-to-air missile (SAM) sites plotted on the briefing slide behind me.

Surgeon's Cuffs

No matter what suit you finally decide to buy, make sure its jacket has what are known as surgeon's cuffs. All of us have seen buttons on the cuffs of a business suit jacket, but what are they for, especially since most are sewn without eyelets, and do nothing? Well, here is your most secret factoid about suits. In ages past, surgeons (medical doctors, generally) needed to tend to emergencies at times without the benefit of preparation. Once a doctor got his hands dirty, he could not take his jacket off without bloodying the sleeve liners. The solution was jacket arms with vented sleeves fastened with buttons at the cuffs, allowing the arms to be opened and rolled up. Buttons then became the fashion on cuffs, vented or not.

Regardless, surgeon's cuffs on a suit jacket are yet another subtle signal of a high quality suit, and of impeccable taste on your part. Now, if you really want to convince the interviewer that you are of near-noble upbringing, unbutton exactly one button on each cuff, the ones closest to your hands. It is the pièce de résistance. Go ahead, be a fashion snob. It might just get you more money.

So, where do you learn such factoids, and whom should you trust to buy all of your clothing? I had a terrific haberdasher named Harley. The man designed entire outfits for me in his mind. He was the employee who outfitted all the displays in the window. That was why I picked him. He was also about my size and build, so I asked him to put aside similar-sized suits and call me when they arrived. He would put together ensembles (suits, matching ties, trouser-braces, pocket squares, and so on) so I could buy them as a set, in one fell swoop.

The Full Break

When having trousers tailored, the physically fit military person will notice something disconcerting. For men, most suits are cut for a physique that is shaped like a barrel. If you are broad-shouldered with a small waist, you will need tailoring. Your shoulders might fit, but the waist of the suit jacket will have to be taken in, especially if have a classic V shape. Similarly, your trousers will probably need the waist taken in, along with some of the seat (especially if you are a runner). This is where it gets tricky. Over the next few years, if your physical activity slows, your body shape may dynamically shift. There are a few things you can do to protect your clothing investment.

The Tailor's Feel

To correctly fit your chosen suit trousers, your tailor has to measure their inseam. To do this he will run a tape measure by the tips of his fingers up the inside of your pant leg to your crotch. If this will be your first such experience, do not squeal, jump, or take violent offense. This minor intrusion is the price of a perfect fit

When it comes to trousers, ask the tailor to cuff the hems. If the styles change, or you change your mind later, your cuffs can be removed. You cannot do the reverse. Also ask for "full breaks" in your trouser legs. Breaks are attractive indentations that form in the razor-sharp front creases of well-ironed fabric just above the cuffs (or plain hems). This means that the trouser legs will be tailored long enough for change in your future physique. Cuffed or uncuffed, full-break trouser legs will be lower at your heels, virtually reaching the floor, to hide your socks in most postures to include sitting. Full breaks can also help if you add weight to your buttocks. With added weight, your pants will ride higher, a look sometimes called "high waters." The breaks in the legs can then fall away without the trousers looking too short, and, if need be, cuffs can be adjusted to add more length later. With that in mind, Harley recommends that your cuff size be 1½ to 1¾ inches.

Shirts

There seem to be infinite possibilities when it comes to buying dress shirts. In white, much less colors, there are limitless off-white shades. Likewise, there are numerous types of collars, cuffs, and so on. I explored relatively few options because of the costs involved, and you will soon see why. To save yourself from too much pain, go with what has worked from time immemorial: simple, traditional, basic white, and good quality. Besides the obvious advantage of keeping a certain level of consistency in your transition, there is also the matter of cost.

The Cost of Simplicity

A good dress shirt will cost about $80 to $100. Yes, good shirts are that much. Sometimes you can catch them at sale prices if you buy three or more. That means you can buy three dress shirts for just under $200. You will need at least seven shirts, plus three more that you will use only for interviewing or special occasions. That means you will need ten shirts total, an investment of roughly $700. Live with the pain. As with previous advice, keep it simple, traditional, white. Go high quality, because you will wear (and launder) each of them roughly fifty times in a year. Do not wear a white dress shirt for more than a single business day (eight to ten hours). Ever. Stressing the fabric by wearing it several days in a row compounds the effect of skin particles collecting around the collar, shortening the life of the shirt. Remember how much it cost to buy them?

Pockets and Collars

I have a couple of recommendations when buying white dress shirts. First, choose only those with a single pocket and with *no* pocket button. Second, only choose pointed collars that do not button down. See the trend here? Although in some parts of the country collar buttons are fashionable (Washington, D.C. included), additional buttons make a shirt more casual. Since you have no control over the business roles you might find yourself in (meeting unexpected VIPs, delivering last-minute presentations), it is always better to be overdressed than underdressed. Unanticipated business encounters are subject to Murphy's Law, so be prepared.

Collar Tabs

Underneath most collars are small hemmed slits. Inside are plastic stiffeners. Do yourself a favor, take them out and throw them away. In military shirts they were sewn in permanently so you had no choice. While at the men's store, invest in a one-time purchase of shiny brass-collar stiffeners. They generally run about $25 for about ten pairs, but you will need more than ten pairs to accommodate all your shirts and allow for losses. Prepare yourself to put in and take out these brass stiffeners *each* time you dress, and hope that your dry cleaner is honest enough to return them if you forget. No more will you have plastic stiffeners warping over time and distorting the shape of your collars. Nor must you ever go into a meeting with your collars veering off into odd directions. With brass they will always be nice and straight. If you must have collar buttons to help with your ties, then collar stiffeners are a non-issue. Just make sure to get collars with buttons hidden on the underside; otherwise you will appear too casual for business.

A final note for those who are more force-protection conscientious than your peers, there is no need to worry about wearing brass-collar tabs on airline flights. They should not set off airport-security metal detectors. I have tested them myself, and they have never set off the detector.

Shirt Cuffs

After years of debate over this, I now recommend that after leaving the military, buy your first seven dress shirts with standard cuffs. Save French cuffs for shirts worn for interviews, special occasions, important presentations, and so on. Although French cuffs look terrific, like double-breasted suit jackets, I find they make it difficult to have a relaxed posture on a hot day. With standard cuffs, you can roll up your sleeves more easily than with French cuffs. The other consideration is maintenance. French cuffs require cuff links. A good pair of links will run you $50 to $100. Do not skimp on your cuff links. Since they are meant to be seen, they become a dead giveaway if you are stingy. What is the use of getting a great suit, and wearing French cuffs, if you will be topping them off with cheap set of lousy cuff links? Every part of an ensemble has to support all other parts. The weakest (cuff) links will give you away, and expose vulnerabilities in your body armor. Remember, attention to details.

Ties and Braces

This was the area of clothing that gave me endless headaches. I cannot pick a tie to save my life. I do not know why, I just cannot. Learning that early on, I deferred to my trusted fashion consultant, namely my haberdasher. There are some who will disagree with my view that you should *not* rely on others to pick your ties. By this, I mean do not let your spouse, significant other, coworkers, or friends who claim to have fashion savvy, accessorize for you. Pay for the objectivity that can only come from a professional. Unless, that is, if your spouse, significant other, or friends work in a haberdashery. Some people do have a better fashion eye than others to match patterns and colors, but proving it on your dollar is a risky proposition. One reason is that a good tie costs about $100. I know what you are thinking: "I can buy ten ties for $100." Go right ahead, and watch that decision undermine all the rest of your suit investments. A tie can make or break a suit. I did not believe it myself, but it is true. Rarely do I ever get compliments directly on my suits, including the best ones, but people will go out of their way to pay my tie the compliment it deserves. Good ties make the outfit. Great ties can land you the job.

Certain tie brands (like suits) consistently run on the expensive side. I have spent upwards of $150 on a tie. These are good silk ties, and it shows. Some of those ties have lasted more than seven years and still look sharp. They are soft to the touch and supple to fold. Lesser-quality ties feel stiff, fold like canvas, and begin to disintegrate after only a couple of seasons. In the end, the investment pays off, as always. But, the investment will be a big one. Pick out roughly three ties per suit, and then coordinate them with the trouser braces and pocket squares, which we will talk about shortly. In total, about ten ties are sufficient for your initial wardrobe. At $100 a piece, that will run you $1000. Some have asked about bow ties. I do not do bow ties, but I envy those who can pull it off. If you can, it will certainly make a signature statement. Make sure it is the correct statement.

The Art of Ties

Ties speak like art. A word of caution, however, before you go out and buy ties with art prints. I have never seen an art print work well on a tie, except at holiday and theme parties. Instead, the art is specific to the print or woven pattern of a tie. A tie sold on the street usually has a generic print, simple and straightforward. Stripes angled at degrees are a popular theme. These kinds of ties are basic, very basic. Your shirts should be basic, to facilitate interchangeability. You have been conservative and basic about virtually every other aspects of the suit ensemble thus far. Now, with your ties, it is time to make a statement. The tie is your own personal way to broadcast your suit. As with the suit, your skin complexion, hair color, and eye color all play to your ability to pull off a splash of color with a tie. If you have bright blue eyes, you can experiment with blues as few others can. For me, this stage of the suit buying was always the most difficult. When I deferred to Harley's judgment, he always picked out colors and patterns that I never would have chosen. In fact, after buying them, I was reluctant to even wear the ties. When I finally did break down and wear them, however, that is when the compliments started coming in. Professionals, who really do know fashion, know how to make bold statements. Where a tie is concerned, buying great ties sometimes requires a level of trust that may make many in the military uncomfortable. If you want your operation to succeed, you have to trust your advisors. Correctly buying your ties is no different, and no less challenging a proposition.

Re-enter the Haberdasher

So, whom should you trust for all of your accessories? The haberdasher, of course. The best approach to the purchase of ties is to acquire them, and other accessories, with the suit. Buy them as a package deal. The reason to buy them together is because you need to coordinate the ties with other ensemble elements that will be discussed below. Buying them together will ensure that your ensemble is well coordinated, complements the suit, and brings out different colors and accents, and your complexion. In addition, and with traditional white dress shirts, you will have numerous tie options for the same suit over several days.

Care for Ties

When I was a child in Catholic school, I had to wear a tie virtually every day. It took so much work and effort to get the tie to turn out just right that I never wanted to untie them when I had succeeded at getting the tie's proportions to fold out perfectly. Untying, hanging, and retying a new tie every day would just create more (unnecessary) work for me in the morning. Point taken, but that was childhood. This is adult reality. After spending more than $100, the last thing you ever want to do is leave a tie folded at the end of the day. A knot is not good for the fabric. It pulls and tugs the silk and then, over time, the tie falls apart, and you have to *pay* to replace it. Buy a tie rack that looks like a coat hanger. Untie all your ties at the end of the day and diligently hang them on your tie rack. The alternative to poor care and maintenance is costly.

Braces, not Suspenders

Suspenders are elastic bands with alligator clips on the ends to hold up sagging pants when a belt is missing. Braces are what captains of industry wear to look devastatingly fashionable and in-charge when executing corporate takeovers. Huge difference. Braces are fabric that button to the inside of your pants waistband from the small of your back, over both shoulders, and then button again in front. Where they button on the brace is usually made of leather. To wear braces, you will need to have waistband buttons put into all of your pants. Have it done when you buy the suit. Some have suggested that belts are preferred in the business world. That may very well be true but, regardless, I try to ensure that all the suit pants I own can accommodate either braces or a belt. The ability to be used reliably in virtually all frontline combat conditions is what made the Kalashnikov (AK-47) not only useful, but also one of the most prolific assault rifles on the planet. Accommodating belts or braces ensures that I can wear either depending upon my mood. Power meeting tomorrow? I will wear braces. Casual work week? I will wear a belt. Hot date after work? Definitely braces, and take no prisoners

Nothing oozes power like braces. Do not ask me why, but they do. Countless women have told me that they feel an irrational and almost subconscious urge to grab the braces worn by a man with his suit. But do not take my word. Go ask a woman what she thinks. Wearing braces seems to make all the difference in the aura that is given off by a suit. The trick is that your braces need to support the splash being made by your tie, along with all the other elements of your body armor ensemble working together as a high-speed team. For example, although they do not necessarily have to match, braces will bring out certain colors in the tie's patterns, and vice versa.

Braces can be expensive, so buy basic colors and patterns. A good pair of braces will easily run $50 to $100. To add flair to the suit, depend on the tie to do the heavy lifting and use the braces as a base. I would recommend the following kinds of colors and patterns: a rich royal blue to bring out blue-colored ties, and a black-and-grey pattern to bring out dark red-colored ties. Three to four different braces are sufficient, and get two to three different ties to go with each.

Maybe this is stating the obvious, but I do not assume anything at this point: do not wear a belt *and* braces at the same time. It is one or the other, but never both. Enough said.

The Square

What the hell is a pocket square, and why should you care? As the name suggests, this business suit item is a square piece of silk that is folded up and tucked into the lapel pocket of your suit. It is *not* a handkerchief. A handkerchief is something you dry a geisha's tears with, or blow your nose into. You never let anything touch a pocket square. You treat it like you would a tie. So again, why should you care? It might sound a little extravagant to go to this level of detail, but a square conveys that the wearer takes the time to put a little more sophistication into his appearance. It is like using the correct glass for a martini, or using shaped Semtex versus bulk explosives. The effects of using a specialized piece of equipment can be devastating. Clothing is no different, and the square is no exception.

Pocket squares are usually patterned in flat colors. The reason for this is because they are supposed to accentuate ties—not compete with them. The two are allowed to match, but only if by *accident* or by a miracle of closeness in otherwise divergent designs. To achieve this is to truly be sublime in one's personal fashion expression. In all cases, though, the tie must win the contest of tension between the two. The square is the tie's wingman.

Expect each square to cost roughly $25. Since they come in a full array of colors, make sure the colors you buy accentuate the colors and styles of the ties and braces that you have. To have one or two squares for each of your braces will mean that you will need a total of about six squares. Your grand total will come to about $150. Not too bad.

There are two main problems with squares. The first is how to hang them at your home. The system that worked best for me is a plastic clothes hanger with alligator clips on the horizontal bar. Clip an extreme corner, or better yet, the manufacture's label, and let the square hang down. Do not leave a square folded, or left in a lapel pocket. Either will just wrinkle the square to death. The second problem with squares is folding them correctly. Unlike a handkerchief, which is folded and pressed into a crisp fabric origami, the whole point of a square is to be fluid, floral, almost like wearing a flower on your tuxedo lapel.

The fine art of square folding is not really art at all. It takes ten seconds to learn, and then you can look James Bond-cool for the rest of your business meetings. Imagine two diagonal lines from corner-to-corner and corner-to-corner, forming an X on the square (see figure 17.1).

Pick any corner as your starting point. The line extending from that corner will be the main diagonal line. Pick three points along the main diagonal line. The first point is the midpoint on the main line, between *that* corner and the center of the X. The second point is the center of the X, and the third point is the midpoint on the main line between the center of the X and the far corner. Then, pick a fourth point on the *other* diagonal line. It will be at the midpoint between the corner and the center of the X. Pluck all four points. Those four points will extend out of your lapel pocket. Bunch the rest of the square into a long tube and feed it gracefully into your lapel pocket. Voilà, you have now accessorized your suit to a T. Now ask for $10,000 more in salary.

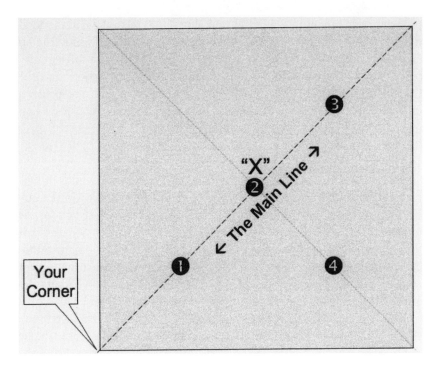

Figure 17.1 Folding the Square

The tie, braces, and square are not supposed to match, but they must coordinate well together. The subtle difference between matching and coordinating may sound like splitting hairs, but in the fickle world of fashion the fine line between clashing and catastrophe is precarious. The costs involved with such purchases make it only prudent to seek an expert opinion. When in doubt, try to remember some basics. The patterns can be (slightly) different, so long as the colors accentuate aspects of one or more of the other elements. When colors work well, they bring out a particular color that you desire. One of the best colors to work with (especially for ties) is the color of your eyes. It is important to embrace your natural skin tones, hair, and eye colors, and only buy the clothing items that work for you.

Shoes

Prepare yourself for a shock. If you have been in the military for a number of years, and buying your shoes at military clothing sales, you have probably been buying and wearing your shoes incorrectly. One of the good things about a uniform is that it *dictates* what to wear. Military shoes are no exception. The hard-leather basic-training dress shoes and soft-squishy "earth shoes" that military clothing sales make available to troops for their Class-A dress uniform and Class-B duty uniform are usually inexpensive, unfashionable, and equally detrimental to feet. My Veterans Administration (VA) disability claim will pay testament to that fact.

The Cost of Comfort

Like a good automobile, quality footwear will cost you. After years of wearing inferior shoes in the military, however, your feet will thank you for the upgrade. Good shoes cost more than $100. In fact, when I first bought a pair of designer Italian leather shoes for $200, I thought I had lost my mind. Then something odd happened: I enjoyed wearing them. More than that, I enjoyed walking again. The firm fit of good shoes, and the proper lift of solid arches, had me up and around on my feet, without pain. Then I had to confront a more acute pain. To keep one's feet in good standing, and keep one's shoes in better shape, you must wear a different pair of shoes for each day of the week. That means you need at least five pairs of shoes.

Pain and Problems

There is an important reason for buying so many pairs of dress shoes. The reason has to do with how much our feet sweat, and the detrimental effect the sweat will have on one's shoes. Just like with combat boots, the more you wear leather, the more it works in. The sweat gets into the leather and softens it over time. That is fine for combat boots, but not expensive dress shoes for suits. In fact, if you wear the same pair of shoes over and over again, the effect of your sweat on the leather becomes additive. The leather never gets a chance to dry and return to its original supportive shape. You might notice the lace holes getting closer to one another over time. That is because the leather is stretching permanently, and soon you will not be able to tie your shoes tight enough. Eventually, your feet might begin to hurt again, despite the arch supports. This is because nothing is holding your foot together in the shoe and it collapses around the arch support.

Between the limited varieties of librarian-style shoes the Air Force made available at clothing sales (and via regulation), and running in combat boots, I walked away from the service with a bad case of what is known as plantar

fasciitis. This funny-sounding condition is no fun to have. It is an unyielding and shooting pain in the heels. There are two remedies for this affliction:
better shoes and better arch supports. The better shoes will cost you dearly.
The better arches are something you might have to purchase for every single pair of shoes you own. Arch supports need to be hard, very hard. I tried
soft, squishy foam arches, and even gel heel pads, but it just did not seem to
help. It might sound initially counterintuitive, but behind it was some simple engineering sense. I needed supports that would hold up my injured
arch, prop it up to its correct curvature so that it could heal properly. A soft
cushion, or gel pad, relieved my initial pain and made my feet feel a little
better, but they did not help the problem. For my arches to heal, they
required a real solution to the underlying condition. Solid arch supports
were the answer.

Shoe Rotation

One of the best preventions for prematurely wearing out your shoes is to set
aside Monday's shoes to dry while you wear Tuesday's shoes, and so on with
your other shoes for the other days of the workweek. In the long term, the
costs will all balance out. If you take care of a high-quality pair of leather
dress shoes, you should be able to resole them about three times. That gives
you a shoe-life of more than three years. If, however, you wear the same pair
of shoes continuously day after day, you will probably have to replace them
in six months. You do the math.

In the end, they are your feet. You can buy a great suit, accessorize to a
T, but have shoes that undermine all your attempts at separating from the
military. If you look cheap, your salary will reflect it. The choice is yours.
Invest in good clothing, or save a few bucks in the short term, and pay for it
later with big podiatry bills.

Shoe Trees

The preceding discussion of shoes and your feet should have conveyed a
persistent theme, namely that care and maintenance will go a long way.
Good shoes, like everything else in the clothing world, are expensive. Taking
care of clothing is an age-old art in the military, so why should this be any
different? Boot camp was about discipline, and one of the most persistent
themes in that discipline that all recruits learn is care and maintenance, of
their boots, shoes, equipment, and each other. Care and maintenance go a

long way, especially on finite resources and combat conditions. You might
be transitioning out of the military, but *some* lessons are worth holding
onto. This brings us to the subject of shoe trees. If you have just spent
$1,000 on five pairs of good quality dress shoes, why wouldn't you want to
care for and maintain them? Of course you know how to polish them, and
keep them shiny. You now know to rotate them so the leather can dry. You
know to buy them with good arches, or even supplement the existing arches
with hard arch supports. But what should you do about the structure of the
shoe? How do you keep your investment well maintained? The answer is
shoe trees.

When I asked Harley, his response was, "One can get a lot more
longevity out of shoes if cedar shoe trees are used after each wear. They have
to be made of an absorbent wood to remove moisture and keep the shape
of the shoe as they dry overnight." Like everything else, shoe trees are expensive, almost $30 per pair. For five pairs, your cost increases another $150.
That is practically the cost of a new pair of shoes. It will be worth it, because
without the shoe trees it will be the earlier-than-expected cost of replacing
five pairs of shoes instead. A final note, if you wear arch supports or other
inserts in your shoes, remove them before you insert the shoe tree. This has
been a public service announcement.

Dress Socks

A simple approach to dress socks is probably the best approach. To start
building your business attire, choose dark socks, in plain colors, without patterns. Plan to buy two pairs for every day of the week (at least 10 total pairs).
Wear dark brown dress socks with a brown suit, and dark gray (or black)
dress socks with gray, black, blue, or dark green suits. Obviously, as soon as
they develop holes, replace them immediately. Getting dressed in the gym
after a power-racquetball session with peers or the boss, only to advertise an
exposed toe, constitutes a major loss of cool points. Do not let this happen.
Have plenty of socks available. Peace.

Belts

Even if you do not buy belts for your suits, I mention them now in the shoe
section for basic fashion sense. This is so simple, I will not waste any further time on the subject: shoes and belts should always match in color.
Move out.

Wardrobe Purchase Requirements

When all was said and done, my shopping adventure for a wardrobe to take me from military to the business world cost me handsomely. From August through December of 1999, I spent a whopping $7,200 on my new wardrobe. Thank goodness I had all that terminal leave saved up. Below is an estimate of what a baseline executive business wardrobe will cost you today.

The point of this chapter was not to turn you into a stylish, power-suit wearing captain of industry. That will only come with time, as you develop your own style. Styles change, but whatever they are must reflect your own

Table 17.1 Wardrobe Purchase Requirements and Costs

Item Type	Cost per Item	Number Suggested	Notes	Final Costs
Business Suits	$1,000	3	Do *not* go cheap	$3,000
Dress Shirts	3 / $200	10	7 standard cuffed, plus 3 French cuffed required	$700
Cuff links	$50 / pair	2 pairs	Do *not* go cheap	$100
Brass Collar Tabs	$20 / 10 pairs	15 pairs	Will *not* "set off" an airport metal detector	$40
Ties	$100	10	Adds style and flair to suits	$1,000
Braces	$50	3	A base for your tie's patterns	$150
Squares	$25	6	The tie's wingman	$150
Shoes	$150	5 pairs	One for each day of the week	$750
Shoe trees	$30	5 pairs	Care and maintenance for shoes extends lifespan	$150
Gross Total	—	—	Basic wardrobe of business attire starting cost	$5,940

emerging post-military sense of self. Buying name brands might help get you started, but it might not help you ultimately define who you are.

Your style has to be internally generated by your own tastes. If you think that you do not have *any* sense of taste, a few trips to a good haberdasher or clothing store might surprise you. Your own sense of personal expression is in there, buried for years under your battle dress uniform (BDU) and polyester. When you see what is out there, and the range of choices, your comfort level will gradually increase. Try not to let it be dictated solely by costs. You can probably buy everything cheaper somewhere. Having suits tailor-made overseas is even better.

In the end, do not sell yourself short. You do deserve better, and now is the time to begin expecting it. Part of that is to not look at the business-suit shopping experience with dread. It can be a frightening prospect to confront insanely

> "The poor girl accessorizes in black."
>
> —T. Rush, 1993

high prices and a seemingly infinite number of possibilities and combinations of styles and colors. So when in doubt, go simple.

Look at buying your business suits as an educational experience. Do not buy the first thing you see, or the first great deal. This is an opportunity for you to *learn*. If you find something you like, put it on hold. You can keep hard-to-find sizes on hold long enough to keep shopping around. Clothing manufacturers will bend-over-backward to help you in this process because, ultimately, they want to make the sale. You are their customer. Let them educate you.

CHAPTER EIGHTEEN

Interviewing as Reconnaissance
They Are Not Interviewing You; You Are Collecting Intelligence about Them

"The secret of all victory lies in the organization of the non-obvious."

— Marcus Aurelius

The purpose of an interview is for your employer to answer two questions about your candidacy:

1. What can you do for the organization?

and,

2. Can you get along with everybody?

If you are invited to a job interview, someone has *already* decided that you possess qualifications for the job. Now, they want to find out what you can contribute, and if you can fit into the organization. In essence, your résumé has succeeded in attracting an employer.

Think of your résumé as a fishing lure. It is baited to attract a particular kind of fish. You have tried to match the size of your hook with the size of the fish's mouth. You have cast it out to where you think the fish are biting. Now you have a tug on the line. You tug back, and sink in the hook. Then the line tugs back, and now you are ready to reel in your catch. It all seems simple, but from an intelligence perspective the analogy is actually a little more complicated. This is not just a case of you and your rod, reel, a line, and a hooked fish. It is actually you and your rod, reel, a line and another *fisherman*. That other fisherman likes the lures you make, and now wants you to make a few thousand more—and haul in as big a profit for his organization from your work as possible. So the two of you have been reeling the other in for the catch.

Personal Questions

Before you do anything, you need to ask yourself the following:

1. What can this organization do for *me*?

and,

2. Do I want to work with these people?

For a military person, these kinds of counterquestions might seem a bit selfish. If you feel selfish asking yourself these questions, do not worry. These *are* selfish questions, and they are selfish for a reason. Now, more than ever, as you redefine your new life you must protect yourself. You must protect yourself from succeeding in the job search, but failing to find the right job. If you need a job because you have to make money, that is relatively easy to accomplish. Under the worst situations we can take work just to pay the bills, but your job does not have to be like this. Expediency is indicative of want, need, fear, or greed. You do not have to be needy, afraid, or greedy while you are still able to make choices for yourself. Why not be a little demanding while you are at it? If you are not selfish at this stage of the game, you may only succeed in securing a source of income, only to find later that you are unhappy.

So, back to the really big, important question that only you can answer:

What do I really want?

Your job is to establish the absolute, no-kidding, deal-breaking requirements for what you want in your life. You may say you want money, but no sympathy will come to you when you are drowning in stress, facing impossible workloads, and existing in the total absence of a life. If you are okay with that, then money may be your goal. For others, life is about more than what you can buy. Remember, you only need a pleasant, enjoyable, suitable job to pay the bills to get on with the rest of your life. You just have to make sure that there is enough time and the right means to get on with the rest of your life. You also have to make sure that you have a "rest of your life."

For those in "the 20 percent," careers have a tendency to get in the way of your life. Your mission is therefore a little more complicated—as always. You must figure out what you can and cannot live with, especially since you derive your self-worth from your job. The process of separating from the military may require a multistep approach, where you first learn how not to work yourself to death. Then, when you can leave your job at "normal" hours, you have to decide what will leave you feeling happy and fulfilled at the end of each day. If you do this right, it will mean being a little selfish. This is not the military anymore. Now *you* decide on everything you want up front, and everything you expect to get out of each and every new job. No more choosing mystery assignments. No more regrets from making bad choices. No more playing passive-aggressive games trying to survive day in and day out. Now you are in control. You decide whether to stay or go. You choose the environment you want to work in, and the job interview is one of your most powerful opportunities to make that informed decision.

> "Reimmersing yourself in a work culture that you dislike doesn't make any sense. It's like moving to a new country whose customs are morally offensive to your sensibilities. You have no one to blame for your resulting unhappiness but you."
>
> —Mavaxiom 181

Interview Collection Requirements

To construct a good set of interview-collection requirements, return to the list of I-dos and I-don'ts from chapter 8. Put these lists into a format that you can work from. You might want to put checkboxes alongside the attributes and annotate good points about each job you are considering. Based on telephone conversations, e-mails, and face-to-face discussions, you can probably begin to fill out a good chunk of the list before you ever get to the interview. This is advisable, because you will be too preoccupied during the interview to fill out any checklists. Certainly right afterward will be the best time to complete your

"Never turn down an interview. You have no idea what you might learn —even if only how to sharpen your skills for the next."

—Marc's rule of interviewing

checklist, even in the parking lot, right after your interview, while your thoughts are still fresh. Do not wait too long, as observations about the job will begin to blur, especially if you have successive interviews. By filling out your interview collection checklist beforehand, you will go into the interview knowing the gaps in your information, and being able to confirm (or validate) already met collection requirements.

Interview Checklist I: Things You Should Look For

Take your own notes and bring them to your interview. Look at your list again, especially right before entering the building for the interview. Watch for red flags. Trust your instincts. See if you feel welcomed at the door, accepted by interviewers, and encouraged to participate in discussions. When you emerge, recall things that annoyed you about the company or the environment, and keep track of aspects of the experience that satisfied you. Like a scorecard, record both positive and negative attributes, along with those hard-to-quantify "gut" impressions. This is more than just an exercise in being a trained observer; this is an intelligence collection mission where you will have to debrief yourself. Maintaining as comprehensive a list as possible will help focus you afterwards when the stress from surviving the experience begins to distract you.

The following is a starter list for basic post-interview debriefing purposes. It is by no means complete, and requires you to insert your own uniquely personal requirements to ensure that this job offer is what you really want. The checklist is organized by specific requirements to be collected, including: corporate administration, management and culture, commuting, work environment, and job satisfaction. Use these questions to navigate though mental blocks and unanticipated distractions. Use them for every interview in your job search. And, above all, good hunting.

Administration

1. Is this a paper-heavy organization? You can usually tell just from the initial application process. If they have you filling out forms, and you do not even work there yet, something is wrong. Get a sense of how much formwork the institution relies on for its basic procedures. Also compare page counts of corporate information handouts, and other company procedures, such as time-card requirements, medical claims forms, reimbursable account rules, and so on from company to company.

2. Will you have to keep track of your own administrative trivia? See how much the company pushes administrative demands down onto its employees. Companies try to direct their employees to all-knowing web pages or 1-800 help numbers. Be wary of such policies, as they disconnect you from interacting with human experts in support services. You will be left on your own, high and dry when you need assistance. This is what you need to find out: Will you have to do everything on your own in that organization's culture?

3. Is the administrative assistance competent, or just taking up space? Organizations run on the abilities of their administrative personnel. These individuals are a direct reflection on the company because they are often the main interface between the company and outsiders. If they are not welcoming, accepting, or encouraging to you when you arrive as a stranger, how friendly will they be to you when you work there? Take special note to see that they are enthusiastic about providing professional-quality products and services. Most importantly, are they reliable? Can you rely on them to tend to your administrative details so that you can concentrate on your job? Ask to know which administrative personnel are assigned to help you, and with how many other people they will be shared. Knowing how much assistance you will receive allows you to anticipate the degree to which you will be able to focus on your job, versus all the other distracting administrative requirements. Those other requirements can add up fast. Having this information upfront can help you adjust your expectations accordingly. Ask interviewers and corporate staff members about the following:

a- administrative forms
b- monthly reports
c- expense reports
d- timecards
e- other reports
f- regular meetings
g- performance reviews

Management and Culture

4. How much of your job will be spent using and cultivating your talent? Are you being hired for your skills and contribution, or will you be the new junior worker bee who has to take up the slack? Employees who uses phrases like, "short-fuse," and "crashing and burning," on more than one occasion to describe projects, or apologize to you for not getting back sooner because "it has been crazy" provide valuable indicators of problematic management practices. Watch for these kinds of warning signs:
   a- emergency meetings
   b- indecisive management
   c- rescue operations
   d- negative customer ratings
   e- reorganizations
   f- policy reprioritizations
   g- constant meetings
   h- corporate takeovers
   i- surges in workloads, or
   j- surges at odd times of the year
5. How much waiting is required of employees (and candidates) for the corporate hiring process (or any process) to go through the system? Slow decision making, and bureaucratic processes are troubling indicators of several problem areas. Because you are leaving a giant bureaucracy, civilian organizations bogged down in red tape might be a bad choice immediately after the military. Any frustrations you had with the government will be extended indefinitely with an inefficient civilian firm. Managements unable to make decisions quickly and decisively may also bring back bad memories of "hurry up and wait." Worse yet are managers who are unsure as to what they want—a very bad sign, especially where business is concerned.

6. How many hoops does a company make you jump through just to get in the door? The focus of this question is ascertaining how a target company filters candidates. Initially, it makes sense for organizations to weed out unqualified candidates, but difficult entrance requirements might also be an indicator of something completely different. Companies might embrace cultural norms contrary to your own, and you might not want to go to an organization with good-old-boy networks, a glass ceiling, or initiation rights. Likewise, if the application process is wastefully bureaucratic, it might be a reflection of the company itself. Do you want to work for a streamlined, high-speed business or for wasteful bureaucrats? You are a grown-up now. You have paid your dues, and you are not looking to join another fraternity. It is time to start looking at work as your job, and a means to an end for paying bills and rebuilding your post-military life.

7. What is your value to the organization? The fact that you are in an interview means that your résumé has communicated sufficient skills to warrant your consideration for the job. The interview is to see what more you can do for the organization, and how effectively you will fit in. As such, having to further *prove your worth* might be a sign of a problem. Your skill level and career competence might be intimidating to managers. Some insecure managers may intentionally make it difficult for you to succeed. To keep you from taking over, artificial barriers might be created to keep you off balance. Ensure that when you are a new employee of the company you will:
   a- be taken seriously
   b- have your opinions valued
   c- make contributions that will count
   d- be heard and consulted
   e- be worthwhile to your team
   f- be sought for your know-how

8. Is the team concept important to workers in this office? It is not assumed that workers in the civilian sector necessarily gel into a high-speed team when required. See if individuals of the interview "team" have even talked to each other about your candidacy. For most, the source of income supercedes all other concerns—even job performance—and work is just time away from more enjoyable activities. Some degree of this is good, but not if it comes at the expense of others in the organization. If you are one of "the twenty," you might become the one always expected to come to the rescue for poor performance. You may be looking for qualities in

potential coworkers such as reliability, competency, trustworthiness, quality performance, a welcoming (accepting and caring) attitude, and a positive approach toward work.

Commuting

9. Really pin down your travel obligations. This can be a deal-breaker. Do not consider just the distance from home to the office, but include all regular traveling you may have to do *between customers*. Where is your desk versus your actual work location? Do you have a desk, or must you "hot desk" from client to client? Do you get an office (with a door) so that you can keep a gym bag or change of clothing on hand? It is important to establish all your expectations up front. Ask:
   a- if you get a parking spot and mileage reimbursement?
   b- what the travel distances and traffic densities are to and from customers?
   c- if you get reimbursement for highway and bridge parking tolls?
10. Are work locations accessible via public transportation? In my view, commuting sucks. Not only that, it is far more likely that you would be involved in a deadly accident driving to work in your automobile (1 in 84) versus flying (1 in 5,051).[1] These issues are only exacerbated in bad weather. Apart from safety concerns, the hours spent commuting represent time utterly wasted staring at someone's bumper. On public transportation, you can at least read a book. Time spent driving equates to *years* of your life thrown away that you can never get back. Moreover, it looks certain now that fuel prices and automobile exhaust will continue to contribute a climate of change towards increased employee anxiety until employers encourage their employees to use alternative forms of transportation. My preference is to work and live in areas that are both near public transportation, and then use my car for pleasure driving. It is a dream for many, but there is no reason why you should not pursue your dreams now.

Work Environment

11. All office environments are not created equal. During an interview, see what kinds of information systems (computers) are present, and ask about future operating system upgrades. It is not a foregone conclusion that the offices you visit will have caught up with the twenty-first century. Prepare yourself. A good poker face might be required to hide your

shock, disappointment, or outright laughter. In essence, you need to establish whether offices are equipped with enough robust computer systems and connectivity to the rest of the world so you can get your job done. *When your home computer works better than your office computer, there is a problem.* Your spy mission is to take mental image snapshots of the following kinds of technologies and equipment:

a- computers
b- Internet connectivity
c- printers, color and monochrome
d- company intranet connectivity
e- copiers, color and monochrome
f- phone connectivity (do not assume anything)
g- sharing of equipment
h- location and number of copiers and printers

12. What other office tools and services are provided? It is important to know because the less you ask, the less potential employers are inclined to volunteer to you. I am constantly surprised by how much equipment is given to those who demand it to accomplish their jobs. If interviewers say, "you can expense equipment to your contract," your reply should be, "what contract am I working?" Ask them to show you the expense form *right there and then.* Do not take "it's on the Internet," as an answer. That is a cop-out, postponing the inevitability of you having to look up everything on the Internet on your own. If an employee does not know how to show you an expense form then something might be wrong. Maybe they never fill one out. Fine. Will you? Also, viable contracts are not a foregone conclusion when you show up. If you do not have direct billing to a contract, then you are on overhead and that can be a corporate death sentence. For these reasons, have a look at an employee expense form while you are there, and ask the interviewer

Photo-Interpretation (PI) Tradecraft Tip

If you have trouble remembering images, try the following trick. While looking directly at the object, close your eyes for a few seconds and allow the image to burn itself on your retina in the back of the eye. With your eyes closed, you will become aware of more details that were allowed to imprint themselves in your memory, without additional visual distractions.

what charge numbers you will be using. As part of your negotiations, your offer letter could be contingent on them providing requested equipment against anticipated charge numbers for:

a- laptops
b- laptop maintenance
c- monthly ISP fees
d- software upgrades, maintenance, and virus scanning
e- mobile phone
f- monthly phone bills

Job Satisfaction

13. What will you be able to learn from your new job? Does the employer provide certificate-granting training programs, educational assistance for advanced degrees, or opportunities with outside academic institutions? The rule of thumb is that a masters degree is worth about $10,000 on top of your base salary, simply because it represents your ability to take on and complete long-term and involved projects. Enhancing your own skills base is not only beneficial to your employer, but also beneficial to the employee.

14. Is there any travel involved in the job? Be very careful with this employment requirement. The term "overseas travel" has taken on new connotations in the post-9/11 world. Many employers doing business overseas, and especially those doing business in hostile areas, look to hire ex-military members because of their perceived willingness to be stationed in harm's way. If you have had enough of combat zones, then you need to express that up front. Some employers will not expressly state that they want you to go into a hostile area. Instead, they may have obfuscating language in their job offer such as: "employee shall perform such other duties as required" or that such travel is "possible" although highly unlikely. Read these employer-employee agreements carefully, especially if they contain such verbiage as, "Responsibilities carried out at the client's work site (in Iraq, Afghanistan, etc.), on a voluntary basis, or at such other places as the employer or client requires." You may need to "red-line" such statements on your job offer, or add amendments, such as, "Employer concurs with the employee that deployment into hostile combat zones (such as Iraq, Afghanistan, etc.), is beyond the scope of this contract." In short, make sure to address any travel or duty requirements to hostile areas.

The unfortunate truth is that troops are not the only people dying overseas. Contractors are being killed as well. Without the protection of uniforms or barricaded fortress compounds, contractors abroad have become the "soft" targets of choice for terrorist kidnappings and blog-aired assassinations. Do not sign up for travel to such areas *unless you are assured of your protection.* The pay compensation can be much higher in such hazardous duty locations than it might be stateside, but so are the risks. Play this kind of contractor roulette at your own peril.

15. Is there any chance of learning about new cultures and languages? Have the company define "new cultures." (See above caution.) The latest design of improvised explosive devices (IEDs) is outside the scope of "new culture." If you are not in a hostile war zone, some so-called "civilized" locations overseas can be hostile *business* zones. As an intelligence professional, I caution those in defense and intelligence contracting traveling abroad for business, especially to former Cold-War "nations of interest" or "nations of concern." This is because former military personnel often draw the interest of the local nation's security and intelligence establishments. Do not be surprised by that weird feeling of hair rising on the back of your neck while abroad. Trust your gut instincts. Watch your personal belongings, and keep an even closer eye on your laptop. Leaving your data unattended, even in your locked hotel room, is an invitation for trouble. With the end of ideological hostilities, many nations are becoming more capitalist than the United States, and part of that involves robust industrial espionage. Forewarned is forearmed.

16. Does the job allow you to exercise creative license? Some companies require candidates to sign employee agreements to control all patented inventions, original works of authorship, developments, improvements, and trade secrets, trademarks, and copyrights made during employment with the company. During the course of employment, if employees incorporate their creations into any company products or processes, the company is authorized to have nonexclusive, royalty-free, irrevocable, perpetual, worldwide license to profit from the creation. For anyone with a creative interest at work, such agreements can be a bit unnerving. Likewise, upon leaving the company, and potentially for years after, employees must not possess, recreate, or deliver any and all devices, records, data, notes, reports, proposals, lists, correspondence, specifications, drawings, blueprints, sketches, materials, equipment, other documents or property, or reproductions developed during employment.

Human Intelligence (HUMINT) Tradecraft Tip

Interrogation has received such a bad connotation lately. Subtle and entirely unobtrusive means of gathering information exist, employing finesse and skill instead of discomfort or suffering. The trick is finding those who want to talk to you. In this sense, do not let potential employers off the hook for not providing the information you seek simply because you did not ask for it. If interviewers do not have satisfactory answers to your questions, find someone who does – and ask them *during* the interview. Strike up a conversation with average employees, and let them fill in the blanks. My best interviews were when busy managers shifted my custody to employees in-the-know who were *more* than happy to give me an unscheduled and unsupervised walk-through of their facilities and office environments. I learned more with them than I did with any manager, because I was getting "ground truth" straight from the locals. One-on-one time with individual employees is when you can elicit some of your most useful intelligence, especially to get a sense of interpersonal atmospheres, office politics, frustrations, and opinions at the worker level.

Talk about a hostile business zone. What if you want to write a novel at that time in your life?

17. Does the job allow you to have any say in how you approach problems, or are there canned approaches that the company wants its employees to use? Like creative license, this is a question of how much "agency" you have over your approaches to your profession. If you are a big-picture kind of person, like me, you may feel drained by jobs that incessantly put you into detail-oriented tasks. Will you have any say in what you really want from your job, or are you an indentured servant?

Probing Enemy Air Defenses

The military's approach to operations is often characterized as "blunt force trauma," but it is not a foregone conclusion that all warfare is about "killing people and breaking things." In the intelligence business, oftentimes, it is much more important just to see what your adversary might do by testing them. By baiting them with something that is too inviting to resist, they may tip their hand and expose their tactics, techniques, and procedures (TTP) that can be exploited later, if necessary. When an adversary reacts to the taunting, the opportunity to watch and take notes is often worth all the effort of the ruse. Over time, the compilation of these notes provides intelligence analysts with a sense of their adversary's thought processes, behavior, and even doctrine. For an intelligence professional, destroying the target is a waste of time and effort because it eliminates an invaluable source of information. Observing the target is much more advantageous in the long run.

Interviewing is no different. Every time I was interviewed, I was focused on collecting as much data as possible on the potential employer. As a natural outgrowth of my intelligence training, I was probing enemy air defenses.

Early-Warning Network

The first line of most air-defense systems is the early-warning network. This network is a massive trip wire, telling a command center that something has either penetrated or is close to penetrating their defensive network. In the business world, this equates to the outer fringe of a company's contact with the outside world. It could be their Internet home page, its media relations department, telephone receptionists, front desk personnel, or others who provide strangers with information. No matter how frustrating they may be, and many are, they are a valuable insight into the company you are targeting. For example, the caliber of their competence, their professional courtesy is an important reflection of the company. Does this company put its best foot forward? Do they even care how they are perceived, or do the real clients never interface with the "little people?"

The same is true when it comes to Internet home pages. Do the home pages work? Are they navigable, or are they confusing to surf? Can you find job postings, or do you need an insider just to guide you through, link by link? Sometimes, in going through the online application process, I found inputting information and résumés to be so awkward that it seemed the real purpose of the web page was to deter everyone except the most committed and patient of applicants. At first glance, the front-end application process should be a filtration system, but the question is, what exactly are they trying to filter? In my opinion, most websites fail at their intended function. Instead of facilitating the process of inviting desired candidates, or providing ready access to information, they simply serve a select group of their own employees—those who live to surf.

I believe the wrong *kinds* of people design websites. Some people are naturally detail-oriented, and others are naturally more creative. Websites are designed by detail-oriented (sometimes antisocial) technicians, and not by socially oriented, naturally expressive or creative individuals. From their front pages, websites inundate the viewer with what amounts to an indecipherable accounting sheet of text. The net effect is to perplex the intended customer, instead of guiding them through the process intuitively and comfortably. Unraveling those cryptic details turns surfing an employer's website into an intelligence collection mission through hostile territory. It would make sense for creative people to design the big-picture intro pages, and for those who are more proficient at details to account for all the link updates. Unfortunately, the reverse is often the case with company websites. The reason that this is important for applicants is made manifest when one considers yet other connection to company information systems. The difficultly in navigating a company's Internet website is often a good indication of what it will be like to navigate the internal *intranet* when you are an employee. Pain before hiring will be prolonged pain after hiring.

Another unfortunate aspect of online application systems is the likelihood of applicants losing hours of work after system glitches dump their inputs. Nothing can be more frustrating to a qualified applicant than an automated process misplacing sensitive personal data simply because the "enter" button was pressed more than once. This goes back to the idea that, although administered and maintained by technicians, websites need to be designed by people-oriented individuals. With unrestricted determination of a company's information systems, imagine what their internal administration will be like?

When I applied for an online job posting at the Central Intelligence Agency (CIA) in 2006, the form required me to restructure my entire résumé into 1,000-character blocks. This was because "the Agency's" system does not allow free text entries or file attachments. Instead, each section of your résumé is segmented into boxes that could accommodate no more than 1,000 characters. A painful lesson learned from the Agency website was to print off the screen intermittently, as well as right before hitting the dreaded "submit" button, so that I had copies of all my inputs throughout the application process.

It may take several attempts just to get an online system to accept your inputs, so is advisable to do all your work in a word document first, and then copy and paste its contents side-by-side into the application input boxes. More importantly, pay attention to how much work *you* have to do just to get their system to work properly. It is likely their internal administration will be no different.

Rules of Engagement (ROE)

Once your data is accepted by the system, it is filed away and filtered through unspeakable algorithmic search engines and bureaucratic evaluation mechanisms. Calling a company human resource (HR) representative at any point in this process may not provide you with the encouragement that you need to keep the process moving. In fact, it may seem that the people designated to help candidates through the process possess precisely the opposite kind of personalities to help. Many of the people I have spoken to throughout my years of job search almost seem chosen specifically for their *lack* of friendliness or customer-service orientation. To them, you are an unidentified calling object, an inconvenience to their otherwise more important office chat. Such phone conversations left me disappointed, frustrated, and deterred from wanting to continue further. However, my advice is to be patient.

Take this part of the intelligence operation slowly. Take notes of how you are treated and compile them with your other observations. If you are hired, it will be both useful and gratifying to validate your notes when you meet the HR person face to face. In the mean time, do not annoy anyone, no matter how incompetent, insensitive, or antagonistic they may seem. Remember, your mission is to probe, not engage. You are in hostile territory and must fly, "alone, unarmed, and unafraid," as they say in the reconnaissance world. There may come a time when you can go "weapons hot." For now, however, maintain a high level of emission control (EMCON) and rely on your abilities to fly quietly as the ultimate stealth bureaucrat.

This part of the process will likely take *months*, so do not wait until separation to start the online application process. Begin six months beforehand. You will have to develop this target gradually and painstakingly, accepting the fact that most HR departments simply are not built to be responsive. Eventually you can engage, divulging your observations, but only when you are:

1. Comfortably safe within the privileged ranks of the company's own walls, or

2. Absolutely sure that you never want to work with that company, and are finished with your interview-search process. Evil people have a surprising capacity to remember you.

Remember, your mission is to see what "lights up" as you penetrate their information space. These indicators are your first clues as to whether this company is the right fit for you. Years after being employed by these companies, you might be surprised by how much was plainly evident about their corporate culture, work ethic, and company functionality during your first encounters on the fringes of the company's application process.

Target Tracking Network

The second line of an air-defense system is the target-tracking network. After the initial trip wire early warning network, the tracking network is the means of locating a target and following it via its latitude, longitude, altitude, and velocity (speed and direction). In the business world, this is a company's means of identifying you and keeping tabs on you throughout the application process. As you become a "known quantity," your desired company will begin to call you, and want further information about you. If your résumé yields interest, the tracking network will begin the process of forwarding information about you to their command and control (C2) management center. From there decisions will be made as to whether you represent a skill set worth engaging via one or more interviews. In effect, this is the phase where your target will attempt to collect further intelligence about you.

Let them collect. Be polite, courteous, and responsive. Pretend you are unaware of their underlying intentions, but all the while take notes on precisely what they ask you to ascertain what kind of skill-sets they may be looking for in candidates. Countless opportunities will arise to see how things work inside their organization. For example, when people identify themselves as managers, they may be calling to see if you would work best with their office, versus another office. You may become the interest of numerous offices. The effectiveness of their coordination process could be telling. Have a pad and paper handy to get their names and information, and make sure you keep track of what each person wants, and which office they represent. It is very possible that every time a new person calls, they will only have your contact information and need to start from scratch with understanding your qualifications. Do not be discouraged. Just take notes. The disconnect between different offices is a window into a company's larger information sharing problems.

Evaluate how effectively the different elements of the employee tracking network function. Do they talk to one another? Are there communication divides between the business sectors? Do they have your most up-to-date résumé, or are they just going off the one you submitted online months ago? All of these actions are indicators of how the company's internal systems function, which will be important to you if you become employed by the firm.

Something else to remember is that the HR department does not just conduct hiring; it also manages employee benefits. This includes a full array of employee concerns, including medical, dental, and optical plans, dependent care, health care reimbursement, short- and long-term disability, life insurance, accidental death and dismemberment insurance, travel insurance, tuition aid, employee assistance, vacation, retirement plans (401K), supplemental retirement plans, and so on. The same people who could not keep track of you in the hiring process will be responsible for keeping track of all those other employee functions. Are you comfortable with that based on your application experiences? Think about it.

References

At some point in this process, you will probably be asked to provide a list of references. This section is a quick guide for generating that list, as well as the different kinds of information that are usually expected by potential employers. There are three kinds of references:

1. Professional only—people you have worked with, colleagues, supervisors, and so on.
2. Personal only—people you have no association with from work, just people you know socially, like friends, neighbors, drinking buddies, classmates, and so forth.
3. Personal and professional—people with whom you have become social friends, engaging in activities outside work, but whom you initially met and interacted with at work.

Include the first, middle (initial), and last name (always confirm spelling) of the person whom you believe will accurately characterize your abilities in complimentary terms. Describe their relationship to you at the time of your interaction, such as friend, coworker, and neighbor. Outline the duration of your interaction from day-month-year to day-month-year. If the person is still a friend or a colleague, then list the end date as "to present." Include where you began interacting, such as the name of the organization or the effort, with an old work address, if applicable. Include their contact information, such as home address, with city, state, and zip code, area code and phone numbers (home, work, cell), theirpersonal@email.com, current work address, phone number, theirwork@email.com, the address if they are deployed overseas, or their family address inside the country.

Some final thoughts on the subject: If you are going to list someone as a reference please make sure you tell that person so that they are not caught off guard by a phone call from an HR representative. You would expect the same courtesy, so show it in return. Likewise, make sure that your reference is someone who knows you, respects you, and can represent your best interests. Having a "drinking buddy" as your reference makes no sense if they cannot speak intelligently and professionally on your behalf. Remember, this is for your new job, and a start at a new life.

Target Engagement Network

The third, and innermost line of an air-defense system is its target engagement network. It is the action arm of the system, tasked with neutralizing threats and confirming the final status of all targets. In the business world, this is a company's means of negotiating and hiring you on *their* terms, or turning you away. This is the showdown. They will be shooting live weapons at you, and you will have to use all your skills to succeed at your ultimate goal: earning a handsome offer letter. It may require you to evade, combat maneuver, absorb shots as you can, perhaps even return fire, and always keep your poker face intact. They will want to see what you are made of, and this is why you have worked so hard to get to this point. If company policies require more than one interview, then this will be the first of many fly-through attempts. In this case collect as much information as you can on your first pass to use for engagement on later missions. Take fire, and keep flying. Your mission is to get that camera footage back to base for processing and evaluation.

People laugh when I describe the interviewing process like this, but rest assured, you will feel like you have been riddled with antiaircraft artillery (AAA) when you get home.

To assist you with that mission, the next section contains a meticulous list of items that are suggested for any interview. If it really was an intelligence mission, you would assemble a "sensor suite" with tools that would help you collect data for later analysis. There are also defensive counter-measures to help you survive hostile engagements. These countermeasures are designed for issues as varied as staying well hydrated to make sure your hydraulic systems continue functioning properly to writing thank you let-ters. You will need all the tools, confidence, and stamina you can muster at this phase of the operation. Like chaff, flares, and decoys, these elements of your interview "combat pack" will get you in and out of adversarial territory with the intelligence you need to make an informed decision on the job that is right for you.

Interview Checklist II: Things You Should Bring (Your Combat Pack, Sensor Suite, and Defensive Countermeasures)

Besides your charming self, well dressed and adequately fed and rested, a couple of other things should accompany you to an interview. The philo-sophical and scientific rule of thumb, sometimes called Occam's razor, is that the simplest solutions are most often best. Under the stress of interviewing, this certainly applies. I have tried to make my list as comprehensive as pos-sible, but you can pick and choose what suits your particular style, mission, or preference. Do not feel limited, but do consider all your options. Remem-ber, Murphy is everywhere.

I. The Briefcase

People can spend years looking for the right briefcase. As with most other rec-ommendations in this section, I advise that you go simple and avoid buying anything too expensive. As long as it does not look cheap, you are probably fine. My first interviewing combat pack was a classic black leather briefcase. After several interviews, I became acutely aware of the weight of leather and chose a very small laptop bag with handles and no strap instead. It was high-speed black and extremely lightweight, like any good combat pack.

The Business-Card Holder

Keep it simple leather or metal. It does not have to be fancy, but it must be small, thin, light, and work well under all kinds of fumbling and stressful social encounters. Be careful with cigarette cases, as they can sometimes make it tricky to remove cards. If you end up spraying the floor with business cards any hopes of maintaining poise will be forfeited.

Marc's 3-Pack

If you think you are genetically superior because you have never needed personal medications, here is an eye-opener for you: you are *not* invincible—especially in an interview. Occasionally Murphy strikes in ways we cannot begin to imagine. For example, let us assume your final duty station is in Florida but you have to interview for jobs in Washington, D.C., as I did. Now imagine that it is winter. You come up for a week of power interviews, and suddenly you are surprised by how cold it is in Washington. How strange, because cold is foreign to Florida. Now imagine a few nights at a friend's house or in a hotel with central heating. Your skin is drying out, joints are aching a little, and sinuses are feeling a little funny. Now imagine thrusting yourself into a power interview session. You are talking about your skills for hours on end, giving a lot of firm handshakes, and showing the best face you can. You are a little tense, a little dehydrated, and feel a little headache coming on, and with all that talking a scratchy throat as well. This is the time you wish you had a cool, soothing throat lozenge handy.

Please allow me to shed some light on why this is important to your interview. The truth is, some interviews are cleverly understated interrogation sessions in disguise. If a company does a lot of interviewing, it may employ planned strategies to see what makes you tick. If they want to see if you can get along with others, maybe they will subject you to marathon shakedown sessions one after another with little down time. If they want to see how you react under stress, maybe they will forego readily providing all that your biology requires, like fluids. Running this kind of gauntlet can prove surprisingly draining, so it is probably best to be prepared.

Some Personal Medications—three things that will make your respiratory system feel better. You only need a few of each, in a subsize zip-lock baggie, to help with unexpected crises. You can partake of one or more, depending upon your symptoms.

Vitamin C lozenges—you can never get enough Vitamin C, and stressful times like interviewing are no exception. These are great for a dry mouth, a scratchy throat, or to satisfy nervous urges without having to resort to gum. Obviously, try not to be chewing anything while speaking or greeting potential employers. Generally, the first lozenge you will chew up and swallow immediately anyway, out of sheer tension.

Menthol lozenges—these are great for opening up all your passages if you succumb to sudden congestion. They also soothe your throat if you have nasal drip.

Non-drowsy antihistamines—you never know when the person leading your interviews will be covered with an invisible layer of pet dander that you are unexpectedly allergic to. Antihistamines are also great for headaches and sinus flair-ups from HVAC (heating, ventilation and air conditioning) units. Make sure they are non-drowsy. Falling asleep during an interview is just plain tacky, and runs you the risk of being posted on the Internet.

Other personal medications—if you have any medical, physiological, psychosomatic, geomagnetic, or cosmic affliction, for the sake of all those at your interview (and your continuing self-esteem), please bring what you need to the interview. For example, if you use an inhaler, bring it. If you must have your dream-catcher handy to make important decisions, and can fit it discreetly into a small briefcase, then bring it. Just do not show it to anyone, and consult it while in the restroom. If you need to take certain medications at certain times of day, bring them, too. If you have a tendency to get cuts at random and inopportune moments, bring adhesive bandages. If you are taking antidepressants or medication to control seizures, for the love of all things good, please bring them. Do not take the risk of doing really well with your interview, only to collapse onto the floor, foaming at the mouth. Poise points aside, you will scare the living daylights out of your prospective employers.

The Day-Timer

You may require a calendar to schedule follow-on interviews, or other actions. You will probably also need it to strategize appointments. My only requirements for a date book are that it be small, professional in appearance, and that it be allowed on the premises. The last point is especially true if you are interviewing in a secure facility that does not permit electronic devices.

Personal Items Sometimes Not Permitted in Certain Buildings

Make sure you ask *before* your interview whether electronic devices can be brought onto the premises. If you fail to do this, you run the risk of something beeping or ringing in the middle of a controlled area, requiring security officers to commandeer your belongings. Imagine your interview starting out like the security check at an airport gate. Not a pretty sight. The following list of items might yield such a reaction, so best check your items beforehand:

1. Cell phone (especially with a camera)
2. Laptop, palmtop, or PDA (personal data assistant)
3. Thumb drive (USB key or flash drive)
4. CD-R / DVD-R
5. MP3 player—music play lists
6. Videogame—why a person might want to bring a videogame to an interview may seem puzzling at first. It seems plausible that some people might want to use a videogame to calm themselves prior to a stressful event, like an interview. Each person is entitled to their own form of stress reduction, just make sure you keep it to yourself. At some point prior to entering a secure facility make sure you can discreetly store it off your person.

Extra Writing Implements

Pens die. It is a fact of life. They succumb to stress and expire, generally right in the middle of an interview. It will happen. There is no escaping destiny, so bring extras:

1. Fashionable pen (black or blue)—nothing too ostentatious.
2. Highlighter—for marking any handouts they give you.
3. Red pen—for scribbling notes on any handouts they give you.
4. Black permanent marker—not only is one useful for writing your name on the adhesive labels or placards given you, but, if you notice a nick on your black shoes or a discoloration on your dark suit, you might be able to effect a temporary, clandestine fix during a bio-break.

Extra Business Cards

You can never have too many, especially when interviewing. If you are not yet employed, create personal cards for yourself. A later section will demonstrate how to create a winning card.

Thumb Drive

A small, cheap, flash memory drive (1.0 gig memory is usually enough). Check to make sure this item is allowed into the facility, and never (ever) try to sneak one (even "accidentally") into (and out of) a secure facility. Use this thumb drive to store electronic copies of:

1. Any presentations specifically requested for briefing, or by your interviewers.
2. Any published articles you have written, letters of recommendation or appreciation.
3. Different versions of your résumé (short versus long, .pdf versus .doc).
4. Other materials you might need while on the road.

II. Inside the Briefcase

Note Pad

Try to have a very thin, black plastic (or nice leather) folder handy for notes, with an inside pocket and 8½ x 11 inch notepaper (white). In the pocket, the following things will help you describe yourself during the interview process (memory-joggers):

1. Extra copies of your résumé.
2. Handout copy (or softcopy CD / DVD) of a presentation you have specifically been asked to deliver during your interview, or requested by your interviewers. Check to make sure this item is allowed into the facility in which you are interviewing.
3. A handout copy of a short published article you have written (as a writing example), or a letter of recommendation or appreciation.
4. A list of accomplishments, articles published, awards, decorations, and so forth.
5. Self-written notes to yourself to describe your strengths, weaknesses, and personality traits. Use this for self-coaching before you enter the building.
6. Clip-on pen (that matches the folder). You can never have too many pens. According to Murphy's Law, the only one you have is bound to die on you, while writing something important, in the middle of the interview. Do not tempt fate; interviews are stressful enough.
7. Check to make sure that anything that you have in this folder is not your only copy, and that you can give it freely to your interviewer.

The "Target Folder"

Use an empty plastic (two-pocket) folder to hold all the intelligence that you have collected on the company. In this folder, compile all the snail mail, e-mail, and other correspondence, newspaper clippings, and handwritten notes. Organize it such that if you need to find something, you can do so quickly and effortlessly. In this game, you get extra credit points for making a speedy retrieval of information under pressure look easy.

Have a separate target folder for each company. On the day of the interview, make sure you have the *correct* folder for the company hosting your interview. If you are doing more than one interview in a day, have different colored folders for the different companies in the same day. This will save you from getting the folders confused. You want to make sure that you have all the intelligence data you need at the interview, and you do not want intelligence data for the *wrong* company at your interview. Color coding will help you stay one step ahead of Murphy.

Just for fun, make the more Republican-oriented company target folder red, and the more Democratic-oriented company target folder blue. See if either company catches on.

The Backup Folder

This is the folder for "other things." Buy a black plastic (two-pocket) folder with three-ring binder clips for inserting plastic top-loading document protector sheets. Store items in these sheets that you do not want to necessarily part with or hand over to interviewers. They include, but are not limited to:

1. A CD / DVD holder sheet. There are four pockets in a standard CD holder. In them, I put ancillary supplies, such as extra thank-you letters (with postage) and cards (in case of mistakes), extra business cards, and room for a CD/DVD (if you need to give a briefing). Check to make sure this item is allowed into the facility in which you are interviewing.
2. Ten top-loading document protector sheets. Use them to safeguard items such as color print-offs of web pages you might have worked on, handouts from conferences in which you participated, color print-offs of articles written *about* you (in a positive light, of course), letters or certificates of appreciation from past efforts or from previous supervisors, your list of references (personal, professional, and both), copies of a past employment application (to help you fill out employee applications during your interview), and finally "recall rosters" from past organizations you worked at for you to use to remember past associates.

3. Business-card holder sheets. Leave room to collect business cards from all the people whom you interview with and meet throughout the process. Remember, as a matter of courtesy, every time someone gives you a business card, you must reciprocate with your own—on the spot. Each business card you receive should also result in a thank-you letter from you to them.

III. A Bottle of Water

Do not assume that the company you are interviewing will have anything that you might need for "normal bodily functions." By law, and for their own employees, they must have a toilet, but thereafter all bets are off. Also, remember that dehydration is a cause for irritability. If your frustrations start showing, it might be because you need water. Few people think of this when they are tense, which adds to further dehydration and exacerbates the situation. Bring plain water. If you spill it on yourself, the floor, or others, it is only water. No harm done. Water might not taste as satisfying, but you can clean a spot on your shirt and rehydrate yourself all at once. If you bring anything with caffeine or sugar, it might just make you jumpy, adding to your tension. Finally, try to bring water in a bottle that has four *flat* sides. That way, if you drop it, there is no way that it can roll away from you. The last thing you want to do is turn your interview into a comedy episode of you chasing around a rolling water bottle in Murphy's office.

The Thank-You Letter

Send a thank-you letter within twenty-four hours of your interview, after every single interview, and in response to every business card you receive— at a minimum. It is the least that you can do after they invited you to their company. The tragic shame is that no one writes thank-you letters anymore. It is a horrible social malpractice. In the seven years I was defense contracting, and in all the interviews I ever did with employee candidates, I *never* received a thank you letter in the mail. Ever. I received e-mails after the fact, but never a handwritten letter. That simple act would have put one person above all the rest. That could be you. Because no one else writes thank-you letters is all the more reason why you should. If you do, you will stand out if only for your consideration, thoughtfulness, and social graces.

In a competition between several candidates, every little bit helps. Receiving your thank-you letter within a couple of days will help identify you in a crowd of candidates. It is also what makes a quick turnaround on your letter all the more pressing. When I left the military I averaged two interviews a day. In between each interview, I scheduled enough time to slow down, relax, get something to eat, and drink a shot of espresso to get me through the next interview. I also made sure that there was enough time between the interviews so I could write my thank-you letters, sometimes right after the interview in the company parking lot, from where I would also mail it before going off to the next interview. Forgetting important details from one interview to the next is easy amid all the stress, so getting a company business card from each and every interviewer you meet can help jog your memory. Sometimes jotting down notes on the back of each card can help, too. Collect as many as you can and then send *each* person a written note of thanks.

To illustrate how powerful a thank-you letter can be, some years after becoming a civilian, a colleague asked me why I had not interviewed with his company. I told him that I had, and even remembered the name of one of the people I had interviewed with—a mutual friend. Then I began to recall how the interview had gone, especially a conversation that had blossomed about World War II. I randomly identified an aircraft painting he had on the wall, and the interviewer shared with me that his father had flown the aircraft, the Lockheed P-38 Lightning, during the war. After the interview, I wrote a thank-you letter and hand drew a P-38 in flight from memory on the inside cover of the card. Then I mailed it to him while still in his company's parking lot, and thought nothing of it.

"I'm not looking for a job. I'm looking for a leader to follow."

—Mavaxiom 182

"Oh my God!" my colleague exclaimed. "That's *your* thank-you letter?" Years later, long after my interview, my thank-you letter was still there sitting proudly on the shelf behind the desk of our mutual friend—who was now a vice president. No wonder he was surprised.

Guidelines for Thank-You Letters

Thank-you letters do not need to be classic works of literature (or art, for that matter). They just need to "be." Not doing them is a mistake, but messing them up can be even more costly. This makes sending the correct kind of thank-you letter all the more important. To prevent inadvertently self-inflicting a mortal wound, follow these simple guidelines:

1. The simpler the card, the better. You can buy any color you want, so long as you choose white. No exceptions. Off-white cards are acceptable, but they may increase the probability of other problems later in this process. Whatever you buy must be simple and very professional. You will be writing a *lot* of thank-you letters, and will have to replace them equally as fast. That means find a simple design that you can buy in bulk.

   Do not buy anything that is too expensive, rare, or hard to find. The fact that they are getting a card from you will be enough of a treat. Convincing an employer that you are a time traveler with overly eccentric thank-you cards will just make them nervous when it comes to salary negotiations. Stick to plain white cards, with plain white envelopes, that have absolutely nothing printed on them. If they must have printing, buy the cheap bulk variety that just say "Thank You" in simple script or nice lettering on the outside of the card.

2. Hand write the card, and do not misspell *anything* on the card. Ever. Absolutely no computer print-off cards are acceptable. It must be in your handwriting. Write in plain letters if necessary. The fewer words you write on the card, the better. It reduces the chances of a mistake. It also prevents you from rambling.

3. If you make a mistake, throw the card away and start over from scratch. Period.

4. Do not try to scribble over a misspelling. Write a whole new card. Destroy the card with the mistake.

5. Never ever use white-out. That is grounds for having your letter posted on a common area bulletin board to be mocked. Do not be that person.

6. Address the recipient of the thank-you letter in the name they preferred that you call them during the interview. If you feel uncomfortable with that, then address them as Mr., Ms., or by their title, such as Dr., or Senator. Either way, make sure you spell their name correctly.

7. End your thank-you letter with "Sincerely," and enough space for your signature.

8. Destroy your letters with mistakes, but save the extra (blank) envelopes. You might need them to replace envelopes that go awry when you are addressing them.

9. Please do not mix-and-match thank-you letters with different envelopes. This is why you want to buy simple, inexpensive, and bulk cards (in ten and twenty-packs). You can make mistakes and still have enough left over to send the perfect thank-you letter.

10. Include another one of your own business cards inside the thank-you letter. If you forgot to give them your card, or you had no business cards left to give them in the interview, this will ensure that they have your business card handy if they need to get in touch with you. Also, one business card is never enough. Strange things happen to business cards that you give to people during interviews. They lose them or misplace them somewhere in the monster paper piles on their desks or in their clothing. A business card or two has been known to meet its fate in a washing machine or at the dry cleaners. Assuming that interviewers have safely tucked away your business card is dangerous. Send another one. Two or more cards will also allow people to forward a second card to someone else they think should also meet you.

To end that last point, the following is a simple (but effective) business-card design. Simplicity rules when it comes to the design of business cards. Probably the best business card I have ever seen is the one I tried to emulate below.

Note

1. Roth, "Ways To Go."

MARC ANTHONY VIOLA
Techno-Anthropologist

*Getting people & technology
to play nicely together ...*

Mobile: (###) ### - ####
Internet: emailaddress@wherever.com

Figure 18.1. The Simple (but effective) Business Card

CHAPTER NINETEEN

Epilogue
Reflections and Feelings on the Job You Make

"Experience is a wonderful teacher, . . . but a costly one."
—Mavaxiom 191

After all that has been said, we are once again at the beginning. Whether you breezed through your separation, or experienced heartbreak leaving behind your life's work, transitioning out of the service leaves a mark on your life. It may seem almost indiscernible at first, but eventually the effects will percolate up through your consciousness. No one in the service of their nation can ever forget that they were once "in." The change back to a normal civilian life reminds us of what we left behind, and why we served in the first place. And now it is the beginning of a new life.

Tuesday
— • Martedí • —
Mars' Day,
Day of the Roman God of War
November the 7th
Two Thousand and Six
— • ~ • —

It is Election Day, seven years after my departure from the military. I have done my civic duty for the day, exercising my right to vote. Today, I was given a choice, a say in what I wanted for the future of my nation. As I awkwardly shuffle through the crowd in St. Thomas Episcopal Church and stroll through downtown Washington, D.C., I struggle to understand a sudden rush of feelings. As I write down these very words, I am overcome with humility, tons of it. It feels as if a 2,000-pound, precision-guided water balloon has splashed its aim point with ruthless efficiency. In one fell swoop I am awash with the knowledge that I have just participated, if only in a tiny way, with something much larger than myself. Although I had rationally understood its significance before, I am finally emotionally connecting with belonging and participating in this important event. Military service had been my contribution to the guardianship of the nation and now, as a civilian, I was contributing in a different way. My participation in the vote would help choose those who would lead us in the future. The two contributions irrevocably linked. I could take pride in both and now, somehow, it made sense of all those years I had served before.

For almost twelve years I fought my way through the quagmire of military culture. All those years are gone. The experience can never be relived, as the transaction is now final. For those dozen years I worked for a few good leaders and a whole lot of bureaucrats. A dozen summers and a dozen winters passed, with red tape to wrap every holiday package. A dozen years of spring blossoms spent completing tasks in windowless vaults so that superiors could make their decisions. It became a balancing act of serving others, and creating opportunities. Throughout it all I believed that it would get better, and that I would eventually find my place. Unfortunately, that never happened. When you do not belong, you do not belong. No matter how hard you try, some things were just not meant to be. Perhaps I could have made it work but in the end, it had to end.

When active duty was too much for me, I tried the reserves. "One weekend a month" did not work either. I was allergic, and resistance became toxic. Every year only prolonged the inevitable as the friction grew to the point of being unbearable. The indicators were all there, right in front of me, but the intelligence officer was trying to ignore the incontrovertible. I believed that my maladjustment was just another challenge I could overcome.

My odyssey began on July the 5th, 1983, but required twenty-three more years before I could write these words because I had not accepted the most important aspect of this entire journey. This struggle with the military was a war with myself. Everything I needed to end the struggle was inside of me. I just had to let it be. Those who knew me just shook their heads, disagreeing with my decision to serve in the military. It was simple for them to see that I just was *not* that kind of person. Perhaps I pursued the romantic ideal of embodying noble virtues. Although the military did take care of me, no amount of awards, or recognition, or acceptance would ever make the ideal a reality. Who I really was and what I really wanted was not in the military.

So, on this Tuesday in November, so many years later, I cast a special kind of ballot. In voting as a civilian, I also resolved to document my transition after the military. Voting marked one small step in ending the struggle inside myself, and putting any lingering disappointments to rest. I was finally letting go, and the act of writing would help me leave the military behind. I was a civilian, and the defense of our nation was somebody else's responsibility now.

Those Who Lacked Wings to Take Us Under

A fellow Air Force captain always mused, "You can't get blood out of a turnip." How much effort, then, should a person reasonably expend before accepting that their pursuit is futile? For those in "the 20 percent," that limit can very well exceed the limits of their health, their well-being, and sometimes their lives. If simply trying harder would yield the results desired, then their actions might not seem in vain. They might have merit in the eyes of desperate circumstances. That is, unless, leaders made other options and opportunities available.

Leadership is the business of providing its people with those options, and a range of alternative opportunities. That is what leadership does. This is why we defer to their judgment, and why we respect their authority. It is a public trust that they must uphold if they are to remain legitimate. We rely on their decision making for the greater good. We hope that they are acting in our best interests, but is such always the case? Those who readily accept the mantle of authority may believe that they have the right to use their power at will, free from their responsibilities to subordinates. We are left asking ourselves if those entrusted with such authority also accept the *responsibility* that comes with their position. Are their actions indicative of the greater good, or do leaders seek a more expedient, Machiavellian end to justify their means?

In short, leadership carries a trust that is all too easily broken. When that trust is broken it also opens a doorway to temptation, and leaders fall prey to opportunistic gain. When things go wrong, many suffer the aftereffects but the few in charge are supposed to be held accountable. How can this be, unless we have allowed responsibility to be diffused, or capitulated to blaming a convenient scapegoat? In my own profession's case, this became the occupational hazard of "intelligence failure."

Ready to serve leaders (good, bad, or otherwise) are a cadre of people loyal to a cause greater than themselves. When they separate from military or government service, they find themselves searching for new causes, and new masters, to serve. What many fail to realize, until they learn it the hard way, is that their service has *ended* and they now need to take care of themselves. They no longer need to seek out the hardship of challenges imposed upon them. Enough challenges exist in everyday life, and new responsibilities that demand attention. Foremost of these new responsibilities is to their own well-being.

We are obliged as adults to take care of ourselves. No institution can ever take up that requirement, no matter how reassuring their motto or the depth of their traditions. At the end of the day, everyone goes home to their own families and their own support systems. Ending the chapter of one's service to their nation, then, means closing more than just a door to the past. It also means leaving behind an old way of being for good.

Spreading Your Wings

Leaders are supposed to inspire with a vision, so imagine the following: Imagine yourself sprouting a set of magnificent wings at the end of your service. With wings large enough to fly, you would probably find yourself unable to comfortably fit inside any standard-sized workspace. In the most ordinary of settings, your unfurled wings would risk injury unless you opened up enough space for your new-feathered appendages. Only the largest indoor rooms, devoid of clutter, would provide enough space for your wings to fully stretch out. You would find a cubicle impossible to sit in for more than a few agonizing minutes. That is the way it felt for me. In the jobs that did not work, I felt that if I could only get outside and find someplace that would allow my wings to reach out and capture the air, I might be all right.

It was a kind of restlessness that I found difficult to describe to others. Most viewed my transition out of the military as a seemingly admirable state of accomplishment, as an achievement in itself. From their perspective, they could not understand why anyone would ever want more, why anyone would ever want to jeopardize the good thing already in hand. Why I would ever want more "room" was beyond them, but they seemed to miss the real point. For the benefit of those people, I will recount a very special experience that illustrated these feelings and why I had to learn the hard way that success is not everything.

Some years ago, I had to get away from it all. On a whim, I flew off to the west coast of Turkey to wander around ancient ruins and cruise the coastline. At the time, I was out of the military and had established my professional credentials as a defense contractor. By all accounts, I was doing very well for myself, but something was missing. Something kept compelling me to run off on trips to ever more exotic and offbeat locations. I went alone, joining a tour group of strangers overseas, thus making the trip completely open-ended and without any expectations. Naturally, that meant that anything could happen, and it did. I met a young, beautiful, and seemingly insanely brave Australian woman who was on her solo, around the world "walkabout." She was halfway through her trip, heading westward into Europe, and it did not take long before the sparks flew. Two magical weeks had to come to an end. She was bravely off to her next destination with her backpack, and I had to return to my cubicle.

Returning from my vacation in Turkey, I felt somehow changed. Everything, and everyone around me, seemed just a little bit "off" from how I remembered them. It was as if my entire world was exactly the same, but had somehow undergone an almost imperceptible shift. Although my thoughts and feelings were somewhere else, that slight shift was becoming more and more evident. Soon I could not avoid it. After encountering the Australian, something important was happening inside of me. I stayed in touch with her via e-mail, and she asked me to rejoin her in Europe. At the time, I had no more vacation left, but despite the warnings of commonsense I felt compelled to action. My drive to go was so strong that I decided to take time off from work without pay.

I remember how strong my feelings were at the time. It was a sudden claustrophobic feeling in a space that I was comfortable in before. I thought to myself that if my company did not let me go on this adventure, I would resign and go anyway. Fortunately, it never came to that. In fact, virtually everyone in my company was eager to hear how this follow-on trip would turn out. I had become the center of an unfolding, real-life, international, romantic adventure-drama through which everyone wanted to live vicariously. I could not let this opportunity go. I put my entire life on hold and headed off to allow my wings to unfurl once more.

We met at Mestre, in the mainland train station of Venice. From there we rode the trains together, backpacking for five incredible weeks across Slovenia and Croatia, in the former Yugoslavia. Every day I spent on the road made it less desirable for me to return to my old life. I never wanted to see another cubicle, sit through another staff meeting, or fight my way through traffic. I was changing in ways I could scarcely understand, and travel was accelerating the entire process. The Australian and I were very different people, drawn into the circumstance as if chance was more than mere serendipity. When she and I talked about what to do after Yugoslavia, it became clear that if we surrendered to these feelings, our lives would never be the same again. I was ready for it. She was not. I had taken her by surprise in Turkey, and now Yugoslavia challenged her expectations further. I wanted more, but she could only give me Yugoslavia. So, like all travel romances, it had to end.

We flew to London where she planned to spend a few weeks with a female friend. I would fly back to the U.S. in the morning. On the Underground the next day, she told me that she would not accompany me all the way to the airport. As the subway train slowed to her station, she silently stood at the car doors, as if to say something but nothing emerged. The doors opened, and my last words to her were, "I wish things were different . . . but I'll never regret falling in love." The doors of the car closed, and the train pulled off. We never spoke to one another again.

When I returned home, my life would never be the same. Backpacking through towns without a clue as to where to stay, and never once worrying, put me into an important state of mind. Like what I sought from the military, during that amazing trip I was alive, thinking on my feet every day, and actively engaged with real people all around me. I conversed in many languages, negotiated for rooms and food at numerous exchange rates, and amazingly it became easy. It became easy because I was there, in the moment, and actualized. Undreamt abilities blossomed as if purely by necessity, and I felt capable of *anything*. For its duration, it was the cheapest vacation I had ever undertaken, specifically because I was part of every decision. I was capable of anything, that is, until I came back to a cubicle.

My real heartbreak, as it turned out, was *not* the Australian. It was trying to fit myself back into my old life. My crushing breakup was nothing by comparison to being asked by my management to kindly retract my empowerment and pack my wings back into the approved dimensions of the office cubicle. Nothing could be more confining, and nothing made me think more about what was really important. I could feel confidence and new-found abilities crashing on the rocks of everyday mediocrity. Those days are a story unto themselves, and until I have written that story, I can only leave you with my hope that you do not let the dimensions of a cubicle define you.

In the end, I realized that I had solved all the practical challenges of transitioning out of the military and into the civilian world, but I had not created the right *kind* of life for myself. I could pay the bills, but I did not have a place that would encourage me to stretch out my wings. Instead of pursuing what I wanted to do with my life, I had succeeded in becoming the misadventure capitalist.

Ultimately, who we are is a choice, an intensely personal and individual choice. If we choose to let others define who we are, then an unfulfilling life is waiting for us. But, if there is even a chance that our place is not among the

"Fortune favors the brave."

—Virgil, *The Aeneid*

herds of "everybody else," then we need to summon the courage, daring, and initiative to be ourselves. Being *that* empowered really does feel like having wings with which we can fly. And if, only briefly, you have felt a gust of your own empowerment you know what I mean. It can be overwhelming, almost frightening. It might seem safer to defer to what everyone else is doing, just because "everyone else is doing it." But this will not leave you happy. In the end, all the dream-catchers in your life will not help you unless you allow yourself to spread your wings and pursue *your* dreams.

Your adventure is out there, right now. Don't let your dreams wait any longer . . .

Bibliography

Adams, Douglas. *The Hitchhiker's Guide to the Galaxy*. New York: Harmony Books, 1979.

Cheney, Margaret, and Robert Uth. *Tesla: Master of Lightning*. Technical editing by Jim Glenn. New York: Barnes & Noble Books, 1999.

Coelho, Paulo. *The Alchemist*. Translated by Alan R. Clarke. New York: Harper Perennial, 1998.

Commission on the Intelligence Capabilities of the United States Regarding Weapons of Mass Destruction. *Report to the President of the United States*. Co-chaired by Laurence H. Silberman and Charles S. Robb. Washington DC: U.S. Government Printing Office, 2005.

Crawford, Craig. "A Nixon Prescription." *CQ Weekly* (July 31, 2006): 2142.

Cunliffe, Barry W. *Rome and Her Empire*. Maidenhead, UK: McGraw-Hill, 1978.

Dahlem, Björn. *Schwarzes Loch (Black Hole)*. Mixed-media artwork displayed at the Hirshhorn Museum. Washington, D.C., courtesy of the artist and the Friedrich Petzel Gallery, New York (viewed December 26, 2006).

Dr. Strangelove, or How I Learned to Stop Worrying and Love the Bomb, directed by Stanley Kubrick. Culver City CA: Columbia Pictures, 1964.

Finley, Bruce. "Intelligence Fixes Floated At Conference." *Denver Post*. August 22, 2006. Voices of September 11th www.voicesofsept11.org/dev/content .php?idtocitems=intelfixesnews (accessed April 20, 2008).

Flax, Dr. Jane. Personal Interview.

Gladwell, Malcolm. *The Tipping Point: How Little Things Can Make A Big Difference*. New York: Back Bay Books, 2000.

Golding, William. *Lord of the Flies*. New York: Capricorn Books, 1959.

Halpin, Bill. "Where is Defense HUMINT in America's New War?" *Defense Intelligence Journal* 11, no. 1 (Winter 2002): 81–89.

Johnson, Matthew M. "A Flawed Marshal Plan." *CQ Weekly* (July 31, 2006): 2084.

Kageyama, Yuri. "At 60, Sony Must Adapt Or Die, Company Chief Says." *Associated Press.* July 31, 2008. The Globe and Mail website. www.theglobeandmail.com/servlet/story/RTGAM.20060731.gtsony31/BNStory/Technology/home (accessed April 20, 2008).

Kübler-Ross, Elisabeth. *On Death and Dying.* New York: Scribner, 1969.

McMaster, H. R. "On War: Lessons to be Learned." *Survival: Global Politics and Strategy* 50, no. 1. http://dx.doi.org/10.1080/00396330801899439 (01 February 2008): 19–30.

National Commission on Terrorist Attacks Upon the United States. *The 9/11 Report.* Chaired by Thomas H. Kean and vice-chaired by Lee H. Hamilton. New York: St. Martin's Press, 2004.

O'Neil, Patrick H. "Complexity and Counterterrorism: Thinking about Biometrics." *Studies in Conflict and Terrorism* 26, no. 6. www.informaworld.com/smpp/title~content=g725841289~db=all (November 2005): 547–566.

Pressfield, Steven. "It's the Tribes, Stupid." Defense and the National Interest website. www.d-n-i.net/fcs/pressfield_tribes.htm (accessed August 11, 2007).

Roth, Siobhan. "Ways To Go." *National Geographic* (August 2006). National Geographic website. ngm.nationalgeographic.com/2007/02/hearts/death-text (accessed April 20, 2008).

Starkweather, Helen. "Interview: David Galenson. Pondering the nature of artistic genius, a social scientist finds that creativity has a bottom line." *Smithsonian* (November 2006): 18.

Interior: Death Star—Conference Room Scene Dialogue, *Star Wars Episode 1V: A New Hope*, VHS directed by George Lucas. San Francisco, CA: Twentieth Century-Fox Film Corporation, A Lucasfilm Ltd. Production, 1977.

Sun Tzu. *The Art of War.* Translated by Samuel B. Griffith. New York: Oxford University Press, 1963.

Tolstoy, Leo. *Anna Karenina.* Translated by Louise and Aylmer Maude, edited by George Gibian. New York: Norton & Company, Inc., 1995.

Waller, Douglas. *A Question of Loyalty: Gen. Billy Mitchell and the Court-Martial that Gripped the Nation.* New York: HarperCollins, 2004.

Index

About the Author

MARC ANTHONY VIOLA has been an intelligence professional in the pioneering, development, and deployment of innovative technologies and tradecraft for the U.S. Intelligence Community (IC) for almost twenty years. He is best known for his work with Measurement and Signature Intelligence (MASINT) at such IC agencies as the National Geospatial-Intelligence Agency (NGA), the National Reconnaissance Office (NRO), and the Defense Intelligence Agency (DIA). He was the director of the MASINT review for the Presidential Commission on the Intelligence Capabilities of the United States Regarding Weapons of Mass Destruction (www.wmd.gov). An aerospace engineer, he expanded the scope of his interests into business, computer and information systems management, strategic intelligence, and national security studies. He is a visiting guest lecturer on intelligence science topics at the National Defense Intelligence College (formerly the Joint Military Intelligence College) in Washington, D.C. As a U.S. Air Force officer, he served almost twelve years in various Air Force intelligence positions before separating from active duty, then served in the Air Force Reserves while becoming a successful consultant. During his years in the U.S. Air Force, Marc Viola was privileged to work with members of the U.S. Army, Navy, Marine Corps, Coast Guard, and the Canadian Forces.